Natasha Walter is author of *The New Feminism*. She is a journalist and broadcaster, and the director of Women for Refugee Women.

Also by this author

The New Feminism

Living Dolls

The Return of Sexism

NATASHA WALTER

virago

VIRAGO

First published in Great Britain in 2010 by Virago Press
Reprinted 2010 (twice)

A CIP catalogue record for this book
is available from the British Library.

ISBN 978-1-84408-484-5

Typeset in Sabon by M Rules
Printed and bound in Great Britain by
Clays Ltd, St Ives plc

Papers used by Virago are natural, renewable and
recyclable products sourced from well-managed forests and certified
in accordance with the rules of the Forest Stewardship Council.

Mixed Sources
Product group from well-managed
forests and other controlled sources
www.fsc.org Cert no. SGS-COC-004081
© 1996 Forest Stewardship Council
FSC

Virago Press
An imprint of
Little, Brown Book Group
100 Victoria Embankment
London EC4Y 0DY

An Hachette UK Company
www.hachette.co.uk

www.virago.co.uk

For Harriet Gugenheim, with thanks

Acknowledgements

Thank you to Cassie Browne and Flo Nicoll, who gave so much time and energy to checking facts and sources with me. I was lucky to meet you at the beginning of what will no doubt be brilliant careers.

I am grateful to everyone I interviewed, as without their insights into so many different areas of experience I could never have written this book. And I am very grateful to the many people who gave me interviews and whose words do not appear here, as they often provided invaluable insights which informed my work even if I was unable to quote them by name. They include Bernice McCabe and staff and students at North London Collegiate School; Charlotte Tan and friends at St John's College, Cambridge University; Lee Eggleston and Sheila Coates at the South Essex Rape and Incest Crisis Centre, Dan Burke, Kimberley Firth Jones, Daisy Leitch, Charlie Little and Flora and Miranda Thomas, and Rebecca Jewell, who sparked one particularly fertile train of thought. Thank you, too, to all those who helped me in contacting individuals to interview, particularly Bernard Bulaitis and Annie Griffiths at City and Islington College, Rachel Bell and Emine Saner.

Thank you to those scientists and academics, including Lyn Craig, Janet Frick, Wendy Hill, Nancy Hopkins, Janet Shibley Hyde, Diane Quinn, Elizabeth Spelke, Sonya Thompson, Ed Tronik and Catherine Weinberger, who patiently answered my queries about their work and checked my references to their research; to Susan Morrissey, who translated sources from the German for me; and especially to Deborah Cameron and Mark Liberman, who read through drafts of the second half of this book and generously gave me the benefit of their knowledge. Above all I am grateful to Melissa Hines, who saved me from some particular errors and gave me invaluable insights into her fascinating field of work. Any errors that remain are, obviously, mine.

Thank you to Lennie Goodings and her colleagues at Little, Brown and to Derek Johns and his colleagues at A P Watt. I am also very grateful to Linda Grant, Liz Jobey and Ruth Walter, who read and commented on drafts of the book with great care and intelligence.

And thank you to Mark Lattimer, whose constant support and interest in the project sustained me.

Contents

Dolls   1

I The New Sexism

1 Babes   19
2 Pole-dancers and prostitutes   39
3 Girls   63
4 Lovers   84
5 Pornography   102
6 Choices   119

II The New Determinism

7 Princesses   129
8 Myths   152
   A Babies   158
   B Words   165
   C Maths   174
   D Hormones   180
   E Brains   189
9 Stereotypes   199
10 Changes   231

   Notes   239
   Give your support   264
   Index   267

Note on Names

Where individuals are identified by first name and surname in this book, this is their real name. Where individuals are identified only by first name, this is a pseudonym.

Dolls

I didn't expect we would end up here, I thought to myself a few years ago during a visit to a toy shop in London. I had moved up through the shop on the escalator, from the multi-coloured bustle of the ground floor, stuffed full of the warm tints and round shapes of soft toys, and into the dream world of the third floor. Here, it was as though someone had jammed rose-coloured spectacles over my eyes, and yet the effect was nauseating rather than beautifying. Everything was pink, from the sugared-almond pink of Barbie, to the strawberry tint of Disney's Sleeping Beauty, to the milky pink of Baby Annabell, to the rose pink of Hello Kitty. There was a pink nail bar where little girls could paint their nails, a pink 'boutique stand' with earrings and necklaces, and dolls in pink boxes that came with pink 'manicure bedrooms' and pink 'salon spaces'.

Many feminists in the past argued that girls and boys should be encouraged to play across the boundaries laid down by their sex, and that there was no reason for girls to be confined to this pastel sphere. But not only does this division between the pink girls' world and the blue boys' world still exist, it is becoming more exaggerated than ever in this generation.

It often seems now that the dolls are escaping from the toy shop and taking over girls' lives. Not only are little girls expected to play with dolls, they are expected to model themselves on their favourite playthings. The glittering pink aesthetic now extends to almost every aspect of a girl's life. The all-encompassing nature of modern marketing techniques means that it is now possible for a little girl to sit at home watching her *Sleeping Beauty* DVD, playing with a Sleeping Beauty doll complete with the same costume, while dressed herself in a shiny replica of Sleeping Beauty's dress. She can then trip off to school with Barbies or Bratz on everything from her knickers to her hair clips to her schoolbag, and come home to look at her reflection in the mirror of a Disney Princess dressing table. The brilliant marketing strategies of these brands are managing to fuse the doll and the real girl in a way that would have been unthinkable a generation ago.

This strange melding of the doll and the real girl can continue way beyond childhood. Living a doll's life seems to have become an aspiration for many young women, as they leave childhood behind only to embark on a project of grooming, dieting and shopping that aims to achieve the bleached, waxed, tinted look of a Bratz or Barbie doll. The characters they watch in romantic comedies are women who make such exaggerated femininity seem aspirational, and the celebrities they read about in fashion and gossip magazines are often women who are well known to have chosen extreme regimes, from punishing diets to plastic surgery, to achieve an airbrushed perfection.

The fusion of the woman and the doll at times becomes almost surreal. When the singers in Girls Aloud launched Barbie doll versions of themselves in 2005, you could look – to paraphrase George Orwell – from doll to girl and girl to doll, and it was almost impossible to see which was which. Both real and plastic women were so eerily perfect in their painted skin, nylon-glossy hair and hard bodies. When two young twins entered the reality television show *Big Brother* in the UK in 2007, dressed in identical pink miniskirts and bleached hair, they said Barbie was the inspiration for their lives. The actress and singer Hilary Duff has said, 'When I was younger, I was so inspired by Barbie. She has been a role model for my friends and me. I love her style and her spirit!'[1] Even when the link between women and dolls isn't made so explicit, many of the so-called role models that strut under the contemporary limelight, from Paris Hilton to Victoria Beckham, take the plastic look so far that they seem to have been created by Mattel.

For more than 200 years, feminists have been criticising the way that artificial images of feminine beauty are held up as the ideal to which women should aspire. From Mary Wollstonecraft's *A Vindication of the Rights of Woman* in 1792, to Simone de Beauvoir's *The Second Sex* in 1949, to Germaine Greer's *The Female Eunuch* in 1970, to Naomi Wolf's *The Beauty Myth* in 1991, brilliant and angry women have demanded a change in these ideals. Yet far from fading away, they have become narrower and more powerful than ever. What's more, throughout much of our society, the image of female perfection to which women are encouraged to aspire has become more and more defined by sexual allure. Of course wanting to be sexually attractive has always and will always be a natural desire for both men and women, but in this generation a certain view of female sexuality has become celebrated throughout advertisements, music, television programmes, films and magazines. This image of female sexuality has become more than ever defined by the terms of the sex industry.

Throughout our society, female sexuality now tends to be seen in a very narrow light, often defined by slender exhibitionists with large breasts gyrating around poles in their underwear. The narrowing of what it means to be sexy arises from the way that

the sex industry has become more generally acceptable. The movement of the sex industry from the margins to the mainstream of
our society can be seen in many places – from the unexpected
resurgence of glamour modelling, which means that many young
women have been encouraged to believe that stripping to their
knickers for lads' magazines is their best possible route to success;
to the sudden growth of lap-dancing clubs in town centres; to a
new fashion for the style of dancing associated with those clubs,
pole-dancing; to the popularity of memoirs of prostitution that
suggest selling sex is a great way for a woman to earn her living;
and, above all, to the much greater presence of pornography in
the lives of many young people, driven by the internet. This latter
development has affected magazine and newspaper publishing,
advertising, television and music, many areas of which have
begun to share the aesthetic values of soft pornography. The
messages and values of this revitalised sex industry have reached
deep into the hearts of many young men and women.

This association of femininity and sexiness starts early: while
it's hardly new for women to want to be sexy, it's new that even
childhood playthings should look so sexy. Although feminists in
the 1970s deplored Barbie's tiny waist, large breasts and perfect
features, she could be marketed to girls as a pilot, a doctor or an
astronaut, with accessories to match her roles. Bratz dolls, who
recently toppled Barbie from her throne as the best-selling fashion doll, were created with a wardrobe for clubbing and
shopping, dressed in fishnet and feathers, crop tops and
miniskirts, with heavily painted faces that look as if they have
been created by Jordan's make-up artist.[2]

When you wander into a toy shop and find this new, altogether more slutty and sultry ideal pouting up at you from a
thousand figurines, you realise that there has been a genuine
change in the culture aimed at young girls. While girls have
always been encouraged to see self-decoration as a central part
of their lives, today they are also exposed to a deluge of mes-

sages, even at an early age, about the importance of becoming sexually attractive. These dolls are just a fragment of a much wider culture in which young women are encouraged to see their sexual allure as their primary passport to success.

This highly sexualised culture is often positively celebrated as a sign of women's liberation and empowerment. It was indeed an aim of the women's liberation movement of the 1970s that women should be released from conventional morality around sex, which had confined them to idealised chastity on the one hand or contemptible promiscuity on the other. The fact that women can now be sexually active and experienced without being condemned is a direct result of second-wave feminism. And this is clearly something to be celebrated. But it is strange that all aspects of the current hypersexual culture are often now seen as proof of women's growing freedom and power. So the renaissance of glamour modelling is seen by many who partici- pate in the industry as a marker not of persistent sexism, but of women's new confidence. For instance, as one ex-editor of a lads' magazine said to me, 'It's the women who are driving this. It's all changed. . . . I think that to people of my age, it's bizarre to see young women being so confident sexually at such an early age.' Similarly, the fashion for pole-dancing classes is talked about as if it were liberating for women. The website for Pole Dancing Hen Weekends states that, 'Pole dancing classes are all about freeing yourself from the restrictions imposed on you in your everyday life and empowering yourself.'[3] Even occupations such as lap dancing and prostitution are often now surrounded by this quasi-feminist rhetoric. One young lap dancer quoted in an interview in *The Times* in 2008 said, 'I have never had a job where I felt so empowered,'[4] and the actor Billie Piper, who starred in a television adaptation of the memoir by 'Belle de Jour', a prostitute working in London, said in an interview, 'When I am playing Belle I have to play a sexually liberated, empowered young prostitute.'[5]

This means that rather than being seen as negative for women, the mainstreaming of the sex industry is now often presented as a culmination of the freedoms that feminists have sought. As one female writer who was looking at the mainstream appeal of pornography put it in an article in the *Guardian*: 'Instead of desperately longing for the right to be seen as human beings, today's girls are playing with the old-fashioned notion of being seen as sex objects. This is not terrible news. In fact, to me, this is the ultimate feminist ideal.'[6]

This equation of empowerment and liberation with sexual objectification is now seen everywhere, and is having a real effect on the ambitions of young women. When I interviewed women who have worked in the sex industry for this book, I was struck to find that some of them had been seduced by the idea that this work could enhance their sense of individual power. Ellie is an articulate, well-educated woman who had gone to private school and a good university, and had been brought up to believe she could do anything in any profession – law, medicine, politics. Instead, she had decided she wanted to be an actor, but when jobs were hard to find and she found herself financially desperate, she took a sideways step in her twenties by going to work in a lap-dancing club in London. She didn't feel, at first, that it would be very difficult. She told me she had picked up messages from our culture that lap dancing was pretty straightforward and even empowering for the women who do it. 'People say that, don't they,' she said to me thoughtfully when we met. 'There's this myth that women are expressing their sexuality freely in this way, and that as they can make lots of money out of it, it gives them power over the men who are paying.'

This was not what she found herself, however. She was shocked to discover quite how demeaning and dehumanising she found the work. In the situation of the club, women became more like dolls than people. 'There's something about the club – the lights, the make-up, the clothes you wear, those huge platform heels, the way that so many women have fake boobs,' she said. 'You look like cartoons. You give yourself a fake girly name, like a doll. You're encouraged to look like dolls. No wonder the men don't see you as people.'

Although the word empowerment is so often attached to this culture, it is a strange distortion of what the term once meant to feminists. When we talked about empowerment in the past, it was not a young woman in a thong gyrating around a pole that would spring to mind, but the attempts by women to gain real political and economic equality. Towards the end of the twentieth century, there was a real optimism that this kind of power genuinely could be within the grasp of more women than ever before, and that women would then be free to attain their true potential without being held back by the weight of inequality.

It may seem strange to say so after the political disillusion of the last decade, but the early years of the Blair administration in the UK and the early years of the Clinton administration in the US were hailed in many places as offering new hope for women who wanted to enter the corridors of power. Naomi Wolf, the American feminist, wrote in 1993: 'In 1992 record numbers of women ran for office in the US . . . The genderquake rattled and reoriented the presidential elections.'[7] And I wrote in the *Observer* just before the 1997 General Election in the UK: 'If we see a six per cent swing to Labour, the number of women MPs should double . . . It's not equality yet, but don't underestimate what it will mean. We'll see the gentleman's club begin to crumble, we'll begin to see a political culture that responds to women's priorities . . . This impending revolution in women's power is one issue that we shouldn't be cynical about.'[8]

This shift towards greater equality in politics meant that feminist arguments that had long been regarded as marginal could be heard in many political debates. During the first five years of the New Labour government, we heard from policy makers about the need to prosecute crimes against women, such as domestic violence and rape, more effectively. We also heard a great deal about the need to change the working world. New Labour brought in the minimum wage, which affected women far more than men, and also expanded parental leave rights, childcare and flexible working. During these early years the Labour government doubled maternity pay, introduced paid paternity leave, introduced free part-time nursery places for three- and four-year-olds, and its ministers discussed how they could push on a workplace revolution.[9] There was an optimism not just about changes in women's lives, but about changes in men's lives too. When Tony Blair took a couple of weeks off work when his fourth child was born in 2000, his move was welcomed, since: 'When one of the world's most powerful men sets this kind of example, the impact on the workplace and parental leave will be immense.'[10]

With this kind of debate happening all around us, it was easy for me to argue in my earlier book, *The New Feminism*, which was published at the end of the 1990s, that even if the women's movement may have quietened down, feminism had become part of the very air we breathed. It was also easy for me to argue, and I was glad to be able to do so, that feminists could now concentrate on achieving political and social and financial equality. In the past, feminist arguments had often centred on private lives: how women made love, how they dressed, whom they desired. I felt that the time for this had passed. I believed that we only had to put in place the conditions for equality for the remnants of old-fashioned sexism in our culture to wither away.

I am ready to admit that I was entirely wrong. While many women relaxed and believed that most arguments around equality had been won, and that there were no significant barriers to further progress, the dolls were on the march again. The rise of a hypersexual culture is not proof that we have reached full equality; rather, it has reflected and exaggerated the deeper imbalances of power in our society. Without thoroughgoing economic and political change, what we see when we look around us is not the equality we once sought; it is a stalled revolution.

Men and women may still be trying to inch towards greater equality at home as well as at work, but the pressure for change and the sense of optimism has gone. The relentless masculinity of British politics is a marker of wider failure in the attempts to create equality between the sexes. While the 1997 election doubled the number of women in Parliament, from 60 to 120 out of 646, the pace of change then slowed to a standstill. The next two elections increased the number of women in Parliament by only eight, and in the Scottish Parliament the proportion of women actually dropped, from 40 per cent in 2003 to 35 per cent in 2009.[11] New Labour gradually began to be associated with a sense of broken promises for women in politics. Many female ministers resigned during the summer of 2009, and one launched a bitter attack on the inability of the prime minister to support women in government, saying that she had been used merely as 'female window-dressing'.[12]

Just as women have not moved forwards as far as was once hoped into the corridors of power, men have not taken the steps into the home that might once have been expected. Although the rhetoric is often spoken about flexible working and shared parental responsibility, in 2009 men were still only entitled to two weeks' paternity leave at £123 per week. Plans to equalise rights to parental leave by introducing a scheme whereby men and women could share twelve months' leave between them were shelved by the government in response to 'tough economic times'.[13] Given the discrepancy between women's entitlement to spend time at home and men's lack of similar rights, it is hardly surprising that women are still doing the vast majority of domestic work. Even when women work full-time, according to one study, they do twenty-three hours of domestic work a week, as opposed to men's eight hours, while women who work part-time do thirty-three hours of domestic work per week. The authors of that report commented that the domestic workload that still fell on their shoulders was what prevented many women from working the long hours required for higher-paid jobs.[14]

The reality is that although girls still do as well as boys at every level of education, the workplace has not seen the changes that were once expected. While men and women with young children have the right to request flexible working, for women the decision not to work full-time still carries a huge penalty. The hourly pay gap for women working full-time is around 17 per cent, but it is around 35 per cent for women working part-time – in other words, an average woman who works part-time earns only two-thirds of the money that the average full-time male worker would earn each hour.[15] And what is most worrying is that there is evidence that progress on the pay gap has stalled; from 2007 to 2008 it actually widened.[16] For women in senior management, equality may be more elusive than ever, as research carried out in 2007 showed: 'The Price Waterhouse Coopers research found that among FTSE 350 companies in 2002 almost 40% of senior management posts were occupied by women. When that research was repeated for 2007, the number of senior management posts held by women had fallen to just 22%.'[17] One female manager, who was interviewed about why so many of her peers had left, tried to put her finger on the problem. While people may understand the need for equality issues on intellectual grounds, 'It's what they get in their hearts that matters.'

What do we get in our hearts? It is time to make the links between the cultural changes we have seen over the last ten years and this stalled revolution. Although opportunities for women are still far wider than they were a generation ago, we are now seeing a resurgence of old sexism in new guises. Far from giving full scope to women's freedom and potential, the new hypersexual culture redefines female success through a narrow framework of sexual allure.

What's more, alongside the links that are made between this kind of exaggerated sexual allure and empowerment, we have recently seen a surprising resurgence of the idea that traditional femininity is biologically rather than socially constructed. A new interest in biological determinism now runs throughout our society. Indeed, the association between little girls and everything that is pink and glittery is being explained in many places not as a cultural phenomenon, which could therefore be challenged, but as an inescapable result of biology, which is assumed to be resistant to change. Some neuroscientists recently carried out an experiment which, they claimed, suggested that girls are biologically predisposed to prefer pink. This experiment consisted of presenting men and women with differently coloured pairs of rectangles and asking them to pick out their favourites. The researchers found that women liked reddish hues more than men did, and concluded by suggesting that this difference in colour preference could be explained by biological differences between men and women, which would have been created by their different occupations way, way back in the past. Since women, they speculated, would have been more likely to be gathering ripe red fruit than hunting big game under blue skies many millennia ago, women had evolved to respond more enthusiastically to pink than men would.[18]

This suggestion was picked up uncritically by much of the national press. 'Boys like blue, girls like pink, it's in our genes,' was the *Independent* newspaper's headline on their report.[19] 'Pink for a girl and blue for a boy – and it's all down to evolution', was the headline in the *Guardian*.[20] The writer in the *Guardian* linked the study immediately to the accessories of modern childhood: 'The theory is encouraging for Barbie enthusiasts, who have seen the doll attacked for her "anti-feminist" pink clothes and decor.' Yet, as a couple of lone commentators pointed out, there was nothing in the study that could prove that this preference for pink was a difference that had been hardwired into women's brains aeons ago, rather than one that is simply being encouraged by our current culture.

This is just one study, but its suggestions and its reception typify much contemporary research on this subject. There has been a great flurry of research into sex differences over recent years, in disciplines from neuroscience to linguistics to psychology. Some of this work has looked into the structure and activity of male and female brains, some has looked into the influence of differing levels of hormones, some has looked into differences in the intellectual aptitudes and achievements of men and women, some has looked into their abilities to empathise and nurture. Conclusions have been mixed, but the way that such research is reported in the media and by popular writers constantly reinforces the idea that the differences we see between male and female behaviour must be down to biology.

These beliefs have now penetrated much of the culture that surrounds our children. The educational establishment often reproduces them uncritically, so that, for instance, the website of the Girls' Schools Association states that 'Research in the last 10 years or so on brain development suggests that gender differences are as much to do with the chemistry and structure of the brain as the way in which girls and boys are raised. The tendencies of girls to be more contemplative, collaborative, intuitive and verbal, and boys to be more physically active, aggressive, and independent in their learning style seems to stem from brain function and development.'[21] And while teachers and parents are picking up these ideas, toy companies reinforce them with alacrity. As a spokesperson for Disney said recently, when explaining the recent success of the Disney Princess brand, which encompasses dolls, dressing-up clothes and accessories: 'We believe it is an innate desire in the vast majority of young girls to play out the fantasy of being a princess. They like to dress up, they like to role-play. It's just a genetic desire to like pink, to like the castle, to turn their dads into the prince.'[22]

This reliance on 'the chemistry and structure of the brain' and the 'genetic desire' as the explanation for stereotypically feminine behaviour is not only being used to explain how little girls play and learn, it is also being used to explain away the inequalities we see in adult life. Writers such as Simon Baron-Cohen, professor of developmental psychopathology at Cambridge University, have written extensively on how they believe that the differences we see between the sexes in adult life are attributable as much to biology as they are to social factors. In his book *The Essential Difference*, Simon Baron-Cohen argues that having a 'female brain' or a 'male brain' will not only influence the way you behave as a child, but will also influence your choice of occupations as an adult. He starts with anecdotes about a typical girl child and a typical boy child, and tells us that the typical girl is 'into dolls and small toy animals. She would spend hours dressing and undressing Barbie dolls.'[23] He then goes further, and suggests that on average grown-up females also have superior social talents to males, and that this is reflected in the occupations they will naturally choose. 'People with the female brain make the most wonderful counsellors, primary-school teachers, nurses, carers, therapists, social workers, mediators, group facilitators or personnel staff . . . People with the male brain make the most wonderful scientists, engineers, mechanics, technicians, musicians, architects, electricians, plumbers, taxonomists, catalogists, bankers, toolmakers, programmers or even lawyers.'[24]

It's striking that the occupations judged suitable for the female brain, by Simon Baron-Cohen and other followers of biological explanations for gender differences, would have been seen as women's work by old-fashioned chauvinism as much as by fresh research. Indeed, if you look closely at the evidence for this kind of biological determinism, it is hard to escape the conclusion that its popularity often relies as much on bad old stereotypes as on good new science. There is science on either side of this debate, yet it is often the case that the media will rush to embrace only one side. This means that biological determinism is often assumed to be the new consensus throughout the academy. In fact, many scientists are now raising their voices to dissent from the use of biological explanations for the continuing gender divisions in society. If this dissent were more widely heard, we might be inclined to challenge not only those apparently trivial differences between boys' and girls' toys, but also the continuing existence of serious inequality in men's and women's adult lives.

I think it is time to challenge the exaggerated femininity that is being encouraged among women in this generation, both by questioning the resurgence of the biological determinism which tells us that genes and hormones inexorably drive us towards traditional sex roles, and by questioning the claustrophobic culture that teaches many young women that it is only through exploiting their sexual allure that they can become powerful. Of course, it has to be a woman's own choice if she makes a personal decision to buy into any aspect of what might be seen as stereotypically feminine behaviour, from baking to pole-dancing, from high heels to domestic work. I am just as sure as I ever was that we do not need to subscribe to some dour and politically correct version of feminism in order to move towards greater equality. But we should be looking for true choice, in a society characterised by freedom and equality. Instead, right now a rhetoric of choice is masking very real pressures on this generation of women. We are currently living in a world where those aspects of feminine behaviour that could be freely chosen are often turning into a cage for young women.

In examining these aspects of women's experiences, I am well aware there are places this book does not go. I have spent much of the last few years talking to women who come from places outside mainstream Western feminist debate. I have travelled to Afghanistan, Saudi Arabia and Iran to find out how women view their rights in different parts of the world, and in the UK I have been working alongside women who have fled here for refuge from other countries. I have learned, and I am still learning, a great deal from these individuals about the importance of working across cultures. This book does not attempt to cover such ground; here I stay not only within Western culture, but also primarily within British, heterosexual experience. In doing so, I am not suggesting that other experiences are not just as valid and vital.

Above all, this is no time to succumb to inertia or hopelessness. Feminists in the West have already created a peaceful revolution, opening many doors for women that were closed to them before, expanding opportunities and insisting on women's rights to education, work and reproductive choice. We have come so far already. For our daughters, the escalator doesn't have to stop on the dolls' floor.

I

The New Sexism

1: Babes

One spring night in the Mayhem nightclub in Southend, young men and women were moving tentatively onto the dance floor through drifts of dry ice, lit amethyst and emerald by flashing lights. 'Five minutes left!' the DJ's voice rang out over the thumping music. 'Five minutes left to enter the Babes on the Bed competition. We're looking for ten of the fittest, sauciest birds here today. Remember, it's not just about tits, it's about personality too.' To the side of the DJ a large, empty bed, looking like a Tracey Emin installation, sat waiting.

Almost all the women in the club that night, with their tiny hotpants and towering wedge heels, their dark fake tans and shiny straightened hair, looked as though they could be planning to take part in a modelling contest. About a dozen of them began to make their way over to a group of men who were standing by the bed and choosing who should enter the Babes on the Bed competition. There were sixteen of these nights in the spring of 2007, up and down England, Scotland and Wales, and of the hundreds of women who chose to pose on beds in nightclubs, one would be given a modelling contract with *Nuts* magazine. 'I want to do it to make my mum proud,' said one young woman, Lauren, in denim hotpants and tight, yellow crop top. 'She should win,' said her best friend, who was standing with her. 'She works out, she's really keen, and she's gorgeous.' Lauren was given the once-over by the men from *Nuts* and told to go into the changing room to be given the competition uniform – red hotpants and crop top with the *Nuts* logo. When she came out, her friend whooped and started taking pictures of her on her mobile phone.

Just then I saw three young women at the bar wearing Playboy bunny outfits: pink cuffs, black lace knickers and basques, black stockings, stilettos and pink bunny tails. Assuming they too were here for the competition, I went to chat to them. 'What competition?' said one, a smiling, rosy young woman with her bobbed dark hair pushed back under her bunny ears. 'No, we're here for Sam's birthday. She's twenty today.' 'Whose idea was the costume?' I asked. 'Mine!' she said. Two of the women are secretaries, and one is a full-time mother. 'I'm allowed out on Thursday nights,' said the mother eagerly. 'This is my me-time. I get away from the family. I can be myself.' Then they went into the toilets to check their outfits, and got the bathroom attendant, a tall young black woman in a long-sleeved T-shirt and black trousers, to take photos of the three of them on their digital camera. I watched as they stood close together, pouting with hands on hips, breasts thrust out, before they went back to the bar.

I returned to the cluster of young women who stood around the *Nuts* team. One of the girls to be chosen, Tania, was wearing a blue lace dress that started low on her breasts and ended just below her knickers, and was saying goodbye to her friends, Nikki and Katie, who wished her luck and perched outside the changing room. Nikki, in a black minidress and silver wedge sandals, had the face of a Botticelli madonna, with a pointed chin and wide-apart blue eyes. I asked her if she was entering the competition. 'No, I already do modelling,' she smiled. 'I'm in a final for a big competition on Monday. I'm here for Tania – she wants to break in now.' Katie joined in. 'I've been modelling for a couple of years,' she said. 'I've got an agent, he found me online.' In this context, modelling means glamour modelling, the coy words for posing almost naked for men's magazines. 'I've done a shoot for *FHM*,' Katie said. 'My boyfriend's a bit protective of me – he doesn't like people seeing me as an object.' I wondered if she also worried about that. 'I did at first, but you get used to it, honestly.' When I asked who their role models are, their responses were immediate: 'I'd have to say Jordan,' said Katie, naming the woman most famous for her huge breast implants and appearances on reality television. 'I really admire what she's done.' Tania came out of the changing room, her exquisite hourglass body now clothed in red hotpants and crop top. She's already done some modelling, but not yet topless. 'I will do,' she said, 'when the time is right.'

Although sales of *Nuts* and *Zoo* have entered a real decline since their early heyday,[1] their influence is as real as ever. They have contributed to an ongoing cultural shift, in which the business of what is coyly called glamour modelling – in which women may be naked, but won't expose the genitals – has massively expanded in Britain. When *Nuts* was launched in 2004, the belief was that the young men who would buy it would want articles about football and cars, rather than pictures of women – and if there were to be women, they should be the acknowledged beauties of the film and television world. But its direction changed quickly. The editors found that while readers might say they wanted to see Jennifer Lopez on the cover, actually the editions with ordinary-looking girls – girls from reality television, girls who were photographed in their local nightclubs, girls who sent in photographs of themselves in their bedrooms – sold and sold. The magazines began to make images and words far more explicit, with pages crowded with pictures of young women in thongs. *Nuts* became a shorthand for a certain kind of culture, a laddish, explicit culture in which women were seen in their underwear or not at all. Together with its main competitor, *Zoo*, it dragged all the men's magazines in the UK, including the once more restrained monthly magazines such as *FHM*, into a constant competition as to which could be the most explicit, without quite stepping into pornography. The circulations of all these magazines have fallen in the last few years, but in 2009 *Nuts* still sold over 180,000 copies every week in the UK, and the change it has created in the culture around young men and women has not gone away. Much of its energy has shifted over to the internet, and on the *Nuts* website you can find a constant stream of men commenting on the photographs women post of themselves in glamour-style poses.[2]

For Gavin Lloyd, a deeply tanned young man who runs the PR for Mayhem club, *Nuts* epitomises the changing culture in which he swims. 'Girls come in here every night wearing just their underwear,' he explained to me. 'The sort of thing you might expect just to see in your bedroom on a special night once upon a time. They're all getting boob jobs now – 18-year-olds who a few years ago would be saving for their first car, they're all saving for a boob job. I know six, seven girls who've had it done in the last six months. They all think it'll be a route to their fortune. For some girls it is – you look at Jordan or Melinda Messenger or Jodie Marsh. That's what they are all thinking of. That's where they'd all like to be.'

While the phrase 'glamour modelling' may be coy, the culture that its resurgence has spawned is far from coy. As the minutes ticked by in the Mayhem nightclub, men began to get themselves in the right position, near to the big bed, which by then had become half screened from view by photographers with their lights and reflective shades. The first woman to get on the platform was a confident girl with long fair hair, in high-heeled boots and hotpants, holding a microphone. 'This is Cara Brett!' shouted the DJ. 'She's on the cover of *Nuts* this week! So buy her, take her home and have a wank.' The men around me cheered, an animal roar that took me by surprise as it issued from a hundred throats at once.

At that point Gavin Lloyd reappeared at my elbow. 'I think you ought to go now,' he said to me breathlessly. 'I don't think *Nuts* would like you around.' 'Can't I just watch the show?' I asked. The poor man looked as if the last thing he wanted was a confrontation. 'OK – but be discreet.' And I nodded, though unsure what discretion would look like in a club where the style was one of pure display.

The crush around me became intense as the girls got on the bed one by one, accompanied by the constant thump of music. Cara began to direct them into more and more suggestive poses. 'Why not on all fours?' 'Let's see your arse in the air!' You might have thought it would be tricky to get young women to take up openly sexual poses in this brightly lit club in front of this crowd of yelling, drunk young men, but the girls seemed to know what was expected of them, and if they became too reluctant, Cara threw herself into the task of encouraging them with some gusto. 'Let's get those off,' she urged impatiently. 'If you're going to be a winner, you've got to show some skin.' One plump young woman in mauve bra and knickers was one of the first to slip off her bra and joggle her breasts at the cameras. As the display became more sexual, the underwear unpeeling from the smooth skin of teenage women, the men in the club began to chant, heavily and fast, and to press nearer and nearer to the stage, and the women they had come with drifted back, ignored, to the bar area where they ordered more alcohol. The men were using their phones to video and photograph the girls as they took off their clothes. One girl, who was a bit too fleshy around the middle and not fleshy enough around the chest, came in for boos rather than cheers. She looked tearful as she went back into the line.

'Come on, girls,' Cara said fiercely to the next one, Tania, who was defiantly keeping her bra on – clearly that night was not the right time for her to start topless modelling, 'if you're going to be a glamour model, you've got to get your boobs out.' The next girl, with huge, perfectly spherical, siliconed breasts perched high on her slender chest, got the loudest roar. 'Oh, there are two things I like about her!' shouted the DJ. 'How about you, boys? She doesn't swim, but she doesn't sink.'

As the show went on, the women became more ambitious. One jumped on the bed and bent straight over, looking through her wide-apart legs, presenting her crotch in stretchy, tight red pants to the cameras, before pumping her rear at them and slipping off her bra, ending up with the splits. 'This is Angel!' called the DJ. 'Isn't she fit? She's on a porn channel too, so you can catch her on telly too.' The shortlisting was done at top speed – only women who flashed their breasts or their thongs for the crowd were called back for the final four, so Tania wasn't in that line-up, although they all went on standing on the stage, a rejected half-naked chorusline. 'Now we're going to judge your girl-on-girl action,' said the DJ to cheers all round. 'Let's see you get a bit friendly, come on, how about some kissing. What do you think, boys? Some of the fittest girls in Southend getting on with each other.'

The girls clambered on top of one another, looking vaguely back at the camera. 'What about the bra? Is that coming off?' asked Cara Brett. The crowd chanted heavily, breathily, 'Get your tits out, get your tits out, get your tits out for the lads.' They pressed around the stage, roaring as the girls rubbed their breasts against each other. The crowd became so big that I could no longer see the women whole – just flashes of breast and thigh on the screens of the phones that were held high in the air.

'Yeah, Gav's got a stiffy now,' shouted the DJ about the PR manager. 'Come on,' said Cara impatiently, 'let's show some skin, girls. Let me help you out of these.' She dragged the hotpants off one girl, showing her sequinned thong riding precariously on a shaved crotch. The crowd erupted, and that girl was judged the winner. Sweatily, the crowd dispersed. I saw the two young women who had come with Tania. 'Did you enjoy it?' I asked them. 'Not really,' said Katie, running long nails through blonde hair, looking uneasy. 'It was a bit degrading, to be honest.' I would have liked to stop and talk more to them, but the PR manager was desperate for me to leave as he seemed to think the men from *Nuts* would be angry at him for letting me in. He could hardly escort me to the door fast enough. The next day I looked on a club website, www.dontstayin.com, to see if anyone had commented on the night at Mayhem. The only comment was laconic. 'Lots of quality Southend fanny.'

As I saw that evening in the Mayhem nightclub, and as one can see any night of the week in clubs up and down the UK, images that a previous generation often saw as degrading for women have now been taken up as playful and even aspirational. 'Me-time' for a young homemaker now can include dressing as a Playboy bunny; breaking into a respectable career that would make your mum proud can start with stripping for nothing in a crowded nightclub. Although for many people this culture may seem quite marginal, it may be more mainstream than we think. In 2006, a survey was carried out among teenage girls that suggested that more than half of them would consider being glamour models and a third of them saw Jordan as a role model.[3] The growth of a culture in which so many women feel that their worth is measured by the size of their breasts rather than by any other possible yardstick arrived in the UK apparently out of nowhere. When I was at university in the late 1980s, that sniggery British culture of Benny Hill and page three seemed to be on the way out – it looked dated and rather absurd, and young women didn't talk about stripping as a means of empowerment or look to lap dancers for their role models. But the revitalisation of glamour modelling has become the symptom of

a wider change in our culture, in which the images and attitudes of soft pornography now come flooding in at young
women from every side of the media: monthly magazines,
weekly magazines, tabloid newspapers, music videos, reality television, and almost every aspect of the internet, from social
networking sites to individual blogs.

University students are just as likely to meet this culture as are
young women in an Essex nightclub. At Loughborough
University in 2007, the student union held a Playboy night –
House Party at the Playboy Mansion – advertised by posters
with drawings of women in Playboy costumes, no faces, with
their legs apart. The club night promised pole-dancing and live
shows and, according to photos posted on students' MySpace
pages, quite a few young women were keen enough to attend
wearing their bunny ears and pink tails, and not much else.
York University's Goodricke College also hosts Playboy nights
and the university is home to a pole-dancing exercise club. A few
years ago I was struck when I received an email from a student
who was complaining about the sexism she felt she encountered
at her university. She had just received a copy of the 2005 college
magazine for Pembroke College, Cambridge, which announced
that it was to 'celebrate 21 years of women at Pembroke
College'. It did so by giving over page 3 of the magazine to
eleven young women posing in their knickers alone on the 'High
Table' in the college hall. Although the articles throughout the
magazine celebrated the fact that women now outnumber men
at Pembroke, and that in 2004 women at Pembroke got more
firsts than men, the message about the way that women should
be seen was unequivocal.[4] Three years later a student magazine
at the same university, *Vivid*, included a picture of a female
undergraduate in nothing but black thong and stockings, posing
with her legs apart on Clare College bridge.[5]

The aesthetic of this kind of modelling has obviously also
affected the ways that women present themselves socially.

Online social networking often foregrounds similar images of young women. One woman I interviewed, Suraya Singh, said to me, 'Of course we all think, I want to be cool, and the answer to that for so many young women seems to be, I know, I'll have a picture of myself in my pants on Facebook.'

It is not easy to understand how the glamour-modelling culture became so acceptable in such a short space of time. Although dissent is now being articulated in some quarters, it is easy for many people in this culture to dismiss such dissent entirely. Before going to Mayhem I had talked to Dave Read, the head of Neon Management, the agency that promotes these club tours and that represents some of the most successful models in this business. 'Do you ever find people saying that glamour modelling is degrading any more?' I asked him, and he snorted with laughter. 'I haven't heard that for I don't know how long. That argument, that, whatever, feminist thing, it doesn't have anything left in it now. You'd really struggle to find anyone who'd say that now.'

A few weeks later I met up with Cara Brett, the model who introduced the show, in a bar in Islington. Sitting at a scrubbed wooden table, she was a diminutive Barbie with long, wispy hair bleached white and a gold aliceband, a low-cut cream sweater over jeans. She had begun doing glamour modelling eight months previously, and with the kind of peachy body and doll face that is wanted by the industry, she is already top of her profession. Less than a year before, she was stuck in her rural home in the Midlands, wondering how on earth she could fulfil her ambition of being famous without having any obvious talents. 'I knew I was going to be famous,' she said, and I asked if she had thought of singing or dancing or acting, but she shrugged. 'I'm not that good at that kind of thing.' But through a friend she met an agent, and very quickly became one of the half-dozen models in the business who make a good living out of this work.

Her kind of work – posing in white stockings or pink thongs

for the *Nuts* Boob Bonanza or Blondes in the Buff special issues – she describes as 'classy'. 'You shouldn't be doing this job if you're uncomfortable with it,' she said. 'I'm getting my boobs out, but so what?' Cara was spending the day with her best friend, Helen Reynolds, who was at university, studying law, in Leeds. 'We're inseparable. She's been on endless shoots with me, I'm always going to see her in hall.' 'It's a laugh, isn't it?' Cara said to Helen at one point, describing what work it is for her to get ready for a night out clubbing – in order to keep up the glamour-model fantasy, her agency provides her with clothes, hair and make-up. 'Fantastic,' Helen agreed.

At one point I turned to Helen to understand more about how she felt about her best friend's work. She was keen to express her support for it. 'Women are now in much more dominant roles in society, and they can say, you know what, I'm doing this for myself. It's something to be proud of,' she said. And how does that make other women feel? I wondered. 'Well, if you're happy with how you look, why shouldn't you be happy with how other women look? Cara chooses to do this work, and it's in a magazine that people choose to buy – you don't have to buy it.'

This emphasis on choice is key. Anyone who would like to criticise this culture that sees women primarily as sexy dolls will find themselves coming up against the constantly repeated mantra of free choice. At one Babes on the Bed club night in Scotland, the club was picketed by a feminist group, and Cara's nose wrinkled with scorn when she described them. 'I had them – I had them outside one of my club nights, in Scotland somewhere. To be honest, I think it's stupid, the feminists coming round, throwing eggs and that, I think they should grow up. The girls that are entering, are entering out of choice, they are not being forced, and so let them.'

When I spoke to other people who have worked to make glamour modelling more acceptable in the mainstream – the magazine editors and television executives who have driven this shift in our culture – I heard much the same views. These powerful figures are, very often, men and women who came of age in the 1980s. That was the time when young women were going on the early Reclaim the Night marches and reading books such as *Pornography: Men Possessing Women*, in which the writer Andrea Dworkin argued that pornography was a form of violence against women. As the launch editor of *Zoo* magazine, Paul Merrill, put it once in an interview: 'I was at Loughborough University when people were trying to ban the *Sun* because of Page 3. They'd recoil if they knew I was now organising competitions to find the sexiest student.'[6] How did people like him make this journey, from being students in university bars discussing why women shouldn't be objectified, to being executives who make their money out of images of women with big breasts wearing thongs?

They have done it, by and large, by arguing, just like Cara and Helen, that the deluge of these images is a symbol of how far we have come rather than how far we still have to go on the road to equality. They too constantly return to the key word: choice. For instance, Phil Hilton was the editor of *Nuts* when it launched. He is politely defensive of the new direction in the culture that has given him such success. 'You can't put old-fashioned sexual politics from another era on to this generation of young women,' he said to me when we met in the Holborn office where he was working on new magazine launches. 'You have to understand how things have changed. This raucous fun-loving working-class culture, this take-me-or-leave-me attitude, it's really taken off. It's the women who are driving this. It's all changed. Once glamour modelling might have been about some fat sinister guy with a cigar tricking young girls into taking their clothes off, but now women are queueing up to do it – they're as drunk and lairy as the guys. Honestly, I think that to people of my age, it's bizarre to see young women being so confident sexually at such an early age – the amount they drink and the sexual confidence they seem to have. This incredible hedonism. Basically these girls see that before marriage and children, these are their golden years – they want to have a whole bunch of adventures. That's their choice.'

This emphasis on choice allows people such as Hilton to side-step any sense of responsibility for the culture they have helped to create. So although Hilton was the editor of *Nuts* as it moved decisively into this semi-pornographic incarnation, he says the move was decided by readers, not by himself. At first the magazine sold a less sexualised culture – it didn't show nipples and it kept the sex talk less explicit. But gradually the editors found they could increase sales by pushing at boundaries, and since this is a world in which value is determined by sales, they went with the tide. 'It's not that I am abdicating responsibility,' he said, 'but it's not for me to judge. I earn my living by trying to understand what people want, and giving that to them. I've given up on judging people.'

It's intriguing that the men who have powerful roles in this culture are so eager to explain that it has in fact been shaped by the choices of others. When I went to talk to the creative director of *Big Brother*, Phil Edgar-Jones, I thought I would hear some recognition about what they did in selling a new kind of ideal to women during their heyday. *Big Brother* was accustomed to choosing a handful of young women from the thousands who auditioned, and made a habit of picking those who were prepared to continue their careers by posing in a particular way for newspapers and magazines. Of the eleven women in *Big Brother 2006* four posed for lads' magazines after leaving the house: Aisleyne Horgan-Wallace, a model who posed topless for *Zoo*, *Nuts* and the *Star*; Grace Adams-Short, a dance teacher who posed topless for *Nuts*; Imogen Thomas, a bar hostess and former beauty queen who posed topless for *Zoo*, and Jennie Corner, a student who posed topless for *Zoo*. There were also

Lea Walker, a pornography model who was said to have the biggest breast implants in the UK, and Nikki Grahame, a woman with smaller breast implants who had been a glamour model and who entered the house dressed as a bunny girl. More than half of them, in other words, made money from having their breasts photographed, while *Celebrity Big Brother* eagerly promoted glamour models as celebrities.

Phil Edgar-Jones, like Phil Hilton, is a man with an unassuming, blokish manner who engaged politely with questioning when I met him. 'Are we reinforcing this trend?' He pondered for a moment. 'I'd prefer to think we are reflecting it. We have open auditions and it's very interesting – most of the women choose Jordan's autobiography as their favourite book.' He professed to be surprised that so many of the women who went into *Big Brother* seemed to end up following the same path. 'The oddest people end up in newspapers in their bikinis. Kitten – who was in *Big Brother 5* – was a complete feminist, or that's how she presented herself – and then came out and was offered money by a newspaper and appeared in a PVC kitten outfit. I didn't see that one coming.' Just like Hilton, Edgar-Jones was reluctant to sound judgemental; choice was once again the operative word. 'If it is a choice between that, and the glamour of that, and the financial rewards of that, and working in Superdrug for the rest of your life, well, kind of, why not,' he said, 'if that's the choice you want to make for yourself?'

Both Hilton and Edgar-Jones are clearly right about one thing. As they say, this culture can no longer be seen as one purely created by men for men. Just as women are freely entering the live show that is the *Nuts* Babes on the Bed competition, and sending in pictures to be used for nothing in the magazines, so women who could work anywhere in the media are choosing to work at men's magazines that sell themselves on the promise of Big Boobs Special or Blondes in the Buff, or to commission reality television programmes that centre on watching women with big breasts in their bikinis. We cannot pretend that this is all about women as victims, when many women are deeply complicit in creating and selling this culture.

These are the kind of women that the American writer Ariel Levy has called Female Chauvinist Pigs[7] – the women who are happy to work alongside men to promote this waxed and thonged image of female sexuality. I was intrigued when I met a woman who works in this world – Terri White, then the deputy editor of *Maxim* magazine, now editor of *Shortlist*. White is a bright, confident woman in her twenties who comes from a working-class Derbyshire background. She first went to work for Phil Hilton as his PA at a shortlived men's magazine called *Later*, and laughed when she remembered the interview. 'Phil was unsure about whether I was the right person for the job,' she said. 'Because I mentioned to him that I had done my dissertation on black feminist theory. He thought I might not be comfortable with what went into the magazine.' Indeed, a young woman with a degree in English literature and feminist theory is not necessarily the person who seems most likely to take to a culture based on the values of soft pornography. Yet for White, men's magazines turned out to be a very comfortable place to work. In order to succeed, she learned to look at women the way that the men who buy the magazine look at women: 'I say, do you think that's sexy, to the men I work with. But I think I've learnt what works for them and what doesn't.'

In many ways Terri White is what I would call a feminist; she wants to make a good career in an area that she enjoys and finds fulfilling, and she is keen to prove herself as good as the men around her. But rather than trying to discover what sexuality might mean in women's terms, she has trained her eye to see women in the way that the readers of men's magazines see them. When I asked White whether she thought that the women who strip for these magazines are being exploited, she bridled. She insisted that the glamour-modelling world respects and celebrates women, and again returned to the theme of free choice. 'We are never misogynistic about the women who model for us. They sell the magazine for us.' And she added, 'I find it really offensive when people say that. It's their choice. A lot of them have huge ambitions, or they just want to be in a magazine. Who are we to judge them?'

This idea that the growth of glamour modelling and its effect on women's ambitions is all down to the operation of free choice seems to have silenced many potential critics. I can certainly understand why it is that many people would like to believe that the changes we have seen in our culture are a marker of women's increased liberation. My first book, *The New Feminism*, argued that feminists should no longer be too anxious about the sexual objectification of women. I believed that we should concentrate on pragmatic advances in terms of economic and political equality and let people behave as they liked in their sexual and private lives. I honestly believed that as women became more equal, any sexism in the culture would easily wither away, that if such objectification remained characteristic of our culture it would apply to men as much as women. But for the last few years, I have been watching this hypersexual culture getting fiercer and stronger, and co-opting the language of choice and liberation, and I realise that I was wrong to be so nonchalant about it ten years ago.

It is time to look again at how free these choices really are. After all, real, material equality still eludes us. Women still do not have the political power, the economic equality or the freedom from violence that they have sought for generations. This means that women and men are still not meeting on equal terms in public life. And the mainstreaming of the sex industry reflects that inequality. It is still women who are dieting or undergoing surgery on their bodies; still women stripping in the clubs while

the men chant and cheer; still women, not men, who believe
that their ability to reach for fame and success will be defined by
how closely they conform to one narrow image of sexuality. If
this is the new sexual liberation, it looks too uncannily like the
old sexism to convince many of us that this is the freedom we
have sought.

Even many of the people who at first seemed so keen to shrug
off criticism of the glamour-modelling industry gradually began
to talk to me about the ways in which the so-called choices
made by women to join this industry were not always very free
or very informed. Cara Brett herself, who on that night in
Southend strutted the stage looking as happy as anyone with the
feast of flesh that she was serving up, could not be sure that
everything was rosy in her world. 'Once a girl who was entering
a competition said to me, do you think this is a dodgy way to get
into the industry, and I said, yes, it is,' she told me. 'Once they
are up there in their skimpy vest top and the thong, I'm there
with the microphone saying to the guys, give us some encouragement, and they're all yelling, and the girls on the bed
basically get naked, they are so desperate.'

This desperation, she thought, too often led to exploitation.
'So many girls do it for nothing,' she said. 'A magazine says, do
a shoot for us, and we won't pay you, but you'll get the publicity. They just do it. If you sell yourself at a low price, then you're
stuck. There are so many, to be honest. If you go into any club,
I guarantee ninety per cent of the girls in there would go, I'm a
glamour model. You get down to the bottom of it and they've
appeared in the *Sport* once.' She curls her lip. 'That paper, it's
filth, get it away from me. The *Sport* is degrading to women. I
wouldn't touch it, I'd run a mile from it. It makes girls look like
cheap sluts.'

And although Cara Brett was so scathing about the feminist
protests in front of the clubs, at one point, suddenly becoming
thoughtful, she unexpectedly echoed their views. Do you think

this is just what women choose to do, I asked. 'No, not really,' she said. 'A lot of girls don't know how to make choices. They think that because one girl's doing it, and everyone's going wild, they should do it. Maybe that will change one day.'

Dave Read, the head of Neon Management, Cara's agency, is an upbeat man, used to selling his business – but he too could not prevent a tone of realism, which even turned to disgust at times, when he talked about what he's seen in his business over the last fifteen years. For him, too, it is clear that these so-called choices are often fuelled more by desperation than liberation. 'There's this desperation, there are so many girls coming through,' he said honestly. 'They churn them through. They don't have to look like a Pirelli calendar, it's this girl-next-door thing – just a sexy girl who puts pictures of herself in her knickers online or in a magazine. You don't even have to pay those girls. You go to Chinawhites any night of the week and you see all these girls milling around, all desperate to bag a footballer and be a glamour model. They come down to London on the strength of one shoot, with stars in their eyes, and they end up up to their ears in debt, pulling pints, lap dancing, prostitution, you name it.'

Other people in the glamour-modelling industry also admit that many of the women who set out into this industry may have few other routes in front of them which they feel will lead to any equivalent success. As Phil Hilton said to me at one point: 'In reality, if you're a young working-class woman from the provinces who sends your picture into these magazines, you're not likely to become incredibly successful. It's like the young working-class guys who all want to be professional footballers – these are unlikely ambitions. But what I'm very reluctant to do is to judge other people's ambitions and choices very differently from how they would judge themselves.' He recognised that he is often talking about choices that are already restricted, but he didn't see that as the magazine's problem. 'Let's be realistic, and take an honest class perspective here – are you going to say to those girls, why do you want to be Jordan – why don't you want to be a cabinet minister?'

Although Hilton may have said this as a throwaway remark, I think it is telling. The mainstreaming of the sex industry has coincided with a point in history when there is much less social mobility than in previous generations. No wonder, then, if the ideal that the sex industry pushes – that status can be won by any woman if she is prepared to flaunt her body – is now finding fertile ground among many young women who, as Phil Hilton says, would never imagine a career in, say, politics.

That's not to say that everyone who has chosen to go into glamour modelling is being exploited or disappointed. On the contrary, this kind of sexual display clearly does deliver a true charge of excitement and energy to many women who participate. Some women in this industry make a point of emphasising that they have freely chosen the work. Jodie Marsh, for instance, a glamour model and star of reality-television programmes, has drawn attention to her good A-level results and that she could have been a lawyer if she hadn't chosen to strip instead. And clearly many other women who have not had to clamber up through the glamour-modelling industry itself may enjoy taking on some of its attitudes and poses, whether that means singers such as Rachel Stevens or Alesha Dixon posing in underwear for men's magazines, or actors such as Maggie Gyllenhaal modelling in handcuffs and black satin underwear for lingerie manufacturer Agent Provocateur, or women with many other options ahead of them, such as the Cambridge undergraduates, being photographed in glamour-model style for student magazines.

Yet those young women who long for the club competition or the online glamour shot to bring them fame and fortune are likely to find that the huge, beckoning influence of the glamour-modelling industry promises much but, as people such as Phil Hilton, Dave Read and Cara Brett admitted, delivers little. And although women may find themselves individually drawn to this work, the overall effect of the growth of glamour modelling is to de-individualise the women involved, whether they are university students or girls in an Essex nightclub. *Nuts* runs a section on its website called 'Assess my breasts', where people can upload pictures of their own breasts or others' – with no faces – and viewers hit the button, assessing them with marks up to ten. Once the magazine produced a poster to go with the website. Even Terri White, who can see nothing wrong with her career in assessing women's bodies through the lens of the boys who want to reduce women to the size of their breasts, was brought up short when she saw the poster. 'It was . . .' she struggled to put it into words, 'all these rows of breasts without faces – it was so . . . depersonalising.'

The effect of these choices, when we look across society, is now to reduce rather than increase women's freedom. And it is not just the women who are directly involved who find their individuality threatened by the glamour-modelling industry. The marketplace is taking up and reinforcing certain behaviour in a way that can make it hard for many young women to find the space where other views of female sexuality and other ways for women to feel powerful are celebrated. By co-opting the language of choice and empowerment, this culture creates smoke and mirrors that prevent many people from seeing just how limiting such so-called choices can be. Many young women now seem to believe that sexual confidence is the only confidence worth having, and that sexual confidence can only be gained if a young woman is ready to conform to the soft-porn image of a tanned, waxed young girl with large breasts ready to strip and pole-dance. Whether sexual confidence can be found in other ways, and whether other kinds of confidence are worth seeking, are themes that this hypersexual culture cannot address. While no one would express unease if there were a few women expressing their sexuality in this style in a society which was also happy to celebrate with similar verve and excitement the myriad other achievements of other women, the constant reinforcement of one type of role model is shrinking and warping the choices on offer to young women.

2: Pole-dancers and prostitutes

When Ellie came to London in 2002, after graduating from a respected university, she was going to be an actor. This in itself felt to her like a rebellious choice, since she came from a middle-class family who had sent her to an academic girls' private school where the expectation was that she would go into a safe profession. Ellie went to lots of auditions, but work was hard to find. She started to become obsessed with her body for the first time in her life, and by eating very little, taking cocaine and going to the gym every day, she achieved the hard and slender look she wanted. But she still wasn't getting the roles. She was temping in office jobs to make ends meet, but she couldn't put her heart into the work and one day her temp agency fired her.

She had just moved into a new flat in north London, the rent was high and she didn't know how to meet the bills. A friend of hers had worked as a lap dancer, and although this woman hadn't said much about the work to her, she had always implied it was pretty straightforward. What's more, there was a lap-dancing club just round the corner from her flat. One day Ellie saw an advertisement for the club in *The Stage*, saying, 'Table dancers wanted, full training given'. So she went for the audition. 'You just had to stand there and hold the pole and take your clothes off,' Ellie remembered. 'I don't think I'd thought it through. I was surprised when I saw what the other girls were wearing – I was just in a skirt and T-shirt and when they asked me to take my clothes off I was like, uh-oh, I'm wearing really bad pants. But they said, shave your pubes, get a fake tan, sort out your nails, dye your hair, pluck your eyebrows, come back next week. So I said OK, and I went and made myself orange. I did it for about six months, every night.'

When I meet Ellie in her shabby bedsit, I can say for sure that if there is a stereotype of what a lap dancer would look like, she doesn't fit that stereotype. She is a fragile-looking young woman with an unassuming manner, who speaks very thoughtfully about her experiences. For her it didn't feel like a big step at first to go into the sex industry. This is because of the way that lap dancing has become an unremarkable part of British urban life in an incredibly short space of time. When lap-dancing clubs started up in the UK in the mid-1990s, they were seen as so sleazy that few people wanted to promote them or be seen in them. Dave Read, who runs Neon Management, which manages the careers of a number of glamour models, remembers, 'When the first lap-dancing club opened, they asked us to send some models along to the opening night, but no one wanted to go – it was so seedy. Now, of course, everyone wants to be associated with that kind of thing.'

From a handful of clubs in the 1990s, there were an estimated three hundred clubs in the UK in 2008.[1] The way that lap-dancing clubs have been classified in licensing laws since 2003 means that such clubs do not have to register under the same regulations as sex shops, but are simply treated in the same way as bars or restaurants. Although this was not a deliberate policy to relax the regulation of the sex industry, but rather an unintended consequence of plans to simplify licensing laws, the effect has been to make it almost impossible for local authorities or concerned residents to do anything to prevent lap-dancing clubs opening. As they have expanded, lap-dancing clubs have become an unexceptional part of many men's social lives, from city workers to men on stag nights. As one online organiser of stag weekends states: 'No stag night would be complete without a lap-dancing club.'[2] Their ubiquity makes possible the kind of scenes that I watched in Mayhem club in Southend, since girls stripping down to their thongs for nothing in one club is seen as so acceptable partly because everyone knows that just down the road women are stripping fully for a few pounds. The Muse lap-dancing club in Southend, near to the Mayhem nightclub, offers 'fully nude dancing' for £10, and a dress code that is unequivo-cal: 'You keep yours on, the girls take theirs off.'[3]

The way that lap-dancing clubs are now seen so much as part of the mainstream has also filtered through to the new popular-ity of pole-dancing. Pole-dancing is usually offered in clubs where girls dance naked for customers, but it is no longer seen as part of a seedy sex industry – rather, it has become seen more as a cheeky part of the entertainment industry and classes in pole-dancing have sprung up throughout the UK. I'm certainly not going to stand in judgement over any individual woman who chooses to learn any kind of dancing, but it is intriguing how young women have chosen to make fashionable a style of danc-ing that is so closely associated with stripping and sex work. While women who are desperate for cash do a pole-dancing show as part of their work in lap-dancing clubs, successful models, singers and actresses do it to show how daring and sen-sual they are. For instance, Kate Moss did a pole-dance in a video for White Stripes, and the Spice Girls went to a Soho club to learn how to pole-dance for their 2007 comeback tour. As quoted in the *Sun*, a source said, 'The girls all agreed that a pole-dancing section in the show would be fabulous and sexy. And they wanted to get some proper lessons from professional dancers. They chose the Soho Revue Bar with all its fabulous kitsch decor and they liked the idea of something a bit seedy.'[4] Similarly, the Sugababes have been praised in the tabloids for participating in the dance culture associated with sex clubs: 'The Sugababes nipped into a nude lap dancing bar this week – then kicked off their shoes for a go on the poles. The girls got hot and steamy at Boutique gentlemen's club following their after-show party at Manchester's Red Rooms. And it seems the girls are big exotic dancing fans. Gorgeous Keisha Buchanan told a fellow clubber she had blown thousands of pounds in a lap dancing club in Atlanta in the US.'[5]

As we see from these examples, some women are using the dancing associated with 'seedy' clubs to enhance their sexiness in the public eye, while others boast about taking the behaviour of the lap-dancing club into their private lives. The actress Emilia Fox, who has starred in Jane Austen adaptations, said in 2008, 'I've mastered the art of removing my knickers. I wanted to know exactly how to do it in the most provocative way possible so I took striptease lessons. You can't just pull off a pair of knickers. That's not sexy. You have to take off your knickers in such a way as to get every man in the room watching you. You do it slowly. Carefully. You hook your thumbs into the top of your knickers and start to slide up and down, then down a bit more. It's the stepping out of them that is the real triumph. It's like a dance. One leg first, then the other, effortless but naughty. It's something every woman should learn how to do. It's amazing how much confidence you get, how good you can feel about your own body. My husband paid for my lessons. I think he was thrilled that he was getting a wife who wanted to know how to do these things.'[6] Obviously there is nothing unusual about a woman stripping for her partner. But it is notable that for this woman the idea is to perform to her own husband as though she were performing to a room full of men with whom she had no relationship. Clearly, the new acceptability of lap-dancing clubs is having an impact both on women's public and their private lives.

While stripping has become more mainstream through the rise of lap-dancing clubs, there are also much more upmarket strip shows, including burlesque, which cater to a more middle-class audience. The close association of burlesque and stripping is a phenomenon of recent decades – once upon a time burlesque simply meant a comedy show that parodied high art. But now performers such as Dita von Teese and Immodesty Blaize have helped to create an inescapably sexy view of burlesque, even if it doesn't have to involve full nudity. While lap dancing is generally seen as pretty seedy, great claims are made for burlesque as art. The art often seems to centre simply on the use of vintage accessories, such as feathered fans and nipple tassels, huge martini glasses and corsets. But as burlesque dancers can come in various shapes and sizes, and can wear more unusual costumes and construct more complicated narratives around the striptease act, burlesque is often seen as a truly creative way for women to take their clothes off.

No wonder, then, that this is where the undressing-as-empowerment rhetoric really seems to come into its own. Indeed, the word empowerment rarely seems to be far away when burlesque dancers talk about their work. Immodesty Blaize has said: 'I find burlesque empowering because instead of all being told we have to be one type, showgirls all have individual characters and body shapes.'[7] Michelle Baldwin, who performs as Vivienne VaVoom, has said, 'Our performances, persona, costumes, all of it comes from us. Before, women were given their persona and even their stage names by men. This time women are in control of their own image and that's empowering.'[8] When former Spice Girl Mel B starred in a burlesque show, her role was described by promoters as a 'bold, sexy icon of female empowerment'.[9] Such a view of burlesque can be very attractive even to feminists.

Laurie Penny is a writer who was attracted by the idea of

trying this kind of stripping as part of a creative stage act when she started studying English at Oxford University in 2005. Penny had identified herself as a feminist since she was ten years old – since she read Germaine Greer's *The Whole Woman*, she told me. But she had been severely anorexic in her teens – so severe that she was hospitalised – and was still looking for a way to feel positive about her body. She joined a burlesque group that was run by two male students, and at first she found that displaying her body on stage felt both powerful and fun. 'To be honest, people yelling for you to take your clothes off does sometimes feel positive,' she told me when we met. 'We were all young, amateur performers and trying out different ways of playing with our sexuality. To have that appreciated by men and women in the audience can make you feel powerful. It's the one kind of power that is sanctioned for women – the power to look sexy, to draw attention to your sexiness – and it can feel very good to succeed on that ground.'

But gradually Laurie found that far from liberating her, the structure of the burlesque acts began to feel restrictive. She began to realise that the audience's reactions made her deeply uncomfortable. Once she was at the Edinburgh Festival and one of the acts was a Little Bo Peep number in which she, as Bo Peep, ended up in nipple tassels and a sheep's tail. 'After the show some guys came backstage, shouting, "Where's Miss Bo Peep, she's really hot," and I realised I just didn't like the way they were seeing me. It felt creepy. Another time when I was doing a ball in Oxford and the audience just saw it as a strip show, they were shouting "Get them off" through my act, and I felt absolutely awful. Afterwards I got incredibly drunk.' As time went on, the creative, comic acts in the show diminished and the stripping increased. 'That's what they wanted to see. It drew in audiences. But it just began to feel so limiting to me. Even if this power to command attention through stripping can be enjoyed by women, it is such a circumscribed sort of power.

In the end it felt more like we were serving up misogyny with a tasteful package of feathers.'

If burlesque keeps falling back into the same old patterns as classic striptease, lap dancing is even more obviously problematic for women who take part. Ellie, the young woman who went into lap dancing, at first believed what the culture around us suggests, that lap dancing can be sexy and even empowering for women, so the reality she encountered came as a shock to her. 'I was aware that I hated it from the start,' Ellie said, 'but I didn't really reflect on it. As soon I started to reflect on what I was doing, I left. I don't think that my feeling of hating it is that unusual. For all the we-love-it, it's-empowering talk, I think that most women who do it don't feel anything positive about it. You just feel you can't make money any other way, that the most important thing about you is the fact that you are a sexual object, and that's what men want, and that's all you are.' Her friend who had also worked in a lap-dancing club was not supportive of her doing it, but to this day they have never talked honestly with one another about the work. 'I think that people who have done it have something very big invested in pretending that it is all right, because to say anything else is embarrassing,' Ellie says thoughtfully. 'The reality is so not what the perception of it is. If you say it's really degrading, and you did that, it says so much about you, or it feels as if it does. But it is degrading.'

The structure of the club Ellie found exploitative to the very core. The women didn't get paid unless they made money directly from the customers, and they would pay the club to be there, so there were nights when Ellie actually went home with less money than she started with. She would turn up to the club and just hope it would be busy, but at times there would be ten women to every man. 'You'd all be sitting around, drinking, and a man would come in and everyone was like, ooohhhh, a man, but you had to wait till he'd ordered a drink, and then the woman nearest to him would go over. You'd have inane and boring chat – which was all about you trying to get him to ask you to do a dance.' What the women were after, Ellie explained, was to talk the man into sitting with them for an hour for £250, which included as many dances as he wanted, or to give him individual dances for £20. And each woman also had to go up to do a pole-dance at least once a night, sometimes more. 'I never did it sober,' Ellie said sadly.

Ellie never felt in danger in the club, but she constantly felt degraded. 'It made me really begin to hate, or despise, the men who came in – that they'd pay money for this, this transaction, and it really isn't sexy. There is a lot of touching that goes on – it becomes a part of what you do, to get more money. It's a sales technique, and the more you put out, the more you get.' I ask her to explain this a little more, because obviously the ostensible code for lap-dancing clubs is that no touching should go on. 'That's right,' she says, 'the culture is that all the men know they aren't allowed to touch, but the game is that you go OK then, just for you, you can do it – and so they feel special.' What struck Ellie is that although being touched on her breasts or genitals was clearly sex work, the lap-dancing club was masquerading as something more innocent than that, and so men who would never think of going to a prostitute would go to a lap-dancing club. 'It's the same as going to a prostitute,' she says, 'but they wouldn't think of it like that. They just think, it's what lads do, and their girlfriends think it's OK, and society thinks it's a bit of fun, a bit of cheeky fun. And it isn't. But because everyone thinks it is, how can they see it isn't?'

It has now been shown over and over again that, as Ellie says, many lap-dancing clubs do not keep to the purported rule of no touching.[10] And it has become increasingly clear that some lap-dancing clubs are straightforward routes to prostitution. For instance, in an investigation for one *Dispatches* programme in 2008 the reporter was offered sex in more than one lap-dancing club. The very presence of lap-dancing clubs in the high street

also appears to have negative effects on women in the local communities. A report by the Lilith Project, an organisation that
works against violence against women, looked at lap dancing in
Camden Town, north London, and found that in the three years
after the opening of four large lap-dancing clubs in the area, incidents of rape and sexual assaults rose in the area.[11]

The fact that lap-dancing clubs have been associated with
prostitution and sexual assault means that this shift in our culture has not gone quite unopposed. There have been protests
against the opening of lap-dancing clubs in various areas, and
campaigners, particularly the organisation OBJECT, have now
forced a concession from the government so that, at the time of
writing, new and proposed lap-dancing clubs will soon be reclas-
sified as 'sex encounter venues'. This will allow local people to
have a greater say over whether clubs can open in that area, and
probably result in a reduction in the numbers of such clubs in
coming years. But even so, it will now be extremely difficult to
take the ripple effects of the fashion for lap dancing out of our
culture. The expansion of these clubs throughout many town
centres and their increasing acceptability among men of all ages
and occupations have changed cultural attitudes to the objectification of women. When the journalist Catherine Bennett saw
an advertisement for a lap-dancing club, 'a heap of predominantly naked women' glued to a hoarding outside a sixth-form
college, she complained to the Advertising Standards Authority,
whose guidelines state that 'ads must not prejudice respect for
human dignity'. The ASA did not uphold the complaints, and
stated that 'in the context of an ad for a table-dancing club, the
image was unlikely to be seen as unduly explicit or overly
provocative.'[12] Even if the growth in lap-dancing clubs is now
rolled back, it seems that the explosion of these strip clubs on
the high street has normalised the sex industry in a way that previously would have been unthinkable.

For individual women who have found themselves seduced by

the idea that working in a lap-dancing club is straightforward and even liberating work, the effects can go deep. Ellie discovered that the whole set-up was the opposite of empowering. 'You are totally and utterly pleasing – that's the game, to be impressed by them. It's not necessarily the best-looking women who do the best, but it's about how much you can convince them that they have the power.' And although Ellie stopped lap dancing a couple of years ago, she hasn't shrugged off its impact. 'You get all this positive affirmation about your appearance, of a totally superficial nature,' she said, 'and in a way that feels good. But it's affirmation of something I already believed, that I am an object, and now I will probably always struggle to see myself sexually in any other way.'

When I ask Ellie how she feels when she hears people say that lap dancing or glamour modelling are free choices made by women and therefore beyond criticism, she responds thoughtfully. After all, she knows that she was not forced into this work, and she worked alongside other women who were students or looking to move forwards in other occupations, whom she wouldn't want to paint purely as victims. 'I don't wish to identify myself as a victim,' she said. 'I did make a choice. It was a self-destructive, damaging choice, like taking drugs, but nobody forced me. At the end of the day I was lucky, I'm well educated, I'm from a middle-class background, and deep down I do fundamentally know I can do something else, that I will do other things.' But she can see that other women's choices are not necessarily as free. 'I do feel angry that women who could do other things, who are bright and intelligent and driven, but not as well educated, live in a culture now that encourages them to think that this is the best thing they can do, that makes them want to aspire to this, and says this is all you are worth.' When Ellie went for her audition at the club, she met two sisters who wanted to be glamour models. 'Their dad had dropped them off for the audition, and they were doing it hoping it would help them into glamour modelling. It was the only route they could see towards wealth, their only opportunity.'

Ellie feels that dissent is being muffled by the identification of sexual liberation with this hypersexual culture. 'Now, women get told they are prudes if they say they don't want their boyfriend to go to a club where he gets to stick his fingers in someone else's vagina, or if they say they don't want to watch porn with their boyfriend. But being sexually liberated . . .' Ellie paused for a while as she thought about it. 'Well, I don't think it means that we have to enjoy and accept the forms of sexual entertainment that were invented by men for their own pleasure.' Above all, Ellie feels strongly that the rhetoric we hear now is far from the reality of what goes on in the sex industry. 'People say it's cool, it's empowering, but I'm not going to put lap dancing on my CV, I don't feel comfortable telling most people about it. I think women need to start speaking up about this, being a bit more intelligent about these things. We hear a lot about choice or liberation, but it just isn't equal – you know, you just look at the lap-dancing club, and it says so much about our culture. The men in there are respectable, they are in suits, they have bank accounts, the women are not respectable, they are naked, they have debts.'

Stripping in various styles is not the only element of the sex industry that has become far more acceptable in recent years. Prostitution has also moved from the margins to the mainstream of our culture in a development that one can track in the popularity of bestselling memoirs of prostitutes. Although people have been intrigued by fictional and factual memoirs of prostitution for centuries, there is a new and hugely popular genre dealing with prostitution, which presents a striking shift in the way this work is perceived. The genre includes *Diary of a Manhattan Call Girl*, by Tracy Quan, *The Intimate Adventures of a London Call Girl* by Belle de Jour and Miss S's *Confessions of a Working*

Girl.[13] Although we have always had glossy accounts of prostitution in popular culture, the difference between the *Pretty Woman*-style fairytale and current tales is that today we are asked to believe that these are genuinely honest accounts of what it is to sell sex. They have a matter-of-fact tone, and tend to emphasise how very normal the occupation is and how close to any liberated woman's sex life.

These books show how the image of the prostitute has changed radically over the last two hundred years, and how this change has been driven by women as much as by men. Look at the difference between fictional nineteenth-century prostitutes, as described by men, and the prostitutes who now describe their own lives in these bestselling memoirs. Those prostitutes of the past might be either glamorised or degraded, but their experiences were definitively separate from those of other women. There were glorious femmes fatales such as Nana in Emile Zola's eponymous novel, a 'force of nature, a ferment of destruction, unwittingly corrupting and disorganising Paris between her snow-white thighs . . . She alone was left standing, amid the accumulated riches of her mansion, while a host of men lay stricken at her feet . . . her sex arose in a halo of glory and blazed down on her prostrate victims like a rising sun shining down on a field of carnage.'[14] Or there were tragic fallen women, such as Nancy in *Oliver Twist*, who is agonised by the sense of her utter degradation when a virtuous woman tries to save her: '"Lady," cried the girl, sinking on her knees, "dear, sweet, angel lady, you are the first that ever blessed me with such words as these, and if I had heard them years ago, they might have turned me from a life of sin and sorrow; but it is too late, it is too late!"'[15]

The tone of these recent writers' work, in contrast, is utterly nonchalant. For instance, as Miss S, a young woman who worked in a brothel while she was a student, says of her choice of work: 'At least I wasn't getting blind drunk like the rest of the student girls in the dorms and going off with strangers, waking up in strange places, not knowing where they were or how they got there! Hell, I could have just as much fun. I didn't need to get plastered to lose my inhibitions – and I got paid.'[16] While prostitution has always been with us, this casualness about what it means to work in the sex industry is an unexpected development. When a television series was created out of one of the most popular books in this genre, Belle de Jour's *The Intimate Adventures of a London Call Girl*, the series and its promotion showed how prostitution has become so normalised in the last few years. One of the most striking aspects of this series was how little it differed from every other television drama about the lives of young women. Here was a young woman who was smartly dressed, with a circle of chic friends, drinking lattes in cafes and cocktails in hotel bars, having sex with strangers – sometimes good, sometimes weird, sometimes bad – without much emotional engagement. There was little to distinguish it from the groundbreaking American drama about promiscuous single women, *Sex and the City*, or the lesbian equivalent *The L-Word*, or the male equivalent, *Californication*. Rather than being seen as shameful, prostitution can now be seen as an aspirational occupation for a woman. 'My body is a big deal' ran the advertising caption for the television series based on Belle de Jour's book over huge images of the actor, Billie Piper, in underwear.

It would be naive to assume that the promotion of such a view of prostitution in the mainstream media does not have an effect on the real-life behaviour of men and women. One day in 2007 I went to visit a woman I'll call Angela, who has been working as a prostitute for four years. Although in some ways Angela was quite formal, and uneasy about sharing the details of her life, from time to time her rage would burst out in a torrent of words. In the sitting room of her chilly, scrupulously clean flat in Middlesex, where there were no comfortable chairs, but where there was a metal pole running floor to ceiling with a pair of patent high heels next to it, she explained to me how she had come to this point.

She first began to think about charging for sex when her marriage broke down. As a woman in her thirties who had not dated for a long time, she was eager to look for new experiences. 'When we separated I needed to find my way again,' she said, frowning a little. She realised that finding one's way as a single woman, in our society, seemed to be associated with having a lot of sex. Her friends said to her that she should go out, have a good time, find a man and have sex, and she began to use internet chatrooms to meet men. When she met up with them, she found that the norm was that 'they would expect me to just get on with it, in the name of sexual liberation and fun'. These experiences in the new world of unemotional sex surprised Angela, as things had changed so much since before her marriage. 'When I had had relationships with men in the past, I have to say that they were usually equal and pleasurable experiences. There wasn't the surround sound, the cultural imperative that it was all about sex, only about sex. What men expect you to do has really changed – anal sex, threesomes, even when you've just met them.' But at first Angela did not question what she was experiencing. 'I believed what everyone said, that all this promiscuous sex was so empowering.'

Angela was intrigued by this new view of feminine sexuality, and how it intersected with the values of the sex industry. 'I was interested in pole-dancing. I went to a class. At the school, the teacher would say, we'll keep the sleaze out of it, but then she'd say, this is what a stripper would do, this is how she would do it. I was thinking of becoming a dancer myself. A male friend of mine went quite often to a pole-dancing club and told me he thought I'd enjoy it. I was still thinking along the lines that it's hot shit that I'm such a woman that I can do all this.'

As she went on having sex with men without much emotional engagement, Angela thought at first that it would not be a huge step to begin charging for sex. Since none of the men she met wanted a relationship, she felt that they could give her something in exchange. She was on her own, and needed the money. Although she is well educated, with a degree from an American university, she had married young and had relied financially on her husband for years. Because she had been out of the job market for so long, she found it difficult to get back into work that was decently paid, and on top of that she was experiencing health problems that made it hard for her to hold down a full-time job. 'I was pretty desperate to find a way to survive, to be honest. It dawned on me that I could get paid for this. I thought that it would be fun – I remember seeing a documentary on television about kids of rich Hollywood stars and there was one girl who said sometimes she went down to the Sunset Strip and got paid for sex as a bit of fun. I thought, OK, there's no harm in it. When I went into it, I thought it would be easy. That's what you're asked to believe, isn't it? I thought, OK, if this is empowering, let's suck it and see.'

The matter-of-fact way that some women enter prostitution is also connected to the way that many men are now much more open about buying sex. Many men in the public eye talk easily about their decisions to visit prostitutes. For instance, in his autobiography the comedian and television presenter Russell Brand described how he saw buying sex from prostitutes as a sign of normal sexual maturing. He was taken to Thailand by his father when he was seventeen. 'In the course of that holiday, I fucked loads more prostitutes, always got a hard-on, never wore a condom, and never fell in love. In Bangkok when bar girls in Pat-Pong left their posts to follow me down the street, cooing and touching my hair, I felt that I had my dad's unequivocal approval. When I came back from Thailand, I was much more comfortable around women – sure in the knowledge that I had "come back a man". Some of the attributes of a man included, "I have now had a prostitute stick her finger up my arse while sucking my cock" . . . After that, I started to get a bit more confident about sex.'[17] Brand visits a Greek strip bar which is a 'misogynistic den of iniquity' and encourages his friends to join him. 'I was wanking and drinking and touching, it was disgusting . . . I jostled a few of the others into giving it a go.' For him, there is nothing degrading or secret about buying sex; quite the opposite, it is a straightforward part of his holiday activities. And although this may have always been the case for a certain number of men, what is new is the casual way that he puts this view into the public domain, without fear of censure.

Although the tabloid media still tend to write in a disapproving tone about men who visit lap-dancing clubs or buy sex from prostitutes, their constant return to this theme makes it seem an almost inescapable part of young male behaviour. These activities are associated with celebrities; men such as the footballer Wayne Rooney, and the television presenters Jamie Theakston and Angus Deayton. These men had to go through a process of being shamed and repenting when they were found to have visited prostitutes, but the reports of their behaviour often suggested that it was seen as normal in their circles to buy sex. This behaviour is also seen as an accepted part of life among men who are not celebrities, who are just like their readers. For instance, in one recent report in the *Sun*, a prostitute talked about how she had felt used and abused by the men who came into the brothel, but alongside her words ran an interview with a man who had bought sex himself on a stag night. 'Mutual friends had been to Riga in Latvia months previously and loved it. They said it was cheap and more importantly that the girls, including the prostitutes, were gorgeous. . . . No one said it but we were planning on having sex when we got over there. . . . I reasoned it was no different to a one-night stand – except I was paying her. The sex was protected and she seemed to be enjoying herself. . . . I read about sex trafficking in the papers but it didn't cross my mind when we were over there. We were out to have a good time and didn't force the girls into anything they didn't want to do.'[18]

The internet has been particularly useful in allowing men to believe they need not feel ashamed about buying sex from prostitutes. There are places on the internet where reviewing sex for sale is taken as naturally as reviewing books on Amazon. On these sites, men can discuss without hesitation how to satisfy their various tastes for larger, or older, or younger, or smaller women and where to find, say, a 'girlfriend experience' – a prostitute who will kiss and give oral sex without a condom.

Some research suggests that this casual attitude to shopping for sex has now become very widespread. One man recently told researchers in London, 'It's just like going to Tesco's,' and another said, 'I just think it's like we live in a consumer society. And I think that's become a bit of a commodity now, really . . . just the whole sex thing. Because the internet's there and magazines are there and you've got images all the time.'[19] Statistics suggest that such developments are part of a wider cultural shift. A survey of 11,000 British adults carried out in 1990 and 2000 found that the number of men who admitted paying for sex rose in that period from one in twenty to nearly one in ten men. The men most likely to pay for sex were single, living in London and aged between twenty-five and thirty-four.[20] The author of the report, Dr Helen Ward, linked the phenomenon to the general mainstreaming of the sex industry, saying that among the reasons why more men admitted paying for sex was that, 'There has been a more liberal attitude towards commercial sex and increasing commercialisation of sex. Lads magazines are bombarded with images.'[21] It's easy to see her point. When I accessed the report on this on the *Guardian* website, I found that under 'related links' I was directed to a site called 'They have to pay for it', which turned out to be advertising 'hardcore videos' and 'free porn'.[22]

This cultural shift which has made prostitution more acceptable has, in some places, been seen as an advance for women. This is understandable. There are sex workers who insist that they have chosen the work they do and that they would like to be given the rights and protections that any other workers enjoy. Many people, listening to those arguments, shy away from sounding too judgemental about prostitution in case they are seen as condemning women's choices. But the casual attitude towards prostitution that suggests it can be an aspirational occupation for women glosses over much of the reality of this work.

One thing that the currently fashionable vision of prostitution has to forget is the fact that, to her clients, Belle de Jour is not 'a big deal'. If we were really moving into a strange new world in which men and women had decided they wanted to buy and sell sex rather than give it freely, then we would expect that men who make a habit of buying sex would speak with ordinary respect about the women who sell it to them. One study carried out in Middlesbrough among men arrested for kerb-crawling found that more than three-quarters saw women who sell sex as dirty and inferior.[23] Those internet spaces where prostitutes are discussed may seem welcoming to the men who participate in them, but any woman who eavesdrops on them is likely to form a very different view.

The misogyny in those spaces is ugly, as this selection of reviews – reviews that include contact details for the prostitutes in question – from Punternet will show: 'Tired old haggard whore. Must have been in her 40s and had saggy tits and a saggy gut. Hairy minge as well . . . Shite punt. She was not into being fucked hard. Finished with her wanking me as she said I hurt her too much . . . waste of money.' 'Chose Jessica, and soon as there was some movement with the pecker on went the condom, still quite limp but she carried on with the oral until he was up. Very little words spoken started to suck her nipples and then she let out a shriek: "That hurt – don't like it." Just seemed to go downhill from then, she lay flat on her back, eyes shut, no sound or movement, until I shot my load, then cleaned me up and off she went. She could not even come to say ta ta when I went. Once again another crap Eastern European shag.' 'Small petite blonde. Size 8 32a tits. 18 years. Very good looking with hair extensions. A poor punt indeed! Wouldn't open her legs to give full penetration. I just drilled her until I finished, cleaned up and left.' 'Pretty poor all round, . . . not very talkative and seemed she did not really want to be there. Onto mish – she just lay on her back staring at the ceiling with a blank expression which was very offputting, eventually filling the raincoat I departed.' From the point of view of the men who write these reviews there may be nothing shaming about seeing women's bodies in this way. But if you read their words from the point of view of the women, whose reluctance, pain and unhappiness is being observed from the outside, the effect is traumatic. 'She said I hurt her too much,' says the man. 'She did not really want to be there.' 'That hurt, I don't like it,' cries the woman, but he never stops, he 'drills her' till he finishes.[24]

Beside this sort of casual misogyny, there is the actual violence and abuse that runs, like a forgotten nightmare, through every survey carried out among women who actually sell sex. One study found that two-thirds of prostitutes had been assaulted by clients, but that fewer than a third of these crimes were reported to the police.[25] Other researchers have looked at the violence that forms the backgrounds of many prostitutes, with one study finding that as many as 85 per cent of prostitutes in their samples reported physical abuse in the family, with 45 per cent reporting familial sexual abuse.[26] Yet others have looked at how women become pulled into prostitution at an early age – too early to make any kind of informed choice – with one researcher finding that a majority of prostitutes interviewed had become involved with prostitution before the age of sixteen[27] and another that a majority started before they were seventeen.[28] Researchers have found that all young women in their samples who were involved in prostitution had a problem with alcohol misuse,[29] and that a majority used hard drugs – one study in Merseyside found that 96 per cent of the women working in street prostitution were using heroin and 81 per cent crack cocaine, and that 84 per cent said that their reason for going into prostitution was to get money for drugs.[30]

When apologists for prostitution mention this strand of violence, abuse and addiction that runs through the lives of women who sell sex, they try very hard to separate it from the rest of the industry. At the moment there is great interest in trafficked women; women who are tricked or forced into working in prostitution and who come from abroad. I wouldn't for a moment want to dismiss the exploitation of women who are crossing borders to sell sex, whether from eastern Europe to western Europe, or from any other part of the globe. It is vital that charities and campaigners continue their work to highlight their situations and to assist women who are experiencing such abuse. But we should be careful that the attention we currently pay to trafficked women does not prevent us from seeing the violence experienced by women who have, apparently, chosen the work – who know that when they go and stand on a street corner or turn up to work in a massage parlour they will be expected to sell the use of their mouths and vaginas and hands for men to reach orgasm. Despite the fact that they have not necessarily been forced into this work, these women are not exempt from levels of abuse that make a mockery of the normalisation of prostitution. About six prostitutes are murdered every year in the UK, and the standardised mortality rates for sex workers are six times those seen in the general population.[31]

In 2006, this constant threat of violence was brought home by the news that a serial killer had murdered five women in Ipswich. His victims were all prostitutes aged between nineteen and twenty-nine, women such as Tania Nicol, a teenage heroin addict whose mother had no idea she was working as a prostitute. This

story hit the newspapers with a splash because the killer murdered more than one woman. But such reports of serial killers
can make us forget that even when there is no serial killer on the
streets where they work, women are at risk of violence when
they sell sex. The first time I spent time talking with prostitutes
about their lives was in 1998, when I went to Hull for the
Observer to investigate the story that there might be a serial
killer on the loose after three prostitutes were found dead in the
city within ten months. 'New Ripper fear' and 'Talk on the streets
has been of a serial killer' ran the headlines and stories in newspapers for a few weeks.

But what I found in Hull was that the dismembered body of
25-year-old Natalie Clubb actually had little in common with
the corpses of 29-year-old Samantha Class and 20-year-old
Hayley Morgan, all found within a few months of one another.
Although they had all died violent deaths, it was not one man
who had murdered them all. The awful truth was that it was just
chance that three prostitutes had been murdered in such a short
space of time in a single city – or, rather, not chance, but the
result of the violence to which women who sell sex are constantly exposed. All the women whom I interviewed in Hull
bore witness to this constant threat, telling me about clients
who had threatened them or beaten them up. Those memoirs of
prostitution that have become mainstream successes tell stories
of a way of life that readers would like to see as totally separate
from this kind of violence and abuse. The writers are prostitutes
who are also, by and large, educated women working in small
brothels and through escort agencies. Yet even these books
cannot sidestep the threat of abuse. And, horribly, the ability to
deal with this abuse, not by challenging or stopping it, but by
accepting and dissociating from it – is seen as success. For
instance, Miss S's *Confessions of a Working Girl* was sold as an
enjoyable account of a prostitute's life, with a pretty pastel cover
showing a young woman in underwear. Yet as soon as you begin

to read it you realise that there is an ugly strand of violence to her work, and that Miss S has to learn to accept this violence in order to continue. In her first shift as a prostitute, she had three clients, one of whom 'forced my head down on him with his hands . . . I gagged time and again' while he shouted 'Suck it, bitch,' and another who 'slapped my breasts until they turned pink' while she was determined not 'to give him any indication that it hurt like hell, as he probably would have got off on it and would have gone on just to spite me.'[32] Gradually you realise that you are reading the memoir of a woman who is teaching herself to dissociate herself from her body. On another occasion after an evening's work Miss S's vagina is so damaged that she has to visit a clinic to be stitched up. 'The doc looked up and said I had a lot of small internal tears and, as I was still so swollen, she could not sew them up. The longer one nearer the entrance was a different matter and seemed to be the cause of most of the bleeding.' But Miss S is soon back at work deciding that, 'I would use the red condoms, so the guys wouldn't notice any spots of blood.' Although the reader might feel physically sick after reading these descriptions of sexual violence, Miss S seems to see her ability to allow her own abuse to continue as a sign of her own strength of character.

When I interviewed prostitutes in Hull during that time when women were being murdered, I was shocked by the way that violence was so close to their lives, stalking them as they worked. But it wasn't just the physical trauma they talked about, it was also the psychological trauma of having to accept the dissociation of sex and emotion. I spent a long time talking with a prostitute called Melanie, who had known all the dead women, and who had been working on the streets for three years. What remained with me was the way that she had learned to dissociate from her own experiences to get through the nights. 'The first time I did it I hated myself so much. I threw up and then I got in a bath and scrubbed myself for hours. Now,' she said sadly, 'I just get on

with it. You learn to switch off. You do manage. I can do it now.'
For her, undoubtedly, heroin helped her to switch off. But it
wasn't just the drugs. She had become inured to a situation in
which she had to remove herself from her body rather than listening to her own desires and needs. The ease with which
prostitution is presented as an acceptable choice for women dis-
misses the psychological trauma that actually seems to be not the
occasional, but the inevitable, result of selling sex.

When Angela, the woman who had been tempted into prostitution by the idea that it might be reasonably easy, actually
started to sell sex, she was shocked by what she discovered
about both the physical and the psychological impact of the
work. 'I saw,' she told me unequivocally, 'it's not empowering,
it's very disempowering. It's harmful. It narrows how you value
yourself, how you define yourself. It's very dangerous to define
yourself through the eyes of these men who are buying your
body. I see that now – I wish I could get other women to see it.
I feel as though this hypersexualisation of society – everyone's
falling for it, and more and more young girls think that prostitution is about being Billie Piper, being Belle de Jour, and it just
isn't. It really isn't like that.'

Angela has mainly sold sex through the internet, or through
putting advertisements for 'massage' up in small shops. She has
also worked for an escort agency in London, and in the 'brothel'
context of small flats run by a 'madam'. She has found that
there is always the possibility of actual violence. 'There are a lot
of clients who are respectful but it's all over the spectrum,' she
told me. 'Really younger ones want to experiment, they've seen
stuff on the internet, violence and rape. What was extreme five
years ago is commonplace now. I get enquiries about being tied
up, being gagged, they want to tie you up, they want threesomes. I get the feeling that some of the men get off on the fact
that the woman doesn't want it. Basically you've consented to
being raped sometimes for money.'

62 Living Dolls

When I ask her about physical violence, she pulls down the side of her jeans, and I see a huge bruise on her thigh. 'I went to this guy's house last week, twice – he was all coked up, a bit drunk. He said, I'm in love with you, you're so nice, but there was always this violence underneath, and then all of a sudden he bit my leg – he said it was in the heat of passion. It is scary.' What Angela finds most horrifying about her experiences, though, is not the physical violence but the psychological effect, the way that working as a prostitute forces her to dissociate her feelings from her body. 'Even when they are violent, and you are scared, or when you are just repulsed, or just not into it – you have to act as though you are enjoying it. How can that not damage you? How can that not eat away at your psyche?' Because of the psychological pressure, Angela feels that her ability to form intimate relationships has been damaged for ever. 'To be honest, I don't think I'll be able to have a relationship again. I can't trust men now and I can't see them other than the way they behave to prostitutes.'

The experiences of a prostitute may be discounted by many women as untypical of normal experience, but there is a resonance to Angela's words as she looks at a society that has successfully told many women that there can be something liberating about working in the sex industry. 'If women resist now, and start fighting back and saying, this isn't power, this is slavery, I think we will be crucified,' she told me. 'All this push to get women to buy into porn and its values – it's turning all women into paid or unpaid sex workers. Is it really empowering? If it was, wouldn't it be empowering for all women? Where are the 70-year-old lap dancers? If I hadn't done what I've done, I don't think I'd see it so clearly. But now I see it, I feel like a goldfish fighting a whale. I've come to the conclusion that most of our culture is dedicated to producing an endless conveyor-belt of women who are there for men's sexual convenience.'

3: Girls

The experiences of women who have actually decided to enter the sex industry can obviously be swept to one side by many people, and women who would never take that step might easily view them with disdain or simple incomprehension. Yet even if we put these experiences aside, the rise of a culture in which it is taken for granted that women will be valued primarily for their sexual attractiveness has become inescapable for many young women.

This culture has even affected the lives of very young girls, from the heroines they look up to, to the clothes they wear, the way they see their bodies, and even the toys they play with. The look of a popular brand such as the Bratz dolls exemplifies the new expectation that young girls will be seen as sexy early in their lives. With their pouting lips and over-defined sleepy eyes, their bling and miniskirts and heels, Bratz dolls look like the young women at Mayhem's Babes on the Bed club night. Those who market Bratz would like girls to see these dolls as relevant to their real lives. As Lisa Shapiro, who is in charge of licensing for Bratz in the UK, said in an interview with the *Guardian*: 'We want the girls to live the Bratz life – wear the mascara; use the hair product; send the greeting card. . . . Bratz is about real life. It has to be.'[1]

When *Bratz: the Movie* opened in 2007 I went to my local Odeon, where a stream of girls aged from four to fourteen, in their leggings and miniskirts, ballet pumps and wedge sandals, bunches and straightened hair, were waiting in the foyer. I started talking to Taylay and Bobbijo, two girls aged five and seven, who were dressed in denim miniskirts and silver ballet pumps. Bobbijo has thirteen Bratz dolls, Taylay has five. 'They go out together,' Taylay explained to me. 'And we dress them up in cool clothes.' 'They love shopping,' said Bobbijo. Another group of girls – 14-year-old Joanne and her friend Jade, and Jade's sisters Courtney, seven, and Demi, four – joined us. Courtney was wearing a dark pink T-shirt stating '95 per cent cute. 5 per cent attitude'. What did these girls want to do when they grew up, I wondered. 'I want to be just like the Bratz,' Courtney said. I asked her what that meant. 'I want to be in films. I want to wear great clothes and look like that.' The film showed the Bratz girls shopping, dressing up, flirting and form-ing a pop group to impress other students in their high school. Afterwards most of the girls seemed happy with the film. 'It's like real life,' said Jade, 'as well as being fun.' Only 4-year-old Demi wasn't sure. 'I wanted them to go on an adventure,' she said.

But there aren't many adventures on offer in this part of our culture, in which the main journey for a young girl is expected to lie along her path to winning the admiration of others for her appearance. Despite the limitations of the narrative, I was struck, during the film, to hear a strong rhetoric of independence and self-expression running throughout. The song performed at the film's denouement, 'Express Yourself', tells girls to be independent and think of themselves, because it is 'your time' and 'you are first in line': 'Baby live your life, 'Cause now we're here to remind you, That no one lives life twice . . . just express yourself.'[2]

It is modern feminism that created this rhetoric that foregrounds self-expression. Feminists encouraged women to cease seeing the good woman's life as defined through service to others, as it had been throughout the nineteenth century, and instead encouraged them to focus on their own desires and independence. But that focus on independence and self-expression is now sold back to young women as the narrowest kind of consumerism and self-objectification.

The belief that even young girls will want to 'express themselves' through perfecting their appearance means that even girls as young as eight or nine are being expected to devote energy to dieting, grooming and shopping. The idea that girls should embark on what the American writer Joan Jacobs Brumberg has called 'the body project' at an early age is becoming more and more prevalent. Brumberg is a historian who has looked at the diaries of young girls to see how the idea of self-improvement has changed over the years. She has found that, 'Before World War I, girls rarely mentioned their bodies in terms of strategies for self-improvement or struggles for personal identity. Becoming a better person meant paying *less* attention to the self, giving more assistance to others, and putting more effort into instructive reading or lessons at school.' This meant that when girls in the nineteenth century thought about ways to improve themselves, they would focus on their internal character and how it was reflected in their outward behaviour. 'In 1892, the personal agenda of an adolescent diarist read: "Resolved not to talk about myself or feelings. To think before speaking. To work seriously. To be self restrained in conversation and actions. Not to let my thoughts wander. To be dignified. Interest myself more in others."' A century later, Brumberg found that girls thought very differently about what bettering oneself meant. From one typical diary entry of contemporary girlhood Brumberg quotes,

"'I will try to make myself better in any way I possibly can with the help of my budget and babysitting money. I will lose weight, get new lenses, already got new haircut, good makeup, new clothes and accessories.'"[3]

It's not just in diaries that we can see this shift. Throughout our culture it is constantly suggested that women's journey to self-fulfilment will inevitably lie in perfecting their bodies. Much of the culture around young women centres on the idea of the 'makeover' – from television shows that focus on the transformation, such as *Ladette to Lady, Britain's Next Top Model* or *From Asbo Queen to Beauty Queen*, to magazines that encourage even their primary-school readers to write in for a chance to be remodelled. The imperative is to better oneself not through any intellectual or emotional growth, but through physical remaking. Such media encourage young girls to believe that good looks rather than good works are at the centre of the good life.

What makes these messages particularly attractive to young women is that they constantly return to the language of empowerment and opportunity. So fashion experts tell girls: 'We'll show you how to be the star of your own show,'[4] while diet gurus exhort, 'Embrace yourself, hold your chin up high and remind yourself who is in charge here – you're gonna make it,'[5] and advice books such as *The Girls Book of Glamour* will state, 'Be confident, be gorgeous, be glamorous.'[6] Susie Orbach, the psychoanalyst who wrote the influential book *Fat is a Feminist Issue* in 1978, returned to an exploration of women's relationships with their bodies in her last book, *Bodies*, in 2009. In an interview Orbach described the way that women are encouraged to aspire to physical perfection through a rhetoric of power: 'It's about transforming that sense of feeling powerless into feeling powerful. It transforms the image of you as the victim into thinking, "Oh, this is a real opportunity! I could do it this time!"'[7]

By drawing attention to this phenomenon, I am certainly not saying that narcissism should be rejected altogether by young girls. In the past, feminists have often seen only the negative aspects of the beauty and fashion industries. I still believe that there is great enjoyment in these pursuits, and when I watch my daughter revelling in her dressing-up box, and changing herself from cat to mermaid to warrior princess, I can sympathise utterly with the pleasure that is involved with transforming one's appearance. As she grows up, I'd be very happy to see her continue that pleasure by exploring the joys of fashion and cosmetics. But there is a huge difference between taking pleasure in such pursuits and believing that the only route to confidence and power for a woman lies through constant physical vigilance.

If we were seeing a growth of individualistic, pleasurable engagement in fashion and beauty, then the culture for young girls would not feel so punishing. Surveys have discovered that nearly three-quarters of adolescent girls are dissatisfied with their body shape and more than a third are dieting[8]; one study found that even among 11-year-olds, one in five is trying to lose weight[9]; another study found that most six-year-olds would prefer to be thinner than they are.[10] It is often shocking to see how narrow the physical ideals held up to young women truly are. I have loved magazines since I was a child, starting with *Jackie* and then graduating through *19* and *Elle* to *Vogue*, but when I look at the magazines aimed at young girls now I can see a definite shift. While the magazines I read at school were never feminist tracts, they were not littered, as girls' magazines are now, with page after page of expensively dressed and made-up young girls exposing such skinny, airbrushed bodies. They did not so relentlessly encourage their readers to measure up to a raft of celebrities whose doll-like looks are seen as iconic and whose punishing physical regimes are seen as aspirational. They did not so viciously dissect other women's failures, as those

magazines do that showcase embarrassing snaps of celebrities'
weight gain and poor clothes choices. And they never touched
on plastic surgery as a strategy towards self-perfection.

Plastic surgery has been boosted in recent years by the rise of
stars such as Victoria Beckham or Jordan who are obviously
reliant on the needle and the knife for their transformations and
by the trend for television makeover shows, such as *10 Years
Younger* and *Make Me Beautiful, Please*, which encourage the
view of surgery as an easy fix for self-improvement. These programmes tend to use the language of choice and freedom; as one
of the plastic surgeons who likes to participate in these shows
put it: 'What's wrong with plastic surgery? It's a matter of
choice.'[11] The influence that this culture has on young women is
such that even teenagers now see plastic surgery as an answer to
their anxieties about their bodies. One survey carried out in
2006 found that one in four girls were considering plastic surgery by the age of sixteen.[12]

The power of this body project is clearly tied to the sexualisation of women. Of course, young girls as well as mature
women are sexual beings, and it is great that young girls need no
longer experience the shame and embarrassment that girls felt in
the past about their sexual feelings. But the liberation that feminists once imagined as involving an honest acceptance of girls'
sexuality has now morphed into something altogether less
enabling. Although there is now a genuine and understandable
taboo around the idea of underage sexual activity, there is para-
doxically a real pressure on girls to measure up as sexually
attractive at a young age. The rhetoric of choice may have bur-
geoned in this generation, but in many ways the range of female
characters and role models available for young girls has narrowed. Sexualised images of young women are threatening to
squeeze out other kinds of images of women throughout popular culture.

Even those heroines that are part of a very childish culture have begun to take on a more sexualised look than in the past. For instance, if you compare the image of Disney's Snow White, created in 1937, to Cinderella, created in 1950, you are moving from a young girl in a high-necked dress to Barbified blonde. But then, if you move on to Ariel, created in 1989, and to Jasmine, created in 1992, the type has become much more exaggeratedly sexy. Ariel and Jasmine have obviously made-up faces and skimpy costumes that show a lot of their prominent breasts. When my daughter was six years old, some other very popular figures for her and her friends – heroines whose DVDs were passed around and whose narratives were played out in the play-ground – were the girls of W.I.T.C.H., five schoolgirls who have inner magic powers. This Disney-branded narrative sounds inno-cent enough, and indeed at least the girls get to have real adventures, with magic and drama and strong themes of bravery and comradeship. Yet the moment they take on their magical personas these girls also transform into absurdly sexy images – they sprout breasts and sprint around in crop tops and miniskirts. I have watched the programmes with my daughter and her friends in puzzlement, wondering why these girls have to look like Lara Croft to appeal to six-year-olds.

Many parents might note these sexy heroines but assume that alongside them will still be a wealth of other female characters for our daughters to identify with, and indeed there are alterna-tives available if one seeks them out. But the clever, brave, physically unselfconscious heroines often require some effort to be found and celebrated, while the narrowness of much popular culture is increasingly obvious. For instance, take a look at these statistics, which I found frankly shocking. In the 101 top-gross-ing family films (films rated G in the US, where the research was carried out, the equivalent to our U certificate) from 1990 to 2004, of the over 4,000 characters in these films 75 per cent overall were male, 83 per cent of characters in crowds were male, 83 per cent of narrators were male, and 72 per cent of speaking characters were male. In addition, there was little change from 1990 to 2004. When the American Psychological Association commented on this research, they said, 'This gross under-representation of women or girls in films with family-friendly content reflects a missed opportunity to present a broad spectrum of girls and women in roles that are non-sexualised.'[13] In this context, in which there is such a narrow range of female characters to identify with, the visibility of sexy female heroines – such as the Bratz or the W.I.T.C.H. girls – has a disproportionate impact.

This narrow view of what a woman must look like to be visible is often reinforced by children's television. The female presenters on children's television conform far more now than they did in the past to a limited vision of what is acceptably feminine, as we saw when Zoe Salmon, a 'full-size Barbie' as the feminist Kate Figes put it in 2006, became one of the presenters of *Blue Peter*. And as Kate Figes furiously said, 'Just before Christmas, in the *Blue Peter* panto, she appeared stripped down to a skimpy bra and knickers, twirling provocatively from male presenter to male presenter singing "Material Girl" in a highly suggestive manner. It was a terrible performance and entirely unnecessary. There are countless Christmas pantomime scenarios without turning a female presenter on the BBC's flagship editorial programme for children into a sex symbol. What sort of an example does this set? . . . Salmon is encouraged by the programme editors to present herself as a sexual bimbo.'[14] Although Salmon is an egregious example, the tendency of many presenters on children's television is to conform to a narrow frame of femininity.

Similarly, the DVD and computer games that children play contribute to a world view in which girls must be sexy to be visible. A recent academic analysis of video-game characters from top-selling American gaming magazines showed male characters are more likely than female characters to be portrayed as aggressive – 83 per cent against 62 per cent, and that female characters are far more likely than male characters to be portrayed as sexualised (60 per cent versus 1 per cent) and scantily clad (39 per cent versus 8 per cent).[15] But you don't really have to look at the numbers to pick up on the narrow way that women are portrayed in computer games. As Jess McCabe, a journalist who loves gaming, put it in an article in 2008, 'Anyone who has played video games with any regularity will know that character design is one of those areas where gender stereotypes run riot. Most pre-packaged characters are white, male and buff. Female characters are few and far between, and when they do appear they are usually highly sexualised or passive, or both. Game architects just don't seem to be able to look beyond those pneumatic breasts.'[16]

The sexual content in the imagery produced by the music industry is just as striking. In one recent analysis of popular music videos, researchers found sexual imagery, usually women dancing very sexily, in 84 per cent of the videos. Seventy-one per cent of women in the videos were seen to be wearing provocative clothes or not many clothes, compared to 35 per cent of the men.[17] But again, you don't really need the number-crunching to know what you are looking at when you see music videos on television or the internet. Most public condemnation of the depiction of women in music focuses on hip-hop musicians with their endless images of women in thongs. But what's perhaps more striking is that almost all the female singers that young girls are encouraged to look up to, from Girls Aloud to Britney Spears, trade so heavily on their sexiness, their raunchy costumes and suggestive routines. Whether they are looking at Cheryl Cole in stockings and a corset for her music videos, or Beyoncé in a leather catsuit for a Pepsi advertisement, or Britney Spears in fishnet tights and hotpants, the young girls who are their fans learn quickly that in order to be visible, female musicians will need to fit into a narrow image of female sexuality.

This culture is not just one that young girls are expected to be spectators in; as young as possible, they are expected to present themselves in a similar way. The online social networking that forms an intrinsic part of almost all young women's lives relies on careful self-presentation, and this often conforms to an aesthetic shaped by the semi-pornographic images they find elsewhere in their culture. 'They are all taking photographs of each other,' one mother of a teenager said to me, 'and it's so often this very sexual, provocative type of photography. These 11-, 12-year-old girls – all of a sudden they look like a 16-year-old advertising herself for sex.'

Many brands of clothing sold to young girls allow them to buy into this kind of sexiness, so, for instance, you can purchase a ra-ra miniskirt for an 11-year-old with 'Golddigga' written across her bottom, advertised by a teenage girl in high heels, one hand on hip, pouting at the camera.[18] One of the most striking ways in which brands have exploited the growing acceptability of the sexualisation of young girls is the new use of the Playboy logo, which once was the symbol of the sexually knowing man. Now, it's used to decorate the pencil cases and erasers of young girls who know there is something a little naughty in the brand but are encouraged to buy into its cheeky, marketable sexuality. High-street stores such as W H Smith and Stationery Box have sold the Playboy logo on all sorts of accessories from pencil cases to notebooks. While many parents have felt disconcerted that their daughters are being seduced by a brand that is based on selling pornographic images of women, teenage girls buy into the brand because it suggests something aspirational. 'I like the brand because it's posh,' 14-year-old Tatiana explained to the journalist Rachel Bell. 'It makes you feel like you're worth something.'[19]

There is now some evidence of real anger about this sexualisation of young girls. For instance, we may hear a sudden panic about, say, the placement of a pole for pole-dancing in the 'toys' section of a supermarket website;[20] the marketing of padded bras and saucy knickers to under-tens in one shop,[21] or T-shirts saying 'So many boys, so little time' to girls under six in another;[22] or we might pick up a sudden unease about a photograph of a 15-year-old star, in a sexy half-naked pose for a particular magazine.[23] But although we hear sporadic effusions of concern about what this pervasive sexualisation is doing to young girls, concerted dissent is absent. I think this is because, just as with the sexualisation of women, these developments are often assumed to be the result of choice rather than exploitation. But when it comes to the sexualisation of young girls, the language of choice seems particularly misplaced. For girls who are still trying to find out what behaviour will bring them approval and admiration, the relentless direction of their energies towards their physical allure is likely to narrow rather than enlarge their options.

Some young women are becoming angry that the culture around them values women primarily for their sexual attractiveness, and they are feeling frustrated that their anger is not being more widely heard and supported. Sometimes their voices come through crystal clear. For instance, a young woman called Carly Whiteley emailed me after she read an article in which I criticised lads' magazines. She was seventeen at the time, and this is what she wrote to me: 'I just wanted to say thank you. I was starting to think it was time to give up and sit in silence while my friends put on a porno and grunted about whatever blonde, airbrushed piece of plastic was in *Nuts* this week. What you said gave me back the will not to give in on it all. It's nice to see someone else saying it, makes me feel like less of a prude type oddball, haha. Keep up the good words.'

Carly and I went on talking by email and one day I visited her home town to meet her. It was a slight young woman with a purple streak in her blonde hair and a silver stud in her nose who met me at the train station. We walked through the town to a bar where she knew we could get in even though she is underage. Over an orange juice, she talked softly but with confidence, and let me into the lonely world of a young woman who doesn't enter into the *Nuts* culture in a world that seems to have gone nuts.

Carly has felt bullied since the age of eleven into joining this culture that values women and girls only for their sexual attractiveness. She distinctly remembered the moment when she changed from primary to secondary school, and how she was expected to fit in. 'I remember my first day at secondary school,' she said, with a note of anger. 'All the girls were suddenly in short skirts and make-up and I was still in trousers and a shirt. Immediately, I started getting trouble from boys and girls. Boys used to follow me home and spit in my hair.' She believes that this bullying stemmed from the fact that she wasn't prepared to buy into the raunch culture that had become the norm. 'They didn't say it was because I didn't fit in with that sexual stuff, but I think it isn't even a conscious thought process – it's just if all the other girls are walking around looking like 18-year-olds, in miniskirts and make-up and I don't, then I don't fit in and they just knew that was unacceptable.'

When she was thirteen, Carly's parents moved to Spain, where she went to an international school for a couple of years. She told me that she felt really happy there, because the peer pressure was so much less and she found a close friend for the first time who also didn't want to buy into the hypersexual culture she had known in the UK. But then her parents returned to England and, having discovered that there could be an alternative, Carly was determined not to go back to her previous school, which she felt had got even worse in the time she was away. So she decided to educate herself, at home. At seventeen, Carly started working as a gardener, with the ambition of studying garden design. No doubt she'll do well, but it seems an incredible waste of this girl's adolescence that she had to leave her education because she couldn't bear the peer pressure in the Essex schools.

This pressure on young women like herself is, she thinks, directly created by the magazine, modelling and music industries that are so keen to objectify women. 'It just starts so early,' she said. 'From when I was eleven or twelve I remember going round with my friend to her boyfriend's – he was older than us – and he would be watching porn on his computer. And then we always had stuff like *FHM* at home. But it's everywhere. I mean, if you put on the television every other music video has half-naked women dancing around. It's just like you don't have any choice – you feel that as you grow up you have to start dressing that way, acting that way – that there is no other way to behave.'

'It's just like you don't have any choice.' This, I felt, was the crux of Carly's experience. Although this hypersexual culture is constantly excused by reference to free choice, that is not necessarily how it is experienced by young women. 'Everything is getting used for one end,' Carly told me. 'There used to be this idea that you could look alternative, indie.' Now Carly finds that even if she dresses the way she does – today, in loose combat trousers and a scoop-neck black top, with a little silver stud in her nose, she can't suggest an alternative to anyone. 'I like expressing myself through what I wear. But now – there's this new Trash Society which sends alternative girls to clubs to do pole-dancing shows and everything. They've taken what the alternative scene offered, and made it into just another part of that same old culture. I got chatting to a guy on the train the other day – it was an amazing conversation, we talked about everything, you know, we were talking about life and death. Then I mentioned I was looking for a job, and he said, oh, you should be a Trash Society girl. Like that was a compliment: you should get your boobs out. Is there nothing else that a girl is allowed to do?'

During the hour or two I spend with Carly Whiteley, I am swept along by this one young woman's anger at having to live in this culture. For her, it is clearly a release to be able to let out all the rage she feels. She hardly ever talks with her friends about how she feels about the culture around her. 'I try to keep it hidden,' she said. 'I think my close friends know how I feel but they would find it too much if I expressed it.' Both Carly's sisters have tried glamour modelling, while female friends have participated in porn videos as well as glamour modelling. In other words, she hardly knows any women her own age who have rejected the influence of the hypersexual culture, and she feels that there are no other options around her.

Carly is uncomfortably aware that this pressure to become sexualised now weighs on younger and younger girls. 'I was on a website the other day, dontstayin, and they had this picture of a very young girl, a little girl in her pyjamas, in the middle of a sexy shoot of women in lingerie, pushing her boobs up and holding a gun. It was meant to be ironic, but it just is so shocking, the pressure on young girls. You look at Pussycat Dolls – they are marketed to kids, it's grotesque. I've seen little girls, five, six, singing those songs, they don't realise what they are singing.' Carly's niece was then just four, and already she saw her copying the culture around her. 'She's into make-up, she imitates the women she sees on *The X-Factor*. It's the only ideal that girls have any more.'

While Carly's is just one dissatisfied voice, adults who work with young girls kept echoing similar views when I talked to them. For instance, Rachel Gardner is a youth worker who lives and works in Harrow, north-west London. She is an enthusiastic, articulate young woman in her twenties, fashionably dressed on the day I met her in a bright tunic top over skinny jeans. She sees herself as a feminist. 'The rise of girlpower – I loved all that,' she said. 'I thought it was great fun – but then I began to see another, negative side of it. I was running a disco in the local church for young kids in the 1990s and one day a nine-year-old girl came in, I can remember it vividly, wearing a black miniskirt, a tiny boob-tube-type top and high boots and heavy make-up. I was shocked seeing this nine-year-old girl like this, a child in a woman's outfit, she still had a child's body.' Rachel remembered that when her mother came to pick the child up, she stopped her and talked to her. 'I said, I just want to question what your daughter's wearing because I think it's drawn attention from the boys tonight and I don't think your daughter can handle that. Her mum said, look, I wear this kind of stuff, and I said, yes, but you're an adult. But it hit me, she was totally unaware that her daughter couldn't deal with it in the same way.'

As Rachel suggested, although adult women may well see the hypersexual culture around them as connected to their liberation and empowerment, it is harder to say the same about teenage girls. It is not liberating for girls who are just on the cusp of sexual exploration to be seen solely as sexual objects. In fact, such a culture may be contributing to a reality in which many young women still feel that they are not in control of their first sexual experiences. In 2006 the National Society for the Prevention of Cruelty to Children and the teen magazine *Sugar* carried out a readers' survey which discovered that nearly half of teenage girls surveyed had had their breasts or bottom groped against their wishes. More than half of girls who had experienced unwanted sexual touching had experienced it more than once. These experiences left girls feeling dirty (47 per cent), ashamed or guilty (39 per cent), worried or insecure (36 per cent), angry (34 per cent), powerless (30 per cent) and frightened (27 per cent). It is telling that, two hundred years after the birth of feminism, so many young women find that their early sexual experiences are accompanied by these negative feelings.[24]

Many people who work with schoolchildren bear witness to the fact that sexual bullying is on the rise. Michele Elliott from Kidscape, a UK charity which aims to prevent bullying and child sexual abuse, said recently that there has been a genuine increase in this problem: 'Certainly over the last four or five years on the Kidscape helpline we used to get maybe one or two calls a year about sexual bullying, but now we are getting two or three calls a week,' she said on a BBC documentary in 2009.[25] Some girls clearly feel that the rise in sexual bullying is tied into this culture in which they are seen as sexual objects. I heard from some young women stories like that of Janine, now aged 17, whom I contacted through her mother who had posted her concerns on a parenting website. She told me that boys in her school started bringing pornography into school from about the age of 13 – on mobile phones, or as printouts from computers. She felt they used this as a way to tease and discomfort girls. When I asked what the teachers did about it, she told me, 'They said, don't do that here, they would confiscate it if they saw it. But we never had any discussion about it, it was as though they were just a bit embarrassed about the whole thing which made us more embarrassed. So when boys would touch you or whatever or tease you about your breasts, it wasn't like you were going to go to the teacher about it anyway. You just learned, let's not talk about that here.'

This idea that sexual bullying is often seen as just something that girls have to put up with was confirmed to me by other women working in this field. Hannah White, who runs a project at Womankind Worldwide that seeks to tackle sexual bullying, told me: 'I wouldn't say it was anything new, I think boys have always behaved in this way. But what I would say is that it's been normalised in this generation in a way that makes it very hard to challenge.' She raised to me the fact that technology has enabled the circulation of very sexualised images of young girls. So, for instance, the rise of what is called 'sexting' – circulating sexual images by mobile phone – bears witness to the strange, sad reality that the sexualisation of young girls often becomes the shaming of young girls. As Helen Penn from the Child Exploitation and Protection Centre told the BBC in 2009, 'We are getting more reports of teenagers being bullied, called names and strung up in front of their whole school.'[26]

Such evidence suggests that the sexualisation of young women is taking place in a world in which old imbalances of power still operate, often harshly. In 2009 the NSPCC worked with researchers at the University of Bristol to uncover truly shocking truths about the sexual experiences of young women. In a survey of young people aged 13 to 17, they found that nine out of ten had been in an intimate relationship, and that of these one third of the girls had experienced sexual violence from their partner.[27] Adults who might once have seen the need to protect girls from sexual bullying and assault may be confused by the way that girls themselves can seem to be complicit in their own sexualisation. At a recent trial of three young boys accused of raping two teenage girls, the barrister who was defending the boys suggested that the way that girls wanted to live up to media and fashion images of sexiness had to be taken into account. 'I am afraid cold stark reality is that things are not the way they used to be,' the defending barrister, Sheilagh Davies, said. 'The clothing available for young girls is so provocative. There is pressure on girls from eight to wear these stomach-revealing outfits, skinny jeans worn way down on the hips. They are learning to be sexually attractive, perhaps before their time. It's about, "Let's try it, let's get on with it." I am afraid information in the media tells us that some girls do comply, maybe to gain attention, maybe to gain affection, and go along with it quite willingly.'[28] The confusion between sexual liberation and the sexual objectification of young girls means that there is a danger that young girls might not be seen as in need of protection from unwanted attention and even assaults.

If this early sexualisation of young women was all about their liberation, and they were in control of it, we would not see large numbers of women saying that they regretted their first sexual experiences. But just as the number of girls having sex early has grown, so has the number of girls who look back with regret. Eighty per cent of girls who had sex aged thirteen or fourteen said they regretted it in a survey carried out in 2000, compared to 50 per cent in 1990.[29] Since one in four girls has sex below the age of sixteen, that's a lot of regrets. Rachel Gardner is trying to encourage girls and boys to challenge this reality through a project she has set up called the Romance Academy, where young people get together to try to work through an alternative view of intimacy. 'I don't talk about abstinence,' Gardner says, 'as that has such negative connotations. We talk about delaying sexual experience.' Abstinence does indeed have very negative connotations. Any voices that have challenged our highly sexualised culture in recent times have generally come from the religious right, which means that liberals have become uneasy about joining them.

One of the young women who has experienced the Romance Academy agreed to talk to me, and we met in a cafe in Harrow. Grace is a talkative young woman who first had sex when she was fourteen, with a boyfriend she had been with for three months. Now, at eighteen, she has had a few sexual partners, she won't say exactly how many. She wishes that she hadn't had sex so young and with so many people. 'It's such a part of our culture to have sex that young. Most of my friends were having sex at the same age. The pressure is there because you are confused. You feel like everyone else is. Now, when I look back I think that was young, that was too young, but I didn't understand that I wasn't ready for it.'

Grace felt the pressure from the media around her. 'There is so much talk about sex. In these magazines – what they don't understand is that young girls read women's magazines – it's all thrown at you – top ten tips to good sex, everything's saying you should be doing it – even in the young magazines, there's nothing saying don't do it, just be a teenager with your friends.' But she also experienced sexual bullying from her peers. 'I'd call it sexual bullying now, but I didn't have the words for it at the time. But it is bullying. That's how I lost my virginity, because my boyfriend was going on about it and all his mates, and you feel like well, I should. It's pressurising, some of the things they used to say, it wasn't nice, they make you feel like a piece of meat. Even little comments like, yeah, are you going to get some of that tonight, they don't make you feel good, because you're vulnerable, it hurts you a bit. But because you're younger you don't talk back. You're not really friends with boys at that age, and to boys you're like a sexual object.'

Grace watched similar things happening with other girls around her, and saw that the pressure came from girls as well as boys. 'My friend, she was a very good girl, she wasn't confident with boys and stuff, but she got a boyfriend, and she wasn't ready to lose her virginity, but one of our friends was putting pressure on her, saying, he wants it, you've got to give it to him, you're so frigid, making her feel bad because she wasn't having sex with him. When you're really being strong, you're seen as being weak, like there's something wrong with you.' She feels that the experience of getting support from the Romance Academy has enabled her to find her own voice. 'Now, I'll speak back,' she told me. 'I'll tell them to shut up, I'll stick up for myself, but that's because I'm older and I've had the Romance Academy experience. It made me a lot more confident in the idea that you don't have to be having sex and you can be a strong person even if you're not having sex. But at school I'd be the girlfriend who'd sit there and smile and giggle. I didn't have a voice to say, don't talk about me in that way. I didn't know that there was something wrong with it. I didn't know I could speak up.'

Although the idea of a Romance Academy that encourages young women not to have sex may sound as absurd as the Junior Anti-Sex League in George Orwell's *Nineteen Eighty-Four*, there is clearly a truth here: that girls need renewed leadership from one another or role models, to be encouraged into seeing themselves as valued for more than their sexiness.

This is not just about giving children more and more sex education, as some feminists argue. Knowledge of the nuts and bolts of sex is important, but we also need to give our children the tools to challenge the culture around them. That will need a change not just in factual messages given in a classroom or by an individual parent, but a more widespread questioning of why we are encouraging our daughters to feel that their worth is so bound up with their physical allure at such an early age, and why there are so few alternatives on offer. It may not be easy for feminists to accept that liberal messages have not always been empowering for young women on the cusp of exploring their sexuality, but it does seem that what was once seen as sexual liberation has become, for young girls, more like sexual imprisoning. As Rachel Gardner says, 'Some of the messages of sexual liberation have actually made it harder for young women to find sexual fulfilment. The younger a teenage girl starts having sex, particularly if it's a negative experience, the harder it is for her to find out what it means to be sexual, and the more likely it is that she'll just see herself as an object.'

A world in which such pressure is put on young girls to value themselves only for their sexual attractiveness is not where feminists once thought we would be at the beginning of the twenty-first century. It is tragic to hear a girl such as Carly saying that she feels entirely isolated on this issue. 'Nobody is speaking out about this,' she told me more than once. She is wrong to say that nobody is speaking up about this situation, but it is true that dissent is often muffled and marginalised. Many young women I spoke to felt that any questioning of this hypersexual culture will only be seen as prudishness, since liberation has become so associated with overtly sexualised behaviour. 'If you say you don't like it, you are just saying that you are uptight and unattractive,' Carly told me. 'That's the problem. Nobody is saying that they don't like it so if you do you sound like an old granny – it makes you sound like some old fart saying, oh I don't think you should wear that, dear.' We need not reinvent the wheel here – there is a great history of feminist argument against the sexual objectification of girls. If we could bring such dissent back into the mainstream, it would give strength to those girls who want to find a different path – girls such as Grace or Carly, who said to me, with sadness, 'There aren't any other options. There isn't anyone speaking out against it. You're just a sex object, and then you're a mother, and that's it. There is no alternative culture. There's no voice saying that girls can be anything else or do anything else.'

4: Lovers

One of the primary goals of the second-wave women's movement of the 1970s was to enable women to feel free to enjoy sex without being held back by traditional social expectations. After *The Female Eunuch* was published in 1970, Germaine Greer said to a journalist from the *New York Times*, 'Women have somehow been separated from their libido, from their faculty of desire, from their sexuality. They've become suspicious about it.'[1] And so Greer attempted to shift women away from the modesty that she felt constrained their natural sexual appetites. This was partly about freeing them from the trap, as she saw it, of monogamy, and encouraging them to move towards a guilt-free promiscuity, which she was certain would deliver more fulfilment. As she wrote in *The Female Eunuch*, 'Possessive love, for all its seductiveness, breaks down personal poise and leaves its victims newly vulnerable . . . Lovers who are free to go when they are restless always come back.'[2] And as she put it when talking about her own sexual relationships, she was proud to see herself as a woman who was not possessive. 'Supergroupies don't have to hang around hotel corridors. When you are one, as

I have been, you get invited backstage. I think groupies are important because they demystify sex; they accept it as physical, and they aren't possessive about their conquests.'[3, 4]

Even if not all writers who are associated with feminism's second wave had quite Greer's cheerleading tone when talking about promiscuity, this was a time when women who had more than one sexual partner were often seen as necessarily more honest and braver than those who chose monogamy. Marriage, which had been sold to so many women for so long as their ultimate ideal, now came under serious questioning. Although there had always been a few independent women who had decided not to follow social pressure to be married, before the 1970s these women had always been successfully marginalised. Now, for the first time, the argument could be heard even in mainstream culture that women could be entirely fulfilled without marriage, and even that women who stayed in marriage had somehow compromised.

This shift towards questioning marriage and monogamy could be seen in magazines, consciousness-raising groups, everyday behaviour and fiction during this period. When Doris Lessing wrote *The Golden Notebook* in 1962, she didn't have the immense optimism of Germaine Greer in *The Female Eunuch* – on the contrary, she communicated a deeply troubled view of sexual relationships. But even then she gave voice to women who were able to state with pride that they had 'not given up and crawled into safety somewhere. Into a safe marriage.'[5] She chronicled their sexual encounters, good and bad, without shame or any attempt to gloss over their reality. Marilyn French's *The Women's Room*, published in 1977, contains a similarly questioning look at married relationships. Although the failure of married monogamy was not to be greeted wholly with joy, it was still seen as a necessary failure. The journey away from bourgeois marriage into freer sexual relationships, even if it was a journey fraught with sadness, was seen as progress.

By questioning monogamy and supporting sexual freedom, the writers associated with the women's movement in the 1960s and 1970s undoubtedly created a real shift in the way that women saw their sexuality. This was a positive shift, in that it allowed women to talk about physical realities and lay claim to their own desires and pleasure. Female sexuality was now discussed with an honesty that had never been seen before, as writers detailed orgasms, masturbation, periods and positions without shame. And alongside this defiant reclaiming of sexual pleasure there was clearly, at that time, a moral charge in the new imperative not to be locked into monogamy. For too long, said the second-wave feminists, and with justification, women had been tricked by romantic ideals into subsuming their own sexual desire into their partner's. They had sunk into marriage instead of claiming pleasure with more than one person. They now needed to learn to take sexual pleasure for themselves and to experiment, and that would necessarily include having sex outside committed relationships.

Feminism is not now always associated with this kind of sexual liberation, as it is often more connected to the thorough-going critique of heterosexuality that was enunciated by some feminists later in the 1970s and 1980s. But feminists who opened out the ideal of freer sexual relationships were part of the whole counterculture of the 1960s and 1970s, and they helped to create a revolution in women's behaviour, one whose effects are still with us.

One day I spent a couple of hours talking to A-level students at a sixth-form college in London. We discussed their ideals for their sexual lives, and I was struck by how definitely they held on to an ideal that few women before the 1960s could possibly have espoused. 'The idea of spending my life with one man, the whole marriage thing, I'm not keen on that,' said Ruby, an articulate young woman with fine features and a tough way of talking, early on in our discussion.

I was faced that day in the sixth-form college with a dozen teenage girls, a mixture of black and white, middle class and working class, British by birth and immigrants. They all, no doubt, had different experiences of love and sex. I do not want to exaggerate the changes in our society by suggesting that all individuals' real lives fall in with the dominant cultural mood. Just as in Jane Austen's time there were women who had sex before marriage and lovers after marriage, so there are women now who hold themselves in readiness for their one true love and seek to remain eternally faithful to him. But just as in Austen's time the promiscuous woman was presented in the dominant culture as marginal and to be condemned, so now a girl who has decided to delay sexual activity until she finds a true emotional commitment can be pushed to the margins and silenced.

Sometimes I felt a range of experience was momentarily apparent; when a girl mentioned that she felt there was too much pressure to have sex, for instance, and another girl chimed in with agreement, 'Yeah, there is pressure – if you're a virgin – and you're at a party, and the college stud muffin is interested, then there's pressure to just do it, just do it.' But it was clear in the group that certain girls' experiences were more approved of and more easily spoken about than others. These dominant experiences belonged above all to three girls; three slender, well-dressed, beautiful white girls whose voices were louder than the others and whose laughter more scornful. 'Mean girls,' I scribbled on my notebook when their laughter silenced the girls who were tentatively describing how they felt pressured into sex too early. Not that they were actually mean, but just like the mean girls in the film of the same name, they were so confident that the other girls in the group seemed subdued beside them. And their sense of certainty clearly arose partly from their sexual self-confidence. While two hundred years ago the girls given the greatest status in a group of unmarried young women would have been those who presented themselves as pure virgins, now the greatest status can be owned by the girls who can boast, as one of these girls did, to having had twenty-two sexual partners – thirteen men and nine women – by the age of eighteen.

When I talked to these three girls afterwards in a cafe, they were easy about telling a stranger quite how uninhibited they were in their happily promiscuous sex lives. Bella, the girl who had had twenty-two sexual partners, was a confident 18-year-old with long, straightened brown hair and bright eyes made brighter with immaculate make-up. She started telling me how she does still sometimes have to prove to men that she really is not looking for love and romance. She told me about how a male friend had come to see her the previous night and got drunk with her. 'Somehow we got on to how much sex I had. He was trying to convince me that I had had a traumatic childhood and that was why I had so much sex. I had to keep saying no, I actually am happy. I like having this much sex. I love it.'

But by and large she felt that her behaviour was accepted by her friends and by the wider culture. Her friend Ruby agreed. 'I don't have boyfriends. I have sex with men, but I wouldn't call them boyfriends,' she said. Is that just how things are now, I asked her curiously, or is that how she wants to run her life? Ruby looked at me with a scornful gaze. 'It's how I want to run my life, basically,' she said, taking another sip of her frappuccino. For girls like these, the romantic ideal that meant so much to previous generations of women, the belief that one day you would find a man who would be the love of your life and you the love of his, has died. 'I did fall in love with my first boyfriend,' said Ruby. 'But it went tits up. It was a load of bollocks.' That was when she was thirteen, but now, at eighteen, these girls are older and wiser.

'We were saying that one week we should go out and try to notch up as many lovers as we can, with the most variety possible – age, gender, jobs, backgrounds . . .' said Ruby. Anna, their

slightly quieter friend, smiled and agreed. 'We should do that.'
Far from feeling isolated by their desire to remain promiscuous,
these girls took heart from the way that the culture around them
reflected and reinforced their behaviour. They liked the sexually
explicit culture in which they moved. 'It means we can talk
about anything we want to when it comes to sex,' said Anna,
'and no one tries to make us feel ashamed or whatever.' They
talked about all the television series and books that reflected this
uncommitted lifestyle back to them. *Sex and the City* was the
first television programme they mentioned with approval. 'You
know that bit when Miranda got an STD and had to ring all the
people she had ever slept with, and she was totting them up and
couldn't believe how many it was – I thought, that's me one
day,' Bella said, smiling. They also mentioned *The L Word*, the
Sex and the City for lesbians, and books such as *Diary of a
Manhattan Call Girl* and *The Intimate Adventures of a London
Call Girl* which chronicle uncommitted and paid-for sex.

For these women, the whole mystique of virginity and first
times has died a death. 'I didn't have an orgasm the first time,'
Ruby remembered, 'but it felt good. Really good. I was the first
person in my group of friends to have sex. It was someone I
really fancied, but wasn't in love with. I knew he was a real slag
and had loads of sex. I really dreaded the idea of a romantic first
time with a boyfriend, you know, that we talked about for a
long time and then it didn't measure up or whatever. I really
didn't want that. I wanted sex. It felt really good. I felt empowered.'

Bella took a while to remember her first time, and then she
smiled: 'It was with a friend of mine, we used to meet up every
summer, it was this camp site I always went to. One summer I
saw him and I thought, wow. We had suddenly grown up – we
were both drinking and smoking. We sat on the beach, we got
drunk, we smoked, it was like, what next. He was only there for
two days.' Did that make her sad, that the first person she had

sex with was only around for two days? 'No, not at all. Another guy I fancied arrived that day.' So you moved on? 'Yeah, exactly. I find it really hard to remember anything about it, to be honest.'

Because they had so successfully subtracted emotion from their sex lives, these young women were perfectly in tune with the culture around them. When I asked them what they thought of the way that magazines published pictures of women purely as objects, Ruby raised her eyebrows and said witheringly, 'What do I think? I think, wow, she's hot. *Or not.*' Similarly, when I asked them if they would ever think of doing something like glamour modelling, pornography or lap dancing if they needed the money, Ruby stepped in again. 'Yes, I would. I wouldn't do it for the money. I don't need an excuse. I would do it for enjoyment. I'd enjoy it.'

For these three girls, the only impediment in their desire to 'run' their sex lives as they wanted was the unfortunate fact that many of the men they met wanted something more. When I asked them, in true *Sex and the City* style, whether they thought that women could have sex like a man, they laughed and decided deliberately to misunderstand me. 'I don't have sex like the men. Men always go soppy on me,' Ruby said, and Bella joined in. 'It's pathetic, they are always talking about love.' 'That's right,' agreed Ruby. 'It's the boys who keep talking about love. They are so emotional and wimpy.' Why is that pathetic, I wondered? 'It makes it difficult for me to run my sex life the way I want,' said Ruby. Bella agreed: 'It just is . . . I met this guy in a pub the other night. We had sex once, and . . . it's pathetic. We're lying there . . . and he says, are you going to sleep with other people? I thought, who are you, why are you asking me this? Obviously I'm having sex with other people. He decided he loved me, he was texting me and phoning me for days. After having sex once! What's that about?'

Isn't it possible he might have felt a real connection? The girls look at me, shaking their heads – that isn't how sex works. 'You don't get so heavy with someone after one night,' says Ruby. 'Yes, for the first three dates or whatever, first month, there are no rules, that's how it works . . . that's the minimum, then you can start talking about whether you want to make it something more.' 'I'm much more attracted to the guys who don't really give a shit,' said Anna. 'God, yeah, there's nothing attractive about a guy who gets all emotional on you,' said Bella.

These women bear witness to a very real cultural shift. The National Survey of Sexual Attitudes and Lifestyles tracks the change between 1990, when the first survey was carried out, and 2000, when the second survey occurred. The average number of partners over a lifetime increased between 1990 and 2000, from 8.6 to 12.7 for men and from 3.7 to 6.5 for women. The average number of partners over the past five years was four for men and two for women. But people under twenty-five had a different pattern of sexual activity: those under twenty-five reported higher numbers of partners in the past five years, with 14.1 per cent of men and 9.2 per cent of women reporting ten or more. The proportion of men and women having more than one part-ner at the same time has also increased. Over 14 per cent of men and 9 per cent of women in 2000 had been in such relationships in the past year, as opposed to 11.4 per cent and 5.4 per cent in 1990. And this proportion was also far higher among younger age groups, with over 20 per cent of 15–24-year-old men and 15 per cent of 15–24-year-old women having concurrent partner-ships in the past year.[6] While self-reporting is a notoriously unreliable way of assessing actual behaviour, what we can see from such surveys – or from the conversations of girls such as Bella and Ruby – is that aspirations have shifted. There has also been a big change in attitudes to one-night stands. In 1990 53 per cent of men and 79 per cent of women considered one-night stands to be wrong. Ten years later only a third of men and half of women held that view. Now, nearly ten years further on, we might wonder if these figures have already fallen by another 30 per cent.

As I talked to Ruby, Bella and Anna, I could see that the attractions of this approach to sexuality are pretty obvious. There is the sex itself, which for these women is neither the scary taboo, nor the uncomfortable duty, that it was for so many women in previous generations, but a reliable, freely chosen source of physical pleasure. And building a carapace around oneself that does not allow too much emotional softness to show is, obviously, part of the sense of empowerment. All three of these young women had learnt, as they saw it, from the vulnerabilities of women of previous generations. 'My father left my mother,' Ruby told me, 'and since then she hasn't really had a relationship. He's had lots of girlfriends. I never want to be in that position. Never.' I believed her; this is a generation of women many of whom have learnt from hearing their mothers cry in the night when their fathers left home, and have resolved never to be so vulnerable.

There are many books, films and television series that reflect the new validation given to a casual attitude to sex. I was intrigued that the media representation of sex that these young women mentioned to me as being most like their sex lives was *Sex and the City*. I had thought its popularity was greater among my peers, thirty- and forty-something women, than among teens who had just started having sex. But it's clear why these girls find it so attractive. Although many other films and novels have foregrounded the experienced, even predatory sexual woman, previously she has tended to be rather lonely and embattled. At the end of the day, Mrs Robinson or Scarlett O'Hara end up alone. And indeed, that was the message of Candace Bushnell's original columns – that women in New York were negotiating a hostile sexual environment in which they were likely to lose out. But the television series changed that, by making these women so popular, with their glittering social lives and close friends, and so beautiful, according to the twenty-first-century ideal of beauty, with their bony bodies and huge designer wardrobes. It was not just that the series allowed sexually frank and sexually experienced women a voice, it was that they made that voice the one that viewers wanted to have; these were the women whose gang you wanted to join. The table where funny, articulate, experienced women were detailing their one-night stands and experiments with bisexuality or group sex was the table that you wanted to be sitting at – not with dull married women or inexperienced girls.

Although most of *Sex and the City*'s heroines were still chasing a committed relationship, there has been a cultural shift towards embracing sex with no emotional commitment, seen in the burst of popularity of sex memoirs by women. While women have written about sex and relationships for generations, what's different about these new books is that they record little or nothing of an emotional journey; they move, typically, through a gamut of experiences from sex toys to threesomes, from orgies to sex with strangers, with extremely detailed records of underwear and positions and physical quirks, but with almost no emotional resonance to each encounter. And yet they are not pornography; they are not written with intent to titillate and communicate fantasies, but in order to present an honest and realistic view of the narrator's sexual experiences.

For instance, *Girl with a One-track Mind*, which started out as a non-fiction blog, was turned into a book in 2006, and became a bestseller. Its pseudonymous author, Abby Lee, who was soon outed as Zoe Margolis, shows herself seeking as varied as possible a menu of sexual encounters, and although she requires these to be mutually respectful, they never seem to arise from any great emotional connection. She includes a number of tips and advice lists that tell us not just how her sex life is, but how she thinks we should all be behaving. These are striking in the way they normalise the separation of sex and emotion. For

instance, the 'Top Ten Guide to One Night Stands – for women'
includes, at number 4: 'Relax, for goodness' sake. It's just sex. It
doesn't have to mean anything', and at number 10: 'If he says,
"We are made for each other" – run.' The adjoining 'Top Ten
Guide to One Night Stands – for men' is almost identical,
together with some strict instructions on not getting too lovey-
dovey, as the north London teenagers would put it. 'Intimacy,'
Zoe Margolis writes stringently, 'can confuse the situation.'[7]

Just as with the teenagers I met in north London, the narrator
explains how she often faces an impediment in running this
uncommitted, easy sex life – and that impediment is the emotional resonance that some men find in sex. For instance, one
day she agrees to have completely anonymous sex with a journalist who is writing an article about having sex with a stranger.
The whole thing is organised through a friend, and a couple of
emails. 'I set out to Ladbroke Grove well armed,' she writes,
'see-through basque, black stockings, tiny g-string, knee-high
boots, condoms and lube.' He opens the door, they immediately
go into his bedroom and take off their clothes. 'I went down on
my knees and sucked his cock. He put a condom on, pushed me
onto my front, slipped his cock into me and began to fuck me
from behind. I was so excited that I came straight away.' After
two more orgasms from her, he loses his erection. 'And pro-
ceeded to tell me that I reminded him of his ex and that he was
too upset to shag any more.' They lie talking for a while, 'not
exactly the aphrodisiac I wanted,' the narrator says scornfully. 'I
did wonder what I was doing there, listening to some guy I
didn't know pour his heart out to me . . . when he should have
been giving me a good rogering.'[8]

Girl with a One-track Mind is not a one-off. Zoe Margolis
was inspired by the blog of Belle de Jour, the anonymous prostitute (who later unmasked herself as Brooke Magnanti) whose
Intimate Adventures of a London Call Girl also became a bestseller when it was published in 2005. That was preceded by

other memoirs of promiscuous sex lives, from *A Round-heeled Woman, my late-life adventures in sex and romance*, by Jane Juska, who was sixty-seven, to *One Hundred Strokes of the Brush before Bed*, by Melissa P, who was sixteen. It has been followed by others, including Wendy Salisbury's *Toyboy Diaries* and Catherine Townsend's *Sleeping Around: Secrets of a Sexual Adventuress*, both published in 2007. These often followed the same pattern as *Girl with a One-track Mind*, which is a pattern of increasingly experimental encounters with little intimacy. Although Catherine Townsend sometimes talks about finding a committed relationship, like the other authors in this genre she is fundamentally unconvinced by the idea: 'Maybe with girls like me, after so many years of à la carte sexual encounters, the thought of a set menu for the rest of our lives makes us panic. Maybe it's not the men we don't trust; maybe we don't trust ourselves to stick to the diet,' she says, or: 'Increasingly, it's women, not men, who are afraid to commit. Though I would love to find someone amazing, on the whole I prefer short love affairs to monogamy. I crave the rush of the first three months.'[9]

This new celebration of promiscuity in our culture exists alongside a continuing attachment to monogamy; we live in a society that still celebrates the big wedding, and the stable family as the place to bring up children. But for women who are not married, having many sexual partners without much emotional commitment is often seen as the most authentic way to behave. What's more, women who celebrate promiscuity are often seen as the true feminists. As one journalist wrote about Zoe Margolis's work: 'Sleeping with whoever you fancy and objectifying men, not just waiting to be objectified. . . . I think she is the voice of third-wave feminism.'[10]

It is wonderful to know that many women, just like many men, do feel that they can now choose their sexual partners and their sexual behaviour with such confidence, and to know that they will not be shamed by old ideas about appropriate feminine

behaviour. You only have to look at societies in which traditional views of honour still operate to know how essential this
change is for women's freedom; it is vital that women who do
not choose monogamy are not made to feel shame. But I do
think it is worth looking again at the equation that is now so frequently made between liberation and promiscuity.

This connection that is often made between the liberated and
the promiscuous lifestyle tells us not only that women can
choose to have uncommitted sex in which both individuals
refuse to invest in emotional closeness, but that they actually
should choose to have sex in this way. Once upon a time many
feminists enunciated the opposite idea; they talked of the idea
that women and men should meet equally in the bedroom,
but rather than seeing this as an equality founded on lack of
feeling, they idealised freely chosen sex characterised by intimacy and emotional connection. Unemotional sex has not been
seen by feminists as a source of power and liberation for very
long.

Western feminism was originally produced by the encounter
of two cultural movements. The first was the Enlightenment of
the eighteenth century, whose leading voices argued that
progress relied above all on reason and science. The second was
Romanticism, whose leading voices at the start of the nineteenth
century emphasised the primacy of emotions and intuition, and
put their faith in the authenticity of an individual's passions
and desires. Mary Wollstonecraft, the founder of modern feminism, wrote her seminal works as the eighteenth century ended
and the nineteenth century began, and she crystallised both the
reason of the Enlightenment and the passion of Romanticism in
her life and work. She produced the influential polemic *A
Vindication of the Rights of Woman*, which argued that it was
by reason that women would progress. Women required the
same education as men, she argued, and should use their
rational faculties to become equal members of society. In that

work Wollstonecraft was scathing about the way that many women saw their lives defined by love. But in her own life Wollstonecraft invested a huge amount of energy and idealism in her romantic relationships. This nearly destroyed her when her first lover left her, and she tried to commit suicide, but she went on to find her soulmate, William Godwin, and to put her faith in her relationship with him. She was condemned during and after her life for choosing to live with men outside marriage, but she did so because she believed in the romantic ideal of total intimacy. She told Godwin that with him she felt that 'the senses are exactly tuned by the rising tenderness of the heart'.[11] She was hardly alone in wanting to move forward women's rights while looking for an authentic, intimate relationship with a man.

At the very beginning of the twentieth century the anarchist Emma Goldman, who at one point went to prison for defending women's rights to contraception, was defiantly in favour of free love even though her position put her beyond the pale of respectable society. She left her husband, and had relationships with a number of men without wanting to be married. But it was free love, not free sex, that she was seeking. As she wrote in her autobiography: 'I have propagated freedom in sex. I have had many men myself. But I loved them; I have never been able to go indiscriminately with men.'[12]

It is even a travesty of much second-wave feminism to suggest that women were then seeking uncommitted promiscuity. Michèle Roberts, the novelist, was a committed feminist from an early age and recently wrote a memoir, *Paper Houses*. In it she discusses what she and her peers were seeking in their emotional lives. 'We believed in passionate sexual love between men and women, as equals,' she wrote nostalgically.[13] Her memoirs detail how difficult that was to achieve, but you never get the sense, as you do with the memoirs of sexually free women today, that it is a journey in which emotional engagement is marginal. When she fell in love with her partner for seventeen years, Jim, she wrote, 'Jim and I were in love. I always compare starting writing a new novel to leaping off the cliff and hoping the angel will swoop down and bear me up on his strong wings, and I think falling in love is similar. You leap into the unknown. And yet you leap at the same time into the known. Your lover knows you, satisfies that deep desire you have to be truly known, and you do the same for him. You discover you are cut out of the same stuff . . . Our minds flowed out and touched. We chose each other. I felt that very deep down we were kin. We were alike. We were soul-mates. We belonged together.'[14] As she said in the same memoir: 'Our belief in free love entailed valuing sex in a way that nowadays, when sex is more commodified and pornogrified than ever, seems perhaps hopelessly romantic.'[15]

The way that absolutely uncommitted sexual encounters are spoken about now suggests that in order to become liberated, a rather cold promiscuity is the order of the day. Some women do not necessarily see this shift as a positive one. Carly Whiteley, the 17-year-old whose words were quoted at length in Chapter Three, is angry that she is growing up in this milieu. 'It's all casual sex now, nobody talks about love,' she said to me. 'I wish I could have a real connection with a man. But there's no courtship any more. That's all dead. It's just immediate. There's no getting to know someone, you're expected just to look someone up and down and make the decision just like that, are you going to have sex or not. There's no time to build up a connection. The idea is that you have sex first, but how are you meant to create the kind of excitement, the emotional connection, after that? I want to have an emotional connection with a man. I want it to be there with the feeling that I am equal to him. I do think I'm as good as a man. But I don't want just this no-strings sex stuff.'

I have heard this kind of sad judgement from many young feminists recently. A woman I'll call Esther, who is twenty-four years old and works in sex education, also feels it is time to challenge this culture in which sex is all performance and no emotional connection. Her desire for something different makes her feel very isolated. 'The group of girls I was friends with at school were all sexually active from a very young age,' she said to me. 'I remember when a friend of mine lost her virginity. It was on a park bench. She was fourteen. There was huge pressure on me to join in with that kind of behaviour, but I didn't. That wasn't what I wanted from sex. That kind of casual relationship isn't right for me, but I was made to feel like a freak right through school and university because of that.' With the young women that Esther works with now, she feels that: 'There is a total detachment from emotion when they talk about sex. I remember one young girl I was working with who told me about how she had lost her virginity in the school field at lunchtime one day. She said she had thought, "The bell's about to go, I may as well do it now or I'll not do it." There was this complete detachment from the act itself and what it means. This isn't rape or sexual abuse, but it isn't a positive experience. In some ways I find it quite disturbing. But people have so normalised this kind of sexual activity – it's totally emotionless. The act itself is no longer about intimacy, it's no longer about communication.'

Esther feels that the culture she sees around her is not a true fulfilment of what feminists fought for in the 1960s. 'People say that this kind of behaviour began in the 1960s, but I'm not sure. I get the feeling that the ideal of liberated sex in the 1960s was about really loving and valuing your body and being proud of it. Now there is a toxic mix, for young girls, of feeling they have to be sexually active but also feeling very critical of their bodies. So they will have lots of sex, but without pleasure or pride.'

Esther herself is not in a relationship and believes that this is partly because of the disjunction between what she is looking for and what the culture around her encourages. 'I just don't want to have a relationship based on this kind of devalued sexual exchange. I know that some of my friends actually think I'm quite extreme in my views, simply because I won't buy into that culture. I'm made to feel isolated. When I read writers from previous times, I feel rather jealous of them. I mean female writers who could explore their sexuality without having to downgrade it. Look at a writer like Anaïs Nin – for the times, she was quite promiscuous, but every sexual encounter was also about emotional communication. When she was with someone she really embraced what they were like physically and emotionally and they did the same to her. I think that's what I'm looking for. It's not because I'm a prude that I don't want casual sex, but I want emotional experience with the sex. I feel that people around me come from a totally different world.'

Esther's point interested me; you may not choose the self-conscious Anaïs Nin, who endlessly dissected her sexual experiences in her detailed journals from the 1930s onwards, as your own heroine, but nevertheless there is something memorable about her emotional engagement in her erotic life. Look at the way that Anaïs Nin insists that every encounter with her lover, Henry Miller, is unique: 'I seize upon the wonder that is brushing by, the wonder, oh, the wonder of my lying under you and I bring it to you, I breathe it around you. Take it. I feel prodigal with my feelings when you love me, feelings so unblunted, so new, Henry, not lost in resemblance to other moments, so much ours, yours, mine, you and I together, not any man or any woman together.'[16] That ease with words such as ecstasy and wonder seems excessive to us now, when set beside the cool, unemotional descriptions of our modern memoirists. In contrast, look at the way that Zoe Margolis explains to men how to approach a one-night stand: 'It's just sex . . . If you want a "Girlfriend Experience", go hire a prostitute.'[17] While for Margolis sexual partners are interchangeable, for Nin her lover is irreplaceable: 'you and I together, not any man or any woman together.' To be sure, in previous generations many women writers had to repress their physical needs and experiences in order to fall in with social conventions, and feminism was needed to release women from that repression. This meant that women clearly needed to break the cage of chastity, but what I heard from some women is that they feel there is now a new cage holding them back from the liberation they sought, a cage in which repression of emotions takes the place of repression of physical needs.

Many young women I spoke to seem to feel that their lives have been impoverished by the devaluation of sex into exchange and performance rather than mutual intimacy. For a long time our culture sustained the ideal that it is not a lowering of the self but a full flowering of the self to become entirely attuned to another's desires and feelings, and that there is a great power, even sanctity, in sex between two individuals who have a deep emotional connection. This new culture of shags and threesomes, orgies and stranger fucks, seems to be replacing the culture in which sex was associated with the flowering of intimacy. Although this is so often associated with liberation, I am not convinced that this is what all feminists were seeking, then or now. I kept hearing a frustration from the young women I interviewed, all the sadder because it is often hidden. As Esther put it, 'I want to be with a man who sees sex as an intense experience, a unity, and people just don't now – sex has become completely devalued.' Or as Rachel Gardner, the youth worker who was quoted in Chapter Three, said to me, 'Feminism is now seen as sexual promiscuity, which is such a narrow view of empowerment. Liberation isn't just about promiscuity. For some women liberation may be about having a new sexual partner every week, but for a lot of women it will be about finding someone to be with for your whole life, growing together over the years, and you never hear about that any more. What liberation means to me is that in any sexual relationship you are cherished, and you cherish.'

5: Pornography

Almost everything that has been discussed here so far is connected, in one way or another, to the new accessibility and expansion of pornography. The huge growth of pornography through the internet is what makes so much of the soft pornography in magazines, newspapers, music and cinema possible; it's hard to object to any of the mainstream aspects of the hypersexual culture, from *Nuts* to lap-dancing clubs, given the great leviathan of obscenity that anyone can access at any time with a couple of clicks of a mouse at a computer. Anyone who wants to put magazines with naked women on the covers back onto the top shelf of newsagents, or to push strip clubs out of town centres, runs up against the fatalism created by the knowledge that the internet has brought all those images and far, far more to everyone's desk.

Many women who would call themselves feminists have come to accept that they are growing up in a world where pornography is ubiquitous and will be part of almost everyone's sexual experiences. Anna Span is the most famous and prolific female porn director in the UK, and she believes that positive effects have arisen for women in the way that pornography has now moved into the mainstream. In her view, this development has encouraged women to be more honest about their own sexuality. When I visited her in her Tunbridge Wells office, I found a matter-of-fact woman in her thirties, who was keen to convince me of the liberating possibilities of pornography. 'Women are exploring their bodies more,' she told me confidently. 'They are learning to orgasm more. Sex shops are now much more female friendly; women can find toys and books and videos that relate to their sexuality.' Span herself decided to start working in pornography when a trip to Soho as a young woman showed her how much there was catering for men's sexuality, and how little for women. She calls herself a 'Nietzschean feminist' for refusing to see herself as a victim of this culture, and instead deciding to join men in producing pornography.

Anna Span's view is no longer seen as that unusual. The mainstream media are often keen to pick up on the voices of women who are positive about pornography – including women who work in pornography. For instance, every Saturday the *Guardian* newspaper publishes a section called Work, which contains advice and tips on different careers. One day in 2007 the main interview was with one Daisy Rock, who spoke about her working hours – 'I don't stop working, except to sleep or go out' – the money she earns, 'anything from £350 to £500' for a scene, adding up to around £64,000 a year, and that the only drawback of the work she does is that 'feature films can be exhausting and repetitive at times . . . much like working on a mainstream movie'.[1] In such an article it seems there could be no better career option for an intelligent, hardworking young woman, than to go into hardcore pornography.

Where pornography is glimpsed in mainstream art forms it now tends to be seen as an unexceptional part of women's as well as men's sex lives. For instance, in one episode of *Sex and the City*, Samantha stars in her own pornographic video of herself having sex with her boyfriend; in Adam Thirlwell's first novel, *Politics*, couples watch pornography together and carefully mimic what they see: 'Into their domestic repertoire, Anjali and Nana had introduced the sexual practice known as fisting . . . They did this, led by Anjali, using tips culled from internet pornography'[2]; in a recent mainstream cinema release, *Zack and Miri Make a Porno*, the hero seduced the heroine by asking her to star in a porn movie with him. While it's quite frequent to see this kind of tolerant reference to pornography in mainstream art, it has become rare to find any condemnation of it.

So we now live in a world in which even many feminists have stopped trying to condemn pornography. This has been a huge turnaround in feminist thought. At one point in the 1980s it seemed that the primary energy of feminists was directed against pornography. The classic feminist critique of pornography saw women only as victims of a male-dominated pornography industry that was based on the degradation of women and encouraged violence against them. As Robin Morgan put it in 1974, 'pornography is the theory, and rape the practice'[3] and as Andrea Dworkin said in 1981, pornography makes men 'increasingly callous to cruelty, to the infliction of pain, to violence against persons, to the humiliation or degradation of persons, to the abuse of women and children'.[4] From the attempts of Dworkin and Catharine MacKinnon, the American lawyer, to legislate against pornography, to the demonstrations by British feminist groups at Soho sex shops,[5] feminists made it known very clearly that they believed pornography was the enemy of liberation.

Yet even at that time there were feminists who dissented from this point of view. These feminists insisted that there was no clear-cut link between pornography and violence against women; although some research suggested that watching pornography encouraged men to hold views that trivialised sexual violence, other research suggested that consuming pornography actually correlated with less aggressive sexual attitudes and behaviour.[6] These feminists said that there was no legislating for sexual desire; what one person saw as arousing and delightful, another might see as exploitative and another as ridiculous.[7] As more feminists with differing views joined the debate, it became clear that the classic feminist critique of pornography had left something very important out: it assumed that women never take any pleasure in pornography. This is clearly wrong. There are intelligent women, choosing and thinking for themselves, who do enjoy watching pornography, and some enjoy making it and acting in it too; we can no longer deny the intense sexual power of pornography for women as well as men.

Now that many women have talked openly about the pleasures of pornography themselves, there is no point trying to return to that classic feminist critique that set all women on one side, and all men on the other side, of pornography. For some feminists, this means that, rather than arguing against the very existence of porn, they are looking more for equality within a world already saturated by pornography. Just as with Anna Span, what we tend to hear from feminists now is not so much a desire to hold back the tide of pornography, as the desire to jump right in. For instance, Charlotte Roche, the German author of the novel *Wetlands*, is a feminist who believes that: 'There is such a nice range for men, they have so much opportunity – porn on the Internet, wanking booths . . . it's a big shame that we don't have that for women.'[8] Or as Zoe Margolis, the author of *Girl with a One-track Mind*, has said, 'If we are to buy in to the sex industry (and let's face it, objectionable as much of it might be, it's not disappearing any time soon) then perhaps it is time women started making demands as consumers, rather than just being the providers.'[9]

I can see why some women are arguing that the way forward

really rests on creating more opportunities for women in pornography, yet I think it is worth looking at why it is that some of us still feel such unease with the situation as it is now. The muffling of dissent about pornography has coincided with a time in which pornography has massively expanded. For a long time I was sceptical about the claim that the internet had really changed people's access to and attitudes to pornography. After all, people who want it have surely always been able to find pornographic material to suit them, whether they were living in fifth-century Athens or the 1950s. But the evidence I looked at for this book convinced me that the internet has driven a real change for many people, especially younger people. If once upon a time someone who was truly fascinated by pornography might have found, with some difficulty, ten, or twenty, or a hundred images to satisfy themselves, now anyone can click on a single website and find twenty, a hundred, a thousand choices of videos and images, with the most specialist and violent next to the most gentle and consensual.

Statistics now tell a story that is hard to ignore. A survey carried out in 2006 found that one in four men aged twenty-five to forty-nine had viewed hardcore online pornography in the previous month, and that nearly 40 per cent of men had viewed pornographic websites in the previous year.[10] But it is the prevalence of pornography consumption among children that is most striking. While 25 per cent of children aged ten to seventeen in a study carried out in 2000 had seen unwanted online pornography in the form of popups or spam, the numbers of children who see pornography this way is rising quite quickly, and in 2005 a similar study found that 34 per cent had seen unwanted pornography when they were online.[11] In this survey, 42 per cent of the 10- to 17-year-olds had seen pornography, whether wanted or unwanted – but this has been dwarfed by results found in other surveys. In another study in Canada, 90 per cent of 13- and 14-year-old boys and 70 per cent of girls the same age had viewed pornography. Most of this porn use had been over the internet, and more than one-third of the boys reported viewing pornographic DVDs or videos 'too many times to count'.[12] While once someone could live their whole lives without ever seeing anyone but themselves and their own partners having sex, now the voyeur's view of sex has been normalised, even for children. For an increasing number of young people, pornography is no longer something that goes alongside sex, but something that precedes sex. Before they have touched another person sexually or entered into any kind of sexual relationship, many children have seen hundreds of adult strangers having sex.

When I spoke to one teenager who is studying for his A levels and quoted statistics to him that said that the majority of young teenagers have looked at pornography, Luke High laughed. 'More like a hundred per cent,' he said. 'It's when you're thirteen and fourteen that everyone starts looking and talking about it at school – before you're having sex, you're watching it. I think that those lads' mags are only read by certain kinds of boys, my friends wouldn't read them, to be honest, just like they wouldn't buy the *Sun*. But pornography – it crosses every social class, every cultural background. Everyone watches porn. And I think that's entirely down to the internet – not just your home computer, but everything that can connect, your phone, your BlackBerry, whatever you've got – everyone's watching porn. Adults have got to know what teenagers are doing, and if you're caught you get told off. But I never had a serious discussion with a teacher or anyone about it.'

Now that the classic feminist critique of pornography has disappeared from view there are, as this teenager noted, few places that young people are likely to hear much criticism or even discussion about the effects of pornography. But this massive colonisation of teenagers' erotic life by commercial pornographic materials is something that it is hard to feel sanguine about. By expanding so much in a world that is still so unequal, pornography has often reinforced and reflected the inequalities around us.

This means that men are still encouraged, through most pornographic materials, to see women as objects, and women are still encouraged much of the time to concentrate on their sexual allure rather than their imagination or pleasure. No wonder we have seen the rise of the idea that erotic experience will necessarily involve, for women, a performance in which they will be judged visually. When I interviewed young women about their attitudes to sexuality, I was struck by one apparently trivial fact – that all of them agreed that they would never want to have sex if they hadn't depilated their pubic hair. 'I would never want a man to see me if I hadn't been waxed recently,' said one young woman from Cambridge University, and her friends nodded in agreement. 'I don't need to have all the hair removed, but it has to be neat,' said another. 'That is definitely tied into porn,' said another. 'We know what men will have seen and what they will expect.'

Where the rise of expectations from pornography result just in depilation, that is one thing, but the rise of interest in surgery to change the appearance of the labia is another, far more worrying development. The number of operations carried out in the UK to cut women's labia to a preconceived norm is currently rising steeply.[13] This development has been covered extensively in magazines and television programmes, often in a way calculated to increase anxiety among female viewers. For instance, in an episode of *Embarrassing Teenage Bodies*, screened on Channel 4 in 2008, a young woman consulted a doctor about the fact that her labia minora extended slightly beyond her labia majora and that this caused her embarrassment. Instead of reassuring her that this was entirely normal, the doctor recommended, and carried out, surgery on her labia. The comments left on the programme's website showed how this decision to carry out plastic surgery to fit a young woman's body to a so-called norm made other young women feel intensely anxious. 'I'm fifteen and I thought I was fine, but since I've watched the programme I've become worried, as mine seem larger than the girl who had hers made surgically smaller! It doesn't make any difference to my life, but I worry now that when I'm older and start having sex I might have problems!' said one girl.[14] This idea that there is one correct way for female genitals to look is undoubtedly tied into the rise of pornography. Indeed, one website for a doctor who specialises in this form of plastic surgery makes this explicit: 'Laser Reduction Labioplasty can sculpture the elongated or unequal labial minora (small inner lips) according to one's specification ... Many women bring us Playboy and say that they want to look like this. With laser reduction labioplasty, we work with women to try and accomplish their desires.'[15] If the rise of pornography was really tied up with women's liberation and empowerment, it would not be increasing women's anxiety about fitting into a narrow physical ideal.

What's more, while interviewing people about their experiences with pornography, I began to realise that despite the absence of much public debate on the issue, many women are struggling with the influence of pornography on their private, emotional lives. Even if they did not accept the classic feminist critique that all pornography necessarily involves or encourages abuse of women, many of them were still concerned about the fact that pornography foregrounds a view of sex that can be profoundly dehumanising. In pornography, there is no before and no after; sex occurs in isolation. In pornography, there is little individuality; every partner is interchangeable. In pornography, there is no communication between the individuals concerned; it is all performance directed at the observer. In pornography, there is no emotional resonance to sex; everything happens on the exterior. When people become imaginatively caught up in pornography, this dehumanised view of sex can clearly have real effects on their own relationships.

One day I found myself taking a taxi in a small town in Essex, and ringing on the doorbell in a suburban street, to talk to a self-confessed pornography addict. Jim, a quiet man in his early forties, was embarrassed by what we talked about over the following couple of hours, but also eager to tell a story that he feels is probably less unusual than one might think. 'I know I'm not the only guy who's like this,' he kept saying. Jim first became aware of pornography when he was just five years old. 'My dad was really into pornography. I was five when I found a copy of his *Mayfair*. I found it quite captivating, to be honest.' When he was about seven Jim discovered hardcore European pornography in his father's wardrobe, and even to this day he can remember some of those first images he saw. 'I found them quite disturbing. I couldn't talk to anyone about it of course, because the whole point is that it's hidden, you know that you're not supposed to know about it.' His fascination with what he had found grew and grew. From then on he would get up before his parents woke, before six in the morning, to look through his father's briefcase and find the porn magazines. 'Then my dad got a Super 8 projector, when I was about eleven or twelve, and he would hire out porn films – he would lock himself in the dining room to watch them. But the real change came when he got a video, and I persevered till I found the films. I was about fourteen, and I would find them and watch them when I was alone in the house. Constantly.'

At this age, Jim did not have any relationships to set against this obsession. He was going to a boys' school and never met girls socially. 'I was obsessed with pornography, I wanted to be pornography, I wanted to live pornography,' he said. 'It wasn't good for me, I can see that now. I knew that even then, I think, but it was an addiction from the start. It had such a powerful hold on me. It had a huge effect on my behaviour with women. I was unable to think of women except as potential pornography. I looked at them in a purely sexual way. I remember one day I was walking to school, I was about fifteen, and I got talking to a girl who must have been about eighteen. I immediately said I wanted to grope her breasts. I had no idea how to interact with women as people.'

Even though Jim did begin to have girlfriends from the age of nineteen, he never managed to shrug off the power of the fantasy world. 'The power of pornography has continued throughout my adult life. Nothing has really measured up to the world of porn, for me. I've seen thousands of strangers having sex. So when I have sex, I am watching myself having sex – it's a performance.' For Jim, the constant presence of pornography in his life has, he believed, threatened his ability to sustain intimacy. 'It has destroyed my ability to have intimate relationships. Its influence on my life has been so destructive. I think my life would have been so different without pornography.'

In his thirties, Jim started a relationship that lasted for seven years. Ali is Jim's ex-girlfriend; a direct-talking, well-read woman whom I spoke to after I had spoken to Jim. 'He did tell me about how much he liked porn at the start of our relationship,' Ali told me. 'He was very honest in that way – at least he was at first. Pornography was completely new to me then – this was ten years ago. It was before internet porn. But I was ready to see what it was like, you know, if it was so much part of his life.'

Jim used to borrow videos from friends, or buy them, and he and Ali would watch them together in the early days of their relationship. 'I could see the appeal,' Ali admits. 'I could see the high you could get from it. But it wasn't long before I realised it wasn't for me. I had been abused as a child. I couldn't stop myself seeing the connections. I couldn't stop asking myself whether these women had really consented, and what it had taken them to consent to this, and whether they were getting pleasure out of it. I wanted to know about their backgrounds, and their feelings. I felt very uncomfortable. I talked about it with Jim and we agreed he would try to abstain from pornography.' When the internet began to be part of their lives, however, he could no longer control his interest in pornography and began to use it again. The relationship finally broke down. 'Pornography has made him only able to see sex one way,' Ali says. 'He has always seen sex as something that has to be performed, not felt. I would say that his addiction to pornography has been the main factor in the breakdown of our relationship.' Ali believes that there is little debate of what she has been going through in the world around her. 'Porn has been so normalised that anyone objecting to it now is just going to be laughed at. I think we need to hear again about how pornography threatens intimacy.'

Ali is certainly not unique in struggling with the impact of pornography in her own relationship. One day when I was visiting a website where parents congregate to talk about parenting and families, I saw a woman I'll call Lara posting about her worries about her husband's reliance on pornography. We went on talking privately by email. Lara has been with her husband for seven years, and married for five years. 'My husband and I had been together as a couple for about six months when I discovered his porn stash,' she wrote to me. 'I wasn't even snooping, it was just in a drawer under his bed. I was shocked, and at first I was just bemused by it – he'd clearly been building this collection up for some time, given the age of some of the magazines.' As this was in the days before everyone had a computer in their homes, they didn't have access to the internet. 'At this point, our relationship was fantastic, we were head over heels in love, had an amazing sex life. I was so in love I couldn't have walked away if I tried. Eventually I brought it up with him, and he seemed embarrassed and said he hadn't bought anything for ages, and was going to stop altogether.' Lara at first believed that they had moved on. They got married and still didn't have a computer, so it wasn't an

issue to begin with, but when they did get a computer at home
the problems began. 'I was pregnant when I found out that he
was looking at pornography online. I caught him at it one
evening, and I was really upset. I also found out he was calling
sex lines. I was gutted. I started looking at his email to try and
find out what he was doing, and my discoveries inevitably led
to major arguments.'

At first Lara tried to get her husband to go to counselling,
with her, but he refused to do so, and the impact on their relationship grew. 'As far as our intimacy goes – it definitely has
been affected,' she wrote. 'I just can't bring myself to be as close
to him as I otherwise would. I always wonder what's going on in
his head – whether he's thinking about a porn site he saw, a particular female or whatever, when we're together. He's very vocal
and specific in what he finds arousing and I believe this comes
from the type of site he likes using. I try not to let this bother me,
but it does.' Lara has looked at pornography with her husband,
but just like Ali, she can't enjoy it, because of the dehumanisa-
tion which seems inherent in it. 'I think about the females as
humans with emotions and lives. I always ask my husband if he
thinks their parents would be proud of them, or if he knows
these women are probably involved with drugs and prostitution, that this surely isn't a well-considered career choice? I ask
him how he would feel if our daughter grew up to be involved in
this industry, and he can't bear the thought of that. I try to
humanise them, to make them something more than a sexual
object.'

Lara has tried to confront her husband about his habits, but
when they argue, he has tried many tactics, from swearing that
he will never again use porn, to telling her to turn a blind eye
and mind her own business, to what she calls the 'old favourite',
that all men do it and it's nothing unusual. 'The upshot of all
this is that it doesn't matter what he tells me any more,' Lara
wrote to me sadly. 'I just don't really believe him. I have never

discussed this with any female friends – I'm too ashamed. I have felt that he is kind of using me when we're together to act out fantasies that he has seen in porn. I wonder whether he's fantasising about some female he likes on the internet instead of concentrating on me.'

Women like Ali and Lara are not alone. It is notable that although their partners first became enthralled by pornography before the internet, it was the internet that encouraged these men to reject their partners' requests that they live out their erotic lives without porn. I do not believe that all pornography inevitably degrades women, and I do see that the classic feminist critique of pornography as necessarily violence against women is too simplistic to embrace the great range of explicit sexual materials and people's reactions to them. Yet let's be honest. The overuse of pornography does threaten many erotic relationships, and this is a growing problem. What's more, too much pornography does still rely on or promote the exploitation or abuse of women. Even if you can find porn for women and couples on the internet, nevertheless a vein of real contempt for women characterises so much pornography.

This is true even of mainstream pornography, let alone all the sites that openly advertise, as many do, images of rape, incest and abuse. 'I find the internet quite disturbing,' Jim told me. 'I've been into pornography for years, I've seen it all. But the internet has pushed things further.' Although he has consumed pornography so enthusiastically for thirty years, he is definite that pornography has become far more contemptuous of women than it was previously. 'Now, porn is way more brutalising than it used to be,' he tells me. 'There is this unbelievable obsession with anal sex – pictures with a woman's arsehole stretched out of all proportion from having sex with two men – that has to be painful. It's far more demeaning to women than in the past.' One might think that someone who has seen as much pornography as Jim would not be shocked by anything, but it is clear that he is shocked with the way that the growing acceptability of pornography is putting into the mainstream a dehumanising view of women. 'People take that for granted now,' he told me. 'This guy who lives over the road said, I'll drop you a DVD – it was all about anal sex, these guys slapping this woman, making her have anal sex with two guys at once and a huge dildo, all up her arse at once. He said, what did you think? I said, it's really not my cup of tea. He grinned and said, yeah, it's horrible isn't it. God, I remember when I saw my first picture of anal sex when I was about sixteen, it was coy in comparison. None of these gaping shots, none of these pictures of what look like a woman in pain. There seems to be such a market for really brutal text, too. The stuff I saw as a kid was what we called hardcore, but the idea in the text along-side was that it was based on mutual consent – mutual pleasure – but what I see now is more male domination.'

Not only is the tone of pornography so often reliant on real or imaginary abuse of women, it is, as we have seen, consumed in increasing numbers by young people who have little real experi-ence to set against it. Jim believes that very young men are beginning to see as normal images which would once have been seen as far beyond the pale. 'So many guys I know are into it. I play a lot of golf and one day I was there and there were these young guys, fifteen, sixteen, looking at video clips on their phones of a girl having sex with a horse, and one of them says, "she died a day later of internal injuries". I don't know if it's true or not, but that's the kind of stuff they want to look at. It's like a bravado, they want to look at worse and worse stuff. When I was a kid what you saw was limited by what you could physi-cally buy on paper. Now it all flashes around so quickly and the taboos have just fallen.' Jim feels that even for young men who don't seek it out, the exposure to these images simply changes their attitudes to sex. 'I think that kind of violence associated with sex lodges in your mind and you never forget it, however much you want to. It's always there.'

Because the old feminist position against pornography has been so discredited, it often feels as though few people are ready to speak out against pornography. I picked up a real sense of hopelessness from those women who have experienced its negative effects in their intimate lives. Ali, Jim's ex-partner, has a young son. She worries that what happened with Jim could be repeated with her son. 'I was first aware that he was looking at pornography when he was fourteen. But how can boys not see it? Unless they make a concerted decision not to look at it, to delete it from their mobiles when it's sent to them, or from their emails. You'd be making a singular, probably a unique decision. Once someone like Jim was unusual, now every boy has seen all of that. I know what it does to young minds, and now it is more and more prevalent. God knows how we can begin to challenge this. Once upon a time kids could experiment, you know, privately, but now all the innocence is lost.'

The tide of pornography is so huge, and so easily accessible, that it often seems impossible to think about turning it back. Yet I don't think we have to slip into despair. There is this idea that 'innocence', once lost, is lost forever, that, as Jim put it, once pornography is viewed, 'You never forget it, however much you want to.' It is true that we cannot turn back the clock and wipe pornography out of our individual experience or the memories of our society. Yet there are still ways to move forwards and to create places where the influence of pornography will be resisted. This will entail giving more support to people who are struggling with pornography's dehumanising effects on their own relationships. Both Ali and Lara feel that it would help them in their own, personal struggles if voices challenging pornography were heard more in the mainstream of the surrounding culture. Lara wrote to me: 'From some discussions I've had online I can see that many wives are struggling with their husband's porn use. If the mainstream media began talking about porn addiction in the same way as they talk freely about drug abuse, gambling or alcoholism, then maybe my husband would see that he's not the only man in the world who has this problem and would see that he should deal with it.' I also heard from teenagers that they wanted more chance to discuss seriously what they are seeing, since they seem to find that this world of pornography is absolutely open to them, and yet is rarely openly referred to.

And even if we cannot censor pornography and shut down the internet, perhaps we have to try again to make spaces that are free from pornography, both public and private. As even Anna Span said, 'It's as though by moving into pornography women have now given men the excuse to sexualise women in so many other contexts,' she says, 'in the glamour world, or using sexy women to sell all sorts of other things from mineral water to cameras. I really don't see that as an advance.' If we are ready to start to challenge the creeping pornification of our culture, this will range from preventing the sale of pornographic images at child height in newsagents to challenging those media outlets which rely on semi-pornographic images in other contexts.

It will also mean believing that we can reclaim a view of sex that is about intimacy rather than exchange. Of course any number of people are creating this experience of sexuality in their private lives, and we can also draw inspiration from those writers and artists who are reimagining sexuality as emotional connection rather than performance, whose acts of imagination can have surprising resonance even in this cynical world. Just to take one – but one particularly fine – example, in her third novel *On Beauty*, the writer Zadie Smith writes powerfully and poignantly about a sexual encounter between a young woman and an older man in which the scripts that the young woman has learned from pornography seem to get in the way of any kind of intimacy. 'At the slightest touch of him to her, she wailed and seemed to quiver with preorgasmic passion, and yet she was, as Howard discovered at his second attempt, completely dry.'[16] But at the end of the novel the man returns to the relationship with his long-term partner, and reclaims a sense of sex based on touch and communication. 'Who cares for technicalities,' Smith asks through her male protagonist, 'when that starburst of pleasure and love and beauty is taking you over?'[17]

6: Choices

The highly sexualised culture around us is tolerated and even celebrated because it rests on the illusion of equality. Since the idea has taken hold that women and men are now equal throughout society, it is seen as unproblematic that women should be relentlessly encouraged to prioritise their sexual attractiveness. The assumption is that this is a free choice by women who are in all other ways equal to men. But if we look more clearly at the current situation, we can see how shaky this illusion of equality really is. To repeat some of the most basic facts: women still do not have the equal political power they have long sought, since only one in five MPs is a woman. They do not have economic equality, since the pay gap is still not only large but actually widening. They do not have the freedom from violence they have sought, and with the conviction rate in rape cases standing at just 6 per cent, they know that rapists enjoy an effective impunity in our society.

There is, of course, nothing intrinsically degrading or miserable about a woman pole-dancing, stripping, having sex with large numbers of partners or consuming pornography. All these behaviours are potentially enjoyable and sexy and fun. But in the current context, in which women's value is so relentlessly bound up with how successfully they are seen as sexually alluring, we can see that certain choices are celebrated, while others are marginalised, and this clearly has a major effect on the behaviour of many women and men.

The hypersexual culture is not only rooted in continuing inequality, it also produces more inequality. When I was talking to Carly Whiteley, the teenager in Chapter Three, I was struck by her view that a focus on individual choice often ignores the effects of those choices. 'I think the thing is that even if they feel that way for themselves, don't they realise what they are doing for other women?' she said of women who decide to go into stripping or sex work. 'It took us a while to get to where we are now, which is basically where men were at – to be able to insist on respect. And these women are breaking it all down. They are putting us back to where we used to be. Like, if you go to a club now it's not unusual that, say, you'll get your arse slapped by some stranger. Of course you can't complain, you can't say anything – all the media are saying that's OK, all you are is boobs and arse.'

This reduction of women purely to their physical attributes stretches way beyond the areas of our culture that I have explored here. If you look at the treatment given to women in political life, you can see how the status of women is now frequently limited by the assumption that they should be judged – often cruelly – on how they measure up to the values not of their work, but of their sexualised appearance. For instance when Ann Widdecombe, the Conservative politician, appeared on the comedy quiz show *Have I Got News For You* in 2007, a large number of the jokes centred on her unsexy looks. The participants quipped about what it would be like to see her pole-dancing, complained that a glance from her would make them lose an erection, and commented freely and nastily on her appearance. Or when Harriet Harman, the deputy leader of the Labour party, commented on the need for more women in power in 2009, one male commentator responded in the *Spectator* magazine, 'So – Harriet Harman, then. Would you? I mean, after a few beers, obviously, not while you were sober . . . I think you wouldn't.'[1] The online version of his article attracted dozens of comments, many along the lines of this one: 'Rod, I wouldn't touch the sanctimonious trollop with yours, let alone mine.'[2]

If a woman in politics does measure up to the right standards of sexiness, that does not make them immune from such bullying. For instance, Sarah Palin, the Republican candidate for the American vice-presidency in 2008, attracted much justified criticism for her political views. Yet nothing justified the torrent of sexual innuendo that she faced at the same time. Manufacturers released a 'naughty schoolgirl' Sarah Palin doll, with a red bra showing through a school uniform blouse,[3] and even a blow-up sex doll. One female commentator in the *Sunday Times* wrote: 'She looks like a porn star, specifically a porn star playing the "good" girl who's about to do something very, very bad. "She's the ultimate MILF," said one friend.'[4] And eventually a porn film was made about a fantasy Palin figure – *Who's Nailin' Palin?*[5] How can young women feel confident about entering public life when they know they are likely to be judged not for their competence and skills, but on how closely they resemble a porn star?

Yet the sexual bullying of women in public life now often goes almost unnoticed, it is so taken for granted. Some of this teasing harks back to a kind of 1950s sniggery nudge-nudge wink-wink, as if the commentators involved were simply amazed to see women, with women's bodies, in public life. For instance, a bizarre furore erupted in 2007 when the then Home Secretary, Jacqui Smith, revealed a little cleavage while speaking in Parliament. It encouraged the *Sun* newspaper to mark a series of female MPs out of ten for the size of their breasts in a feature entitled 'The best of Breastminster'.[6]

Such bullying feels like an old-fashioned throwback, but this attitude towards women has also been taken up by comedians and performers who see themselves as 'edgy'. When female actors and singers seek publicity by going on chat shows such as Jonathan Ross's on the BBC, they simply have to accept comments about their size of their breasts or how much the host would like to have sex with them. When one writer, India Knight, went to interview the broadcaster Russell Brand, she felt that she was a professional doing her normal job. She later tuned into his radio show, and was 'taken aback to find myself named on air as a prelude to Brand discussing my bosoms with, surreally, Noel Gallagher from Oasis, who insistently asked: "Did you sleep with her?", a question that caused Brand to speculate in some detail about what sleeping with me might have been like . . . it was out of order and reductive: woman, ergo piece of meat, fair game, punchline, nonperson.'[7]

This assumption that a woman should be valued primarily for her sexy appearance is having a real effect on women's visibility in our culture. For instance, in sport, it was revealed in 2009 that in the Wimbledon tennis tournament the women selected to play on centre court were being chosen for their looks rather than their tennis rankings. In television in 2009 an older and more experienced woman, Arlene Phillips, was moved aside for a gorgeous but inexperienced young woman, Alesha Dixon, in one of the BBC's flagship family entertainment shows, *Strictly Come Dancing*. In such instances, we can see how a focus on women's physical attributes means that their other attributes, from their sporting prowess to their articulacy to their experience, are devalued. So the equation that is often made between the hypersexual culture and women's empowerment is a false one. Far from being empowering, this culture is claustrophobic and limiting.

This is particularly true of women who may not have other paths towards success and status. The hypersexual culture weighs especially heavily on women with few options in life. For this reason it often seems that the middle classes can dismiss it as being of no relevance to their own lives or the lives of their daughters. It became clear to me that some of the men who create and support this culture do so in the belief that they can protect their own families from its effects. When I talked to some of the powerful people in this industry, I asked them whether they could see their own daughters going into this work. Dave Read, the director of Neon Management, which supplies models to the industry, has a daughter. What would he think if she wanted to be the next Jodie Marsh, I asked, and he was frank. 'I would die to think that she'd try to follow in her footsteps. I want her to have other options.' Phil Edgar-Jones, the creative director of *Big Brother*, also has a young daughter. He started with surprise when I asked how he would feel if she wanted to go into *Big Brother* and do glamour modelling. 'I'm a middle-class parent, so I'd be—' Then he stopped himself. 'If that's what she wanted to do . . .' He paused again. 'I would hope she would have different aspirations. I encourage her to read books. Other people have different backgrounds.'

But it is not the case that this change in our culture only affects women in one area or one class. The emphasis on presenting oneself as physically perfect has an impact on women throughout society. When I interviewed girls who were aiming for good degrees and careers I was constantly struck by the way that they were aware of how their boyfriends' expectations of sex would have been formed by pornography and their expectations of women's appearance by the airbrushed standards of current magazine and celebrity culture. These young women returned again and again, despite their academic and creative achievements, to a dissatisfaction with their looks. I have always believed that individuals can enjoy investing time and energy in their looks and clothes without detracting from their freedom, but in our culture this interest in appearance is often more punishing than pleasurable, and tied into an over-vigilant regime of dieting and grooming.

One day I visited a college at Cambridge University, where I talked to five young women who had just received their degree results; more than one had a First, they were looking into bright futures and were full of optimism and excitement. Yet when we talked about body image, it was as though a cloud passed over the sun; smiles dropped, shoulders drooped. 'I really never eat without feeling guilty,' said one, and another agreed. 'From the age of thirteen to seventeen I couldn't put anything in my mouth without worrying,' said another. This kind of punishing attention to their looks may have an effect on women's ability to fulfil their potential in other ways. There has been intriguing research published recently that suggests that women who are put into situations where their attention is directed to their bodies, by the clothes they wear or the advertisements they watch, score worse on maths tests and are less likely to see themselves as decision-makers.[8, 9] Such studies suggest that the narcissism that is being encouraged so relentlessly among young women may be affecting their ability to take up the roles that they would otherwise embrace.

There has been little questioning of this culture for many years. The tenor of so much of our society has been to exalt the role of the market. If certain magazines sell, if certain clubs make money, if certain images shift products, then dissent about their values is effectively silenced. As Phil Hilton, the ex-editor of *Nuts*, said to me, 'I've given up on judging people.' So many people would say the same. To judge any aspect of our culture or behaviour is now often seen as impossibly elitist; the market is the only arbiter. Television producers and publishers have told me the same story: that in this society they cannot make decisions based on quality or morality, they must make decisions based on sales. Throughout our society, any attempt to complain about or change this culture is often met by fatalism: if the market is so powerful, then how can any individual stand against it?

To be sure, the current hypersexual culture does not impact equally on all women. There are young women following their dreams in anything from music to literature, campaigning to politics, and throughout their private lives, who have truly benefited from the work done by feminists before them. Yet so many women are hampered by this claustrophobic culture, and feel trapped and frustrated by what is going on around them. Through the glamour-modelling culture, through the mainstreaming of pornography and the new acceptability of the sex industry, through the modishness of lap and pole-dancing, through the sexualisation of young girls, many young women are being surrounded by a culture in which they are all body and only body. In the hypersexual culture the woman who has won is the woman who foregrounds her physical perfection and silences any discomfort she may feel. This objectified woman, so often celebrated as the wife or girlfriend of the heroic male rather than the heroine of her own life, is the living doll who has replaced the liberated woman who should be making her way into the twenty-first century.

II

The New Determinism

7: Princesses

I was brought up in a family who pretty much agreed, as many families did in the 1970s, with the idea that was so clearly enunciated by Simone de Beauvoir in 1949: 'One is not born a woman, one becomes one.' So my mother had refused to buy Barbie dolls for her daughters and bought Lego and toy cars for my sister and me; the fight against gender stereotyping began at home. A generation on, I thought that my daughter would be growing up in an altogether freer time. I assumed that the very successes of my mother's generation had made it possible for femininity to be seen as a choice rather than a trap for women. In the same way that I believed that adult women were now free to choose to embrace aspects of femininity that second-wave feminists had once seen as coercive, such as high heels and make-up, so I believed that little girls should now be free to be fairy princesses if they wanted.

But then I realised that, almost without my noticing, the walls have closed in. What should be the freedom to choose a bit of pink often feels more like an imperative to drown in a sea of pink. My daughter is growing up in a world predicated on medieval values, with every girl a princess and every boy a fighter, every girl with fairy designs on her lunch box, and every boy with a superhero on his. This new traditionalism does not just affect what toys children are expected to play with, it also extends to expectations about many other aspects of children's behaviour, from how they will dress to how they will talk, from how they will learn to how they will fight. And what seems strangest of all to me is how few questions are being asked about this return to traditional expectations.

'Come to my princess party!' said the invitation from a girl in my daughter's nursery, next to a vivid illustration of a Sleeping Beauty-style princess in crown and gown. My daughter was delighted, and on the day in question she got me to help her pull on her glittering paste tiara and her miniature nylon balldress sourced from the Disney Shop. When we got to the party we were greeted by the expected sight, a dozen little girls modelling outfits dreamed up from the 1930s onwards for fairy-tale hero-ines. A scattering of boys in their everyday clothes, navy and grey, hung around the edges. The tea table was decorated with glitter and pink plates and cups, with a few plain blue ones thrown in too so that the boys would have somewhere to sit.

My daughter didn't join in for a while. 'She's feeling a bit shy,' I explained to one or two other mothers, as she sat on my lap for a while, watching. 'I wish I had a girl,' said one. 'So quiet. Thomas is such a handful.' Later I heard the same mother in the kitchen, with Thomas clinging to her leg and refusing to speak. 'He's like his dad,' she was saying. 'Grunts rather than talks when he's fed up. Honestly, boys . . .' At one point the party dis-integrated into a fracas. One boy was slow to pass the parcel on. A girl, furious with him, stood up, her tiara askew, and punched him in the face. He screamed and ran from the room and refused to rejoin the game, so the hostess sat him at the tea table while she laid out the cakes. The parents in the kitchen passed judge-ment on why he wasn't in the circle. 'Boys aren't great at playing games at this age,' said one. 'They just can't sit still! It's so much harder for them, I think.' 'Boys are just so much younger than girls in many ways,' said another. At the end the children were handed their party bags, colour coded in pink and blue, with plastic bracelets and hairclips inside for the girls and bouncy balls and plastic spiders for the boys.

Pink girls, blue boys. Princesses, fighters. Shy girls, grunting boys. Good girls, aggressive boys. That's what we want to see, so that's what we see. Even if our children so often diverge from expectations, and the princess becomes the puncher or the fighter wants to chat, this hardly seems to dent the strength of the stereotypes. And the assumptions made by parents are often being backed up by stronger gender divisions in the marketing carried out by toy companies. So our children are now growing up to see that the toy cookers on sale at Marks and Spencer are labelled 'Mummy and Me', while the toy tools and drills are labelled 'Daddy and Me'.[1] On the website of Boots the chemist you can find all the fascinating products from the Science Museum, including a kit for sending secret messages, in the 'boys' toys' section.[2] On another toy shop website, Hiya Kids in Putney, south London, in 2008, the 'boys' toys' page contained various intriguing objects, including a walkie talkie, a metal detector and skittles, while the female section sold only toy kitchens, tea sets, dressing-up clothes, dolls and dolls' houses.[3] One company, Indigo Worldwide, even goes so far as to market one set of magnetic words for little girls learning to read and another for little boys. The girls' words include 'heart, love, cooking, friends, angel', while the boys' words include 'money, monster, scary, running'.[4]

When my daughter was four, I remember taking my first trip to Hamleys toy store in London. There, the floors are absolutely divided; as you rise up the escalator you go into a pink and silver world of Barbies, tutus and fairies. Their catalogue explains: 'Little princesses deserve nothing but the very best: at

Hamleys we've got the finest selection of girls' toys anywhere! We've all the dolls you could dream of and acres of accessories too. There are pony play sets, make-up and beauty boxes and much more to enjoy ... In fact, everything a girl could wish for!'[5] The website's bestselling toys for girls were a baby doll, mouse babies, a changing bag and body glitter.[6] These play into exactly the kind of femininity described by Simone de Beauvoir in 1949: 'The little girl cuddles her doll and dresses her up as she dreams of being cuddled and dressed up herself; inversely, she thinks of herself as a marvellous doll.'[7]

One of the strongest branding exercises for this generation of little girls has been that of the Disney Princesses. What could be more traditional than this theme, which resurrects those heroines, Snow White, Cinderella, Sleeping Beauty, Ariel, Jasmine, Pocahontas and Belle, which were first created by Disney up to seventy years ago and which were relaunched as one pastel, smiling sisterhood in 1999? Yet it has taken off like wildfire; sales of Disney Princess products increased from $136 million in 2001 to $1.3 billion in 2003, and to $4 billion in 2007.[8]

Given its appeal to such an old-fashioned femininity, the surge of this brand's popularity has taken many by surprise. I had never seen a single one of these Disney Princess films until I had a child myself; although my parents didn't try to edit Disney out of my life, it was simply the case that children in the 1960s and 1970s, without videos and DVDs, saw fewer feature films. How intensely and vividly, however, this brand has gripped our children. There must be hardly a little girl alive in Britain today who doesn't have some possession stamped with the brand. If I go into my daughter's bedroom I will see it on a music box, miniature dolls and medium-size dolls, a wand, a cup, a necklace, crayons and stickers. When I open her dressing-up box, I see the crackly nylon Cinderella dress, and the Snow White dress that is so worn it is falling apart, and the Sleeping Beauty shoes with their little pink heels.

Of course it isn't a problem that little girls are dreaming of being little mermaids with sweet voices, or of going to the ball in a puff of silver. I wouldn't want to deny any girl these pleasures – so long as they aren't all expected to do it, and so long as it isn't all they are expected to do, and so long as boys are not seen as being contaminated if they so much as pick up a pink wand. Yet right now it is often assumed that boys and girls will play in absolutely distinct styles. For instance in 2003, Mattel launched ello, a pastel-coloured, curvy building range for girls which was to compete with Lego or Duplo, but 'specifically made for girls'. Mattel's resident psychologist, Dr Michael Shore, explained why girls needed their own building range: 'While "building" is generally associated with boys' play patterns, there are several ways that girls "build". Girls also "build" stories and characters with their traditional doll play . . . The ello creation system . . . stimulates roleplay and storytelling in a way that is relevant to girls.'[9]

Similarly, there have always been books aimed at girls and books aimed at boys, but these divisions are becoming even more vivid in this generation. Now, if you go into any children's section of any bookshop you will find shelves and shelves of books aimed solely at little girls, all with pink glittery covers and an emphasis on fairies and kittens, ballet and theatre. Their plot lines are fantastically repetitive, reinforcing over and over again the traditional femininity of their young readers. Here is one typical heroine of one typical fairy book: 'Evie took off her pyjamas . . . then she put on the blue sparkly dress and matching knickers – which both fitted her perfectly now that she was fairy-sized herself. There was a mirror on one wall and when she went to look at herself she couldn't help smiling – she looked so pretty. Now all she had to do was fix her hair.'[10] Beside such books, there will be examples of a genre aimed specifically at young boys, which feature scarlet and navy covers and scowling heroes. A leaflet published recently by Leapfrog explained to parents how boys' and girls' reading choices would naturally differ. 'Let boys be boys and girls be girls', it urged. It explained that: 'Boys . . . Like reading to have a purpose, for example books that show you how to make things or tell you about things. Girls . . . Enjoy a bit of fantasy, magic and make believe – princesses, castles and so on.'[11]

I am not saying that there are no differences between boys' and girls' preferences, on average, or that what differences there are would entirely disappear if children were given complete freedom in a completely equal world. Whatever parents do, and whatever changes we created in the wider society, it might be that we would never see the boys choosing the dolls and the girls the footballs in precisely equal numbers. But the expectations that we are laying on our children in this generation are failing to allow for their true variability, their true individuality, their true flexibility.

Those parents who find that their children are happy to fall in with these traditional gender divisions often feel no need to question why their daughters' bedrooms are hung in pink, and their sons' wardrobes are unrelentingly sludge and navy; why their daughters' T-shirts proclaim 'Princess in training' and their sons' say '100 percent lazy'. But other parents feel very uneasy about the way that our culture is constructing such limited environments for each child, pink or blue according to their gender. Joanna Moorhead is a writer who lives in south London. She has four daughters. It was after the birth of her third, Miranda, she began to question the way that the whole family had supported such a stereotyped view of girls' upbringing. Because Miranda is a rebel. Given pink dresses to wear, she decided she would prefer jeans; given dolls, she decided footballs suited her better. Instead of fairies and princesses, she decided her heroes were Horrid Henry and George from the Famous Five. She was a classic tomboy, but in a world, her mother thinks, that no longer celebrates tomboys.

'Miranda has lifted the scales from my eyes,' Joanna said to me over a coffee one afternoon. 'Now, I look back on my older daughters' early years, and I can't really believe that I bought into those stereotypes without ever questioning them.' Joanna gave her older daughters the classic upbringing of our times, full of pink and ballet and dolls. 'It's strange that our culture is so insistent that girls should be so girly, even though the opportunities have developed so much for women. You know, I go to work at a newspaper where men and women work together, and I'm usually wearing trousers, and there is no issue about that. We don't assume as adults that we will have totally different interests and ways of dressing from one another. But for young children, it's so much more divided. I do think it is led by the market, it's very commercially driven.' Joanna cited the gender division you can see in television commercials, which will flash up a vivid pink spectrum of dolls to dress up and cuddle, against the active toys for boys.

Many parents believe that these expectations mark a shift towards more rigid beliefs, away from the freer childhoods which they themselves experienced. For instance, looking back on her own life, Joanna Moorhead believes that a generation ago her tomboy daughter, Miranda, would have found it easier to get through her childhood. 'I wasn't a tomboy myself,' she said, 'but I just don't think it was a big issue. There wasn't all this big pink frilly thing about being a girl then. I grew up with brothers, we shared toys, I had a trainset, I don't think that being girlish was something all girls had to fit in with in the same way. Boys and girls had the same toys.'

We can see why it might be tricky for a girl like Miranda to find a way through contemporary culture, but it can be equally tricky for boys who do not fit the mould. Fenella is a 42-year-old mother who currently lives in Belgium; I contacted her through the problem pages of a newspaper, to which she had written for advice. She has one son and one daughter. She was brought up by a mother who was influenced by feminism's second wave and who took it for granted that children could follow their own preferences without pressure to conform. 'Apparently I never played with dolls,' Fenella told me. 'And my brother was quite feminine in some ways – I mean, he did ballet when he was young, he wore make-up in his teens. He is now an artist, and he always was a bit of a rebel in that way. I think people now often assume that means gay, but he isn't – he has a female partner now and has always had girlfriends. My mother was very keen to reject stereotypes; she had been brought up in a conventional way herself but she responded to the feminism around her. She wanted us to cross conventional boundaries – she encouraged my brother to do housework and treated us very much the same.' Before she had children herself, Fenella assumed that this freedom would only have increased for this generation. 'I honestly didn't think that anyone would have a problem any more with a girlish boy or a boyish girl. I thought my children would be living in an even freer time than I did in my childhood.' But she has found the opposite, and for her son, a six-year-old who prefers dolls to cars and ballet to football, the problems are now very real. This is a generation in which many boys are encouraged into a stereotyped masculinity at an early age; for those who resist, life can be uncomfortable.

'He can't be accepted for who he is,' Fenella says sadly. 'My husband, who isn't exactly macho himself, says he will be teased at school if he behaves like this, and he reacts with absolute fury when he sees him being girlish, as he sees it. My son desperately wanted an Ariel Barbie so in the end I bought him one and told my husband it was a present from a friend. My son absolutely loved it, but one afternoon my husband cut all its hair off, in an effort to try to make it a more suitable doll for a boy.' For Fenella, she sees anger at her son's choices coming partly from her husband, and also from the peer group. 'My son will spend the morning dressing up one of his teddy bears like a ballerina and when a boy comes to play he'll show him so enthusiastically and the boy will say, pink is for girls, and my son is so downcast.' For a while her son had a group of female friends at school, but then they closed ranks and wouldn't play with him because he is a boy.

Fenella's daughter is not very typically girlish, either. 'She likes pink and dolls, but she is very physically aggressive. Still, people now accept that more from girls. Whereas my son – he wants to dress up in my scarves and dance around the house. My husband thinks I've encouraged it by letting him watch *Strictly Come Dancing*, and he gets so angry when he sees him. "Why doesn't he go and play football?" he says. But that isn't who my son is, and it's really sad that he isn't allowed to be who he is. My husband will snatch the scarves off him and say, boys don't do that.'

What worries Fenella is that her son, whom she sees as a normal, even talented and creative child, is being made to feel abnormal and secretive about his interests and pleasures. 'I think he could be a talented dancer or designer,' she said to me, 'but I fear it's going to be squashed out of him, that he'll feel he has to spend his time playing sport and he'll end up an accountant like everyone else. And he'll be a secret cross-dresser rather than just enjoying wearing great clothes in public. This culture seems to be making boys feel that certain behaviour is abnormal for boys, when it isn't.'

This is not just about the difficulties experienced by the occasional girl who hates pink or boy who wants to do ballet, but about how we reinforce stereotypes in many, often subtle ways. As we saw at the princess party, girls are constantly assumed to be more verbal and sensitive, and boys more aggressive and socially immature. And this new traditionalism is taking on extra strength by the renaissance of biological determinism: the theory that the differences we see between boys and girls are not created by social influences, but are laid down for them by the time they are born by genetic and hormonal differences.

In the 1970s, during the heyday of second-wave feminism, biological explanations for behavioural differences between boys and girls were often questioned, and explanations from social influences became more popular. It became generally accepted among educationalists then that Simone de Beauvoir had a point, and that if we wanted to move towards greater equality we had to be prepared to challenge the ways that femininity and masculinity were encouraged among girls and boys by the influences around them. Scanning my mother's bookshelves recently, I came across a number of books that would have been unexceptionable in the 1970s and sound weirdly dated now; books such as Mia Kellmer Pringle's *The Needs of Children*, which, according to its cover, was well reviewed on publication in 1974. Aimed at 'students, teachers, social and welfare workers and others caring for children', it took a socially oriented view of how sex differences are produced. 'Clothes, toys, subtle differences in words, play, hugs, rewards, punishments and parental example, surround the child with a world which clearly distinguishes behaviour expected from boys and girls,' it stated plainly. Far from encouraging the view that children are born into their pink and blue boxes, it suggested that children only learn to become masculine or feminine through the way they are treated. 'The gender role is psychologically determined first by parental and then by wider society's expectations.'[12]

This view became pretty mainstream in many schools and playgroups. A guide to non-sexist education published in 1975 shows us what could be expected in a playgroup that tried to put it into practice. The aim was to encourage girls to feel free to encroach on boys' toys and boys' roles. It encouraged playgroup leaders to develop 'non-sexist play situations . . . When we do woodwork, we especially encourage girls to learn to use tools as well as boys, and try to make sure that women help with this.'[13] Such advice was seen over and over again in literature about children's education at this time.[14] And much research that was carried out in this period was very optimistic about the results of such non-sexist child-rearing practice. For instance, in one study carried out in 1984, the researchers found that if exposed to a non-sexist curriculum for just six months, boys and girls aged three to five years showed significantly less preference for sex-stereotyped play, as measured, for instance, by asking them whether they thought certain objects, from cars to tea-sets, belonged to boys or girls, or asking them what activities they liked doing, from looking after babies to sawing.[15]

Marianne Grabrucker was a leading proponent of the ideas about boys' and girls' development that were briefly fashionable in the 1970s and 1980s. Grabrucker is now almost unknown in the UK, but in the 1980s her diary of bringing up her daughter, *There's A Good Girl*, enjoyed huge success throughout Europe.[16] This book speaks to us from a vanished world, in which this politically engaged German mother tried to resist the pressures on her daughter to be a perfect, girly girl. These included pressures from wider society, such as advertisements, toys and clothes, and pressures from within the family, such as Grabrucker's own mother or herself. In the diary, Grabrucker battles with all these influences, trying to create a free space in which her daughter can follow her own desires rather than being pushed to fit in with the expectations of others. Grabrucker's aim was to alert us to how social expectations encourage different behaviour in boys and girls.

For instance, in this passage she is out with her daughter and her daughter's best friend, a little boy, when they call at a friend's house. 'Ingrid's door opens; she is a teacher with a progressive approach to education. Anneli and Schorschi are in front of me. In their snowsuits, with their bright blue eyes and brilliant smiles, they do make a lovely picture. Ingrid says hello and we talk briefly. Then she turns to the children. "Well Schorschi, it's lovely to see you; have you been busy tobogganing?" She speaks in a normal, cheerful tone. Then she bends over Anneli, gives her a brilliant smile, puts her arm round her, picks her up and says, "Hello Poppet, don't you look pretty today? And what lovely curls; they are growing quickly. I've got something for you." . . . Is it surprising that girls can relate to people better?'[17]

In picking apart such situations and showing the impact they had on her daughter, this book explained very clearly what was to turn out to be one of the most vital projects of the second-wave women's movement: the attempt by some parents and teachers to allow girls and boys to grow up free from such stereotypes. In my desire to find out what had happened to this enterprise, I went to Munich to talk to Marianne Grabrucker and her daughter Anne-Marie, about how things had changed since those idealistic days.

Anne-Marie, like her mother, is now a lawyer, and we met in her simple, small flat in Munich. Marianne is now sixty, while Anne-Marie is a confident young woman of twenty-six. Marianne explained to me why she had felt the need to write the book, back in 1985. 'It was Simone de Beauvoir who showed me what I should do,' she told me. 'She was my intellectual mother. She said, a girl is not born, she is made a woman, and when I knew I was pregnant with a daughter I felt, OK, I had to give evidence to see how this happens.' Marianne had herself already rebelled against her extremely conservative Bavarian upbringing, by becoming a lawyer and a feminist activist. The genesis of the book lay in a diary she kept for herself of her day-to-day struggles with the environment around Anne-Marie, and when it was published she was amazed at the response she received. 'I was surprised by the success – the first edition of 10,000 sold in two weeks. So much press, radio, TV shows – loads of lectures – parliamentary debates – all the reaction, or almost all of it, was positive.'

But now, she says, the temper of our culture has changed completely. 'At the end of the book, when Anne-Marie was three, I write about how I and my friends establish a kinder-garten, and we were very serious about this issue, about how boys and girls should be treated equally there. Now, if you started talking about this, people would think you were crazy – you can't even talk to teachers about this issue – they would think you were a bit mad. Then, people were ready to think about how differences between men and women are produced by society. Now the mainstream is that it is all the genes. Even when I talk to the same people who thirty years ago thought along my lines, they have started saying to me, no, it's all genes . . . I don't mean that they say it very emotionally, on the contrary, it's just taken for granted . . . it's in the genes, that's it, no argument.'

Just a few weeks before I met Marianne, an article appeared in *Die Zeit* which showed how much attitudes have changed.[18] The journalist, Burkhard Strassmann, argued that there are differences in the innate aptitudes of boys and girls and that these drive all the differences we see in their behaviour. He mentions Marianne Grabrucker's work and the 'failure' of her experiment as proof that differences between men and women are biologically determined. 'At the beginning of the 1980s, the feminist Marianne Grabrucker deliberately attempted to raise her daughter in a truly liberal and gender-neutral way . . . Marianne Grabrucker's diary reads as a shattering document of failure.' When I asked Marianne about this article, she spoke with resigned irritation. 'He said that I did an experiment to try to prevent these differences, but at the end of it I had to admit there were still differences. He said that this meant that the experiment failed. But what he never mentioned was that I gave an explanation for this. My conclusion in the book was that I can't change everything as an individual, just through myself, because my influence – I said this clearly – on my daughter was not more than one-fifth. The other four-fifths were made up of other family members – grandparents can have great influence – friends and neighbours, educators and other childcarers, and cultural influences, everything that is out there – advertising, films, going to church, television, books.'

So the conclusion Marianne came to after writing her book was not that she should despair, but that it was time for her to work politically. 'I didn't change my mind. The starting point was to ask, is the gender problem caused by education, or genes – and finally I knew, yes, gender inequality is caused by education. I was very optimistic in the beginning, and I was optimistic still in the ending. I thought, now I know: it's not only education in the narrow sense, we have to define education in a very wide sense. Education is more than the personal influence by parents. It's politics. My book was very useful for me. By writing it I came to the conclusion that we have to go into politics and change the wider culture.'

Marianne Grabrucker feels that the ground established by feminists like herself is now being undermined by a backlash in the culture around her. 'I don't think that women are any longer interested in how to create political change.' Anne-Marie, Marianne's daughter, also believes that the current state of our culture has made it difficult to carry on the project her mother began. 'This is a bad time for feminism,' she says seriously. 'There was a peak, then it died down. Then another peak, then it died down again. I am still glad about how things have changed to the extent that they have – I can go to work at a law firm now that wouldn't even have employed women twenty years ago. But if anything, the pressures on young girls are more than before. I think the way they are pressuring them at such an early age is just taking away their choices. There are a lot of very feminine women out there, and some very masculine ones, and I think you should be given the choice and left to your own devices, to see which way you will go.'

It was both heartening for me to meet Marianne and Anne-Marie, and very dispiriting. On the one hand they were still convinced by the experiment that Marianne had undertaken, and they still believed that it had been invaluable for Anne-Marie to have been encouraged from the beginning of her life to feel free to behave as she chose. But they both believe that the culture around them is no longer enabling other women to find freedom in the same way. Biological explanations are currently squeezing out other explanations for differences between boys and girls, and contributing to a fatalism about sex inequality.

In the educational world, biological explanations for differences between the ways that girls and boys play and learn have become ubiquitous. For instance, when one educational consultant published a book on gender equity in 2004, she found herself talking to headteachers who told her categorically, 'One would think there must be something neurological because people have tried very hard to, you know, change things with their girls, to make sure they are playing with trains.' These teachers believed that non-sexist education, or equal opportunities for children, had been tried, but had been seen to fail. 'It's just not on,' said one. 'I used to believe it was possible to have all that sort of equal opportunities.'[19] You can see the same view in the work of the bestselling childcare expert Steve Biddulph, who has written, 'For thirty years it has been trendy to deny masculinity and say that boys and girls are really just the same . . . New research is confirming parents' intuitions about boys being different.'[20] The causes for this difference, he suggests, are 'the powerful effects of male hormones' and 'the ways in which boys' brains are vulnerable'.[21]

This interest in biology – 'something neurological' or the 'effects of male hormones' – as the explanation for differences between girls and boys means that far from exploring how social factors might create these differences, and how they could therefore be challenged, many people are retreating into fatalism about the innate and inescapable nature of these differences. Parents and teachers are now encouraged to avert their eyes from the influences of consumer marketing, parental reinforcement or peer-group pressure on children's behaviour. Instead, we are asked to believe that the exaggerated femininity and masculinity that we often encourage in our children is simply a natural result of their biology.

The current assumptions about how boys and girls differ often overlook the very real variability among boys and girls, and, what's more, the point that Marianne Grabrucker made so strongly to me when I met her still holds good. If we do see differences along the expected lines, it does not follow that these are necessarily produced by biological rather than social factors. It is not the case that a thoroughgoing experiment in non-sexist upbringing was made throughout society in the 1970s and 1980s, and seen to fail. A few parents, a few teachers, made individual efforts to help children to resist the conditioning around them, but while boys and girls were still surrounded by such differing expectations from books, films, friends, toys, advertisements, schools and so on, it is hardly surprising that their efforts often foundered. It is strange that so many people have fallen so uncritically for the idea that the differences we see now must be put down to biology. Since we have not yet created the equal world that Simone de Beauvoir dreamt of, and since girls and boys receive so much encouragement to fall in with traditional expectations, the jury must still be out on whether the differences we see between boys and girls are innate or the result of social factors, or – which seems most likely – a complicated and constantly changing mixture of innate and learned responses. Yet we now constantly hear that the jury has declared, and nature has won the day.

This current fashion for biological determinism purports to rely on new directions in scientific research. Over the last few years there has been a deluge of research studies on the possible biological basis for sex differences, emanating from psychology to linguistics to neuroscience departments of universities, and those studies that seem to back up biological explanations for stereotypes are picked up with enormous enthusiasm throughout the media. For instance, as mentioned in the introduction to this book, even the very association of girls with pink and boys with blue has been put down to their genetic make-up, when researchers at Newcastle University devised an experiment to test the colour preferences of men and women. The experiment consisted of presenting 208 men and women with differently coloured pairs of rectangles and asking them to pick out their favourites. They found that the general preference was for blue colours, but women liked pinky and reddish colours more than men did. There was nothing in the study to show why this might be the case, but that did not stop the researchers suggesting that this phenomenon was created by genetic differences that arose from a divergence in the way men and women had evolved. 'We speculate that this sex difference arose from sex-specific functional specialisations in the evolutionary division of labour,' they said[22], and this was what the media picked up on, from the *Guardian* to the *Daily Mail*.

Here is part of the *Daily Mail*'s report: 'While men developed a preference for the clear blue skies that signalled good weather for hunting, women honed their ability to pick out the reds and pink while foraging for ripe fruits and berries. Professor Hurlbert, of Newcastle's school of psychology, said: "The explanation might date back to humans' hunter-gatherer days, when women were the primary gatherers and would have benefited from the ability to home in on ripe, red fruits."'[23]

Dissenting voices were hardly heard in the mainstream media, except in a 'Bad Science' report by Ben Goldacre in the *Guardian*, who pointed out that even if a preference for pinkier colours was seen among women, the researchers had not screened out the likely explanation that this is a cultural rather than biological difference. We surround girls with pink, we buy them pink clothes, we give them pink bedrooms, can we be surprised if they are readier to say they like pink? The study suggested that this could not be a result produced by acculturation, because it included some Chinese subjects, but as they were immigrants who had been living in the West, it is not clear how they constituted a control group. And although the researchers speculated that the difference was 'hardwired' into our brains because of our foremothers' need to pick out fruit in the ancestral plains of our evolutionary past, as Goldacre pointed out, they did not test whether the preference (that women liked more pinkish colours) was backed up by greater discrimination (that women could actually see pinks more clearly).[24] What became clear in the way the experiment was reported is that there is now such a strong desire to explain the pink-is-for-girls phenomenon as biologically based that this desire can override the need for balanced reporting.

In fact, the current convention to associate pink with girls and boys with blue seems to be a recent and culturally specific practice. Until the twentieth century infants' clothes were generally white, and even once white was discarded for all infants' clothes, the division of boys and girls into blue and pink took a while to get going. 'In the beginning,' Jo Paoletti, a leading expert on children's clothes, writes, 'the rule was just the opposite.' In evidence she cites magazines from 1918 and 1939. The first stated, 'There has been a great diversity of opinion on the subject, but the generally accepted rule is pink for the boy and blue for the girl. The reason is that pink being a more decided and stronger colour is more suitable for the boy, while blue, which is more delicate and dainty is prettier for the girl.' And the second, 'There seem to be more reasons for choosing blue for girls . . . red symbolises zeal and courage, while blue is symbolic of faith and constancy.'[25] Consider, too, the fact that when *Time* magazine reported on the birth of a daughter to Princess Astrid of Belgium in 1927, and the country's disappointment that it was not a son, the reporter mentioned that, 'The cradle was optimistically decorated in pink, the colour for boys,'[26, 27]

If this new determinism just aimed to explain a preference for blue or for pink among girls and boys, then it would be essentially trivial. But biological explanations are now being used to underpin expectations about many aspects of childhood behaviour, and are also being carried through into adult life. The same beliefs about genetic and hormonal differences now underlie the expectation of persistent differences between men and women both big and small, from their readiness to take parental leave to their ability to park a car, from their desire to stand for election to their memory for arguments.

Certain scientists have taken these biological explanations for differences between adult men and women into the mainstream in recent years. For instance, Simon Baron-Cohen is a respected scientist, professor of developmental psychopathology at Cambridge University, whose influential book *The Essential Difference* has given much strength to these arguments. In this book he argues that while women invest more in social relationships, men are more interested in systems. He uses anecdotes that play into these stereotypes. 'One of the women may open a conversation with her female friend by saying something like this: "Oh, I *love* your dress. You *must* tell me where you got it. You look *so* pretty in it. It really goes well with your bag." . . . the two men's opening gambit might go something like this: "How was the traffic on the M11? I usually find going up the A1M through Royston and Baldock can save a lot of time. Especially now they have roadworks just beyond Stansted."'[28] These differences are explained by genes and hormones. 'All the evidence . . . leads us down one path on our journey. Namely to suspect that testosterone (especially early in development) is affecting the brain and thus affecting behaviour.'[29] Overall, Simon Baron-Cohen's thesis is that, 'The female brain is predominantly hardwired for empathy. The male brain is predominantly hardwired for understanding and building systems.'[30]

And alongside Simon Baron-Cohen are many other scientists who have crossed into the mainstream with their views on how we should pay more attention to biological factors when discussing sex differences. For instance, Steven Pinker, the well-known psychologist, wrote in his bestseller *The Blank Slate* that just as girls play more at parenting and trying on social roles, and boys more at fighting, chasing and manipulating objects, so women put more energy into their emotional lives and men compete more with one another for status using violence or occupational achievement. Biology rather than society, he argues, is probably at the root of many of these differences.[31] Other writers have also crossed from academia to the mainstream in writing about these topics, such as Louann Brizendine, a neuropsychiatrist, whose book *The Female Brain* explains how a woman 'tends to know what people are feeling, while a man can't seem to spot an emotion unless someone cries or threatens bodily harm',[32] and Susan Pinker, a psychologist, whose book *The Sexual Paradox* explored the relationship between women's higher levels of the hormone oxytocin and their propensity to drop out of the workforce at the higher levels, and between men's higher testosterone and their apparent ability to succeed in the face of all odds.[33]

All these writers differ, but they all support the same major themes. They argue that behavioural and cognitive differences between girls and boys are observable even at birth, and are not just produced by social factors such as the influence of the peer group or the wider culture. They suggest that these differences will then carry on into adulthood, and are shown particularly in the way that men excel at logical, systematic thinking, particularly mathematical and spatial skills, while women are naturally better at empathising and caring. They explore the idea that such differences are laid down in our genes and hormones because, thousands of years ago, it was evolutionarily advantageous for men and women to occupy different niches in society. And they suggest that we can find proof that these differences are both innate and unchanging – 'hardwired', as these writers often put it – by looking at the ways they are related to differences in hormone levels, and to differences in brain structure and activity among men and women.

The work of such scientists has been enthusiastically taken up by other popular writers. John Gray is a self-help writer whose insight into the difference between men and women is that men are from Mars, and women are from Venus. Ever since 1992 he has been telling couples that they cannot expect their spouse to have similar interests and ways of talking, that instead they must accept difference. The ability to tolerate, even love, difference is clearly a prerequisite of any relationship between any two humans, but in John Gray's universe these differences are assumed to exist only along preconceived lines, in which men grunt and go into their caves and women chatter and wait for romantic gestures. All Gray's books are essentially variations on a theme, but his 2008 book, *Why Mars and Venus Collide*, was new in one telling way; now Gray does not just put forward his ideas as observations of everyday life, he uses explanations from biology, from genes and hormones, to explain these observations. As evidence for his views he now quotes scientific sources, including Simon Baron-Cohen. Mars and Venus are now driven by the hormones testosterone and oxytocin. 'A woman's happiness and energy levels come from the oxytocin-producing acts of nurturing and being nurtured, while a man's happiness and energy levels comes [sic] primarily from the testosterone-producing act of making a difference.'[34]

The media have also taken these themes up enthusiastically, and commentary that supports biological explanations for stereotypes of childhood and adult behaviour can be found throughout print and broadcast and online media. For instance, we can read in the *Economist* that: 'In the 1970s there was a fad for giving dolls to baby boys and fire-engines to baby girls. The idea was that differences in behaviour between the sexes were solely the result of upbringing: culture turned women into ironers, knitters and chatterboxes, and men into hammerers, drillers and silent types. Switching toys would put an end to sexual sorting. Today, it is clear why it did not. When boys and girls are born, they are already different.'[35] Note how the connection of dolls and girls is linked to the fact that women are natural home-makers, the 'ironers' and the 'knitters'. Or, as Rosie Boycott, the journalist who co-founded the feminist magazine *Spare Rib* in the 1970s, said recently in the *Daily Mail*: 'You can see these differences from very early on – and they cannot be "overridden". Nature wins over nurture every time. I've had many feminist friends who have relentlessly presented their tiny daughters with bright-red fire engines to play with, only to be aghast when they throw them aside in favour of a Barbie doll. The converse is true for boys. Above all, the hormones women receive in the womb mean that, by nature, they do not want to be manic, one-dimensional workhorses who invest all their energies in one thing: their job.'[36] We can see the same themes voiced on television, so that the BBC in the UK and ABC in Australia recently ran similar series called *Secrets of the Sexes* and *Battle of the Sexes* which emphasised the biological basis for behavioural differences between the sexes. As the narrator on the British programme said: 'According to science, men are interested in things, women are interested in emotions.' The same ideas are pervading other aspects of the culture around us, from fiction to drama to feature films, and influencing our public, political lives and our private experiences.

It is intriguing to note that just as women are taking on more varied and powerful roles in the wider world, and just as men are being encouraged to take on what were once seen as feminine roles at home, there is this strand of our culture that so intently insists there are biological constraints to male and female equality that will never be overridden. If these biological explanations for the differences between men and women rested on the best evidence, then it would be futile to question them. But as I saw when I looked more closely at the science that is supposed to underpin this narrative, it is far more complicated, nuanced and subtle than we are often led to believe.

8: Myths

In order to see more clearly how we are often presented with a skewed picture of the real state of debate about sex differences, we can look at a controversy that erupted a few years ago. In 2005 Lawrence Summers, then president of Harvard University, got into a much publicised spat about the innate differences between men and women. He had been asked to speak about the under-representation of women on the science and engineering faculty at Harvard. When he came to give his talk at the National Bureau of Economic Research to a group of about fifty academics, he argued that because women naturally see the world in terms of family and human relationships, they will not be as happy as men in high-intensity careers.[1] He also argued that women do not have the same propensity as men to excel in scientific thought, which he called 'different availability of aptitude at the high end'. He said that such innate differences between men and women were more important than any social factors in creating inequality in certain occupations. 'So my best guess,' he said, '. . . of what's behind this is that the largest phenomenon, by far, is the general clash between people's legitimate family desires and employers' current desire for high power and high intensity, that in the special case of science and engineering, there are issues of intrinsic aptitude, and particularly of the variability of aptitude, and that those considerations are reinforced by what are in fact lesser factors involving socialization and continuing discrimination.'

As we have seen, these views have become pretty commonplace today. Many writers, teachers and parents now downgrade the influence of socialisation in favour of biological differences, and assume that women will naturally be more focused on relationships than working life, and less suited to logical and scientific thought. Although this view has now moved into the mainstream, it was very telling that if you look at the way the debate was covered in the British media, it was constantly suggested that Summers was actually breaking down some kind of taboo.

For instance, alongside its news reports the *Financial Times* ran two feature articles about the Summers dispute. In the first article the writer, Christopher Caldwell, stated that 'there is no clear evidence contradicting what Summers said. What there is, instead, is a taboo.' He went on to refer to Summers's 'easy erudition' and the fact that he was a 'first-rate scholar'; his critics, on the other hand, were characterised as 'resolutely obscurantist' and 'anti-intellectual'.[2] In a second article the same writer argued that there were no good arguments against what Summers said, but only the 'taboos that protect professorial privilege and self-regard', and damned the 'political correctness' of Harvard's faculty for arguing with him.[3]

Other newspapers also considered the debate in the same light. The *Sunday Times* covered the debate three times. Once, the conservative commentator Andrew Sullivan wrote, 'Summers is the best thing to happen to American higher education in a very long time. . . . For all the offence he has created, Summers has revealed one important fact: the truth sometimes is controversial.'[4] Next, in a news piece, the reporter said that the problem lay in the fact that 'American academics are renowned for political correctness,' and quoted the views of Steven Pinker, who stated that Lawrence Summers's words were 'masterly' and 'supported in the scientific literature'.[5] Then, editors chose Alan Dershowitz to defend Summers as a new Galileo, suffering from attack by the establishment. 'What if Summers were to be fired and in 10 years genetic research were to prove him correct? . . . It would not be shocking to discover that women, as a statistical matter, may have somewhat different aptitudes than men. We know that girls test higher in certain verbal skills than boys. Galileo, you will recall, was forced to recant the heliocentric theory, to apologise and to promise not to repeat his blasphemy. So, too, with Summers.'[6]

Much of this coverage suggested that Summers's views were controversial, but well supported by the evidence. This made it seem completely baffling when Summers backed down, apologised and put in place a taskforce to look at women's under-representation on the science and engineering faculty at Harvard. Was this really just the result of political correctness gone mad? Or was there a substantial body of opinion that was not being heard in the media, that had convinced him to retract? Summers's critics were hardly heard in the British media, although they were eager to find a public platform for their dissent.

Nancy Hopkins, a biology professor at the Massachusetts Institute of Technology, was the first and one of the leading critics of Lawrence Summers. She had been present at his talk and had left the room during it. When I contacted her soon after the speech I found she was not the kind to try to silence debate. She was happy to speak to journalists who contacted her about the issue, and, along with other academics who had been present at the meeting, was keen to see publication of Lawrence Summers's speech so that it could be debated fully in public rather than worried over behind closed doors. 'I felt that this speech was off the chart, it was so inappropriate, and I wanted to let the public know that,' she told me. 'We have solid evidence that discrimination is real. But despite all the work that is done on biological factors, we still have no solid concept of the genetic factors behind mathematical achievement, for instance, so to say that the brains of women are unsuited to math isn't science, it's just pure bias, it's so unscientific.'

Another of Summers's critics was Elizabeth Spelke, one of the world's leading experts in child cognition, professor in the Department of Psychology at Harvard University and director of the Laboratory for Developmental Studies. Over the last thirty years she has designed a series of experiments that study the innate abilities of young babies to assess their surroundings, to perceive objects and to make inferences about how objects behave. Other academics see Spelke as the prime mover in this field, as Karen Wynn, a Yale psychologist, told the *New Yorker* magazine in 2006. 'Spelke has done more to shape our understanding of how the human mind initially grasps the world than anyone else.'[7] Spelke was categorically critical of Summers's speech, calling it 'wrong, point for point'. And in the aftermath of the furore over his words she took up the challenge of a public debate with Steven Pinker in which she trenchantly argued that there are no differences in intrinsic aptitude for science among men and women.[8] This debate can be read online, and her reasoned arguments, with their constant appeal to the best evidence, contrast forcefully with the press's caricature of Summers's critics.

These scientists still feel frustrated by the way this debate was reported. When I spoke to Nancy Hopkins in 2008, she said that looking back she felt that much of the reportage had been extremely biased. In the *Washington Post*, Hopkins was branded a 'hysteric' who was 'theatrically flurried by an unwelcome idea and, like a Victorian maiden exposed to male coarseness, suffers the vapors and collapses on the drawing room carpet in a heap of crinolines until revived by smelling salts and the offending brute's contrition'.[9] Hopkins feels that these attacks obscured the real debate. 'It was said that we just didn't want to know the truth – I reject that characterisation of my views. I'm a scientist and I have spent my life in pursuit of the truth, and Lawrence Summers was not telling the truth. My fear is that many people have picked up this view, that he spoke out against politically correct women, rather than that we criticised him fairly, for putting forward inaccurate and biased views.'

This skewed coverage by the media when it comes to the science of sex difference is not a one-off occurrence. As we have seen in the last chapter, the work of writers who seem to support the narrative of biological determinism can be sure of a wide airing throughout the media. But when I talked to other scientists and academics who have put forward differing views, I found much dissent which is heard less clearly and less frequently. Deborah Cameron is professor of language and communication at the University of Oxford. She was recently moved to write a general interest book, *The Myth of Mars and Venus*,[10] rather than her usual academic papers, because she was incensed by the way the debate was going in the media. What was missing from the current debate, I asked her. 'Evidence!' she said furiously. 'There is a real debate about some of these issues in the academy. But the popular writers are picking and choosing the evidence that suits them. In all the science around gender difference the findings are very mixed. For instance, if you can find one study that shows differences in the male and female brain you can find another study that fails to find the same differences or that finds differences in the other direction. But these popular writers will only cite the evidence that suits them. And the media follow them.'

Melissa Hines is a professor of psychology at Cambridge, whose nuanced book *Brain Gender*[11] examines whether there are any innate sex differences in cognition and behaviour in humans. Journalists often get in touch with her when they have been commissioned to write stories in support of the popular narrative of biological determinism. When they hear her views, which do not discount the contribution of biology entirely, but look carefully at the full spectrum of evidence and the interplay between innate and environmental factors, sometimes they stop writing the piece, sometimes they ignore the dissenting evidence, and very occasionally they struggle with their editors to get these more nuanced views into print. One journalist from a respected weekly magazine contacted Hines and decided to try to get some of the dissenting evidence into the article she had been commissioned to write about the differences between men and women. I spoke to the journalist after publication. 'I was stunned by what Hines told me,' said the journalist, who wanted to stay anonymous. 'I kept on asking her, but what about this or that, and each time she'd demolish the so-called facts I'd been accumulating.' But when the journalist went back to her editors she found they were seriously reluctant to believe her research. 'I took a real beating from all of my colleagues,' she said, 'because this is a subject that everyone thinks they know a lot about. So everyone was arguing with me. And I just had to keep saying that the science didn't bear it out.' This article was then published next to an editorial by a senior member of staff, which pulled the argument towards the determinist point of view.

When I went to talk to Melissa Hines myself about her work I found a scientist who was becoming more and more frustrated with the way these issues are being reported in the media. 'In the media there is now this trend towards seeing sex differences as biologically determined,' she said, decisively. 'The way it is being conducted makes me uncomfortable, because we scientists are not really managing to have an honest and accurate conversation with people. Newspapers and magazines are trying to sell one point of view.' Having heard these scientists saying that they felt the media were often misrepresenting the state of the debate within the academy, I realised how important it has become to look more closely at these possible misrepresentations. If we are only hearing one side of the story when it comes to differences between men and women, it is time to ask what the story would sound like if we were able to hear the dissenting voices as well.

A: Babies

If we are going to look more closely at whether the current fashion for biological determinism rests on the best evidence, we should start at the very beginning. As we saw in the last chapter, the theory that there are innate differences in behaviour and cognition between men and women is held to apply to children. You can see why those who are convinced that biology forms our behaviour would want to find these differences present even at birth; otherwise, it might turn out to be possible to put these differences down to experience. It is unsurprising then that these writers have argued that even as babies, girls are more responsive to people than boys are. And it is this, they suggest, that lies behind all kinds of other differences between men and women, such as that men are more interested in systems such as cars, football scores and higher mathematics, while women are more interested in friends, families and relationships, which also plays out in men's dominance of the corridors of power and women's greater investment in domestic life.

One famous study suggests that this basic difference between boys and girls can be observed even in newborn babies. In an experiment published in 2000, a psychologist who worked with Simon Baron-Cohen, Jennifer Connellan, leant over day-old babies so that they could see her smiling face, and also showed them what was termed a 'mechanical mobile' (a hanging ball painted with human eyes in the wrong position). Boys looked for longer at the mobile, and girls looked for longer at the face.[12] When Simon Baron-Cohen published his book *The Essential Difference* in 2003, he took this study as one of the key pieces of evidence for the argument that the female brain is hardwired to relate to others, while the male brain is hardwired to work with systems rather than people.

In his book Baron-Cohen described this experiment at length, and concluded from it, 'The fact that this difference is present at birth strongly suggests that biology plays a role.'[13] The study has been frequently retold, sometimes in articles by Simon Baron-Cohen himself, in the *New York Times* and the *Guardian*,[14] and also by other writers. For instance, in the *New Statesman* the journalist Nick Cohen wrote that men are more likely than women to systemise the outside world, and quicker to see patterns, while women are better at empathising with others and producing a sympathetic response. As evidence he mentioned this experiment: 'Simon Baron-Cohen found that newborn boys, untouched by culture, were more likely than girls to look at a mobile than a human face.'[15] In the *Guardian*, the philosopher Helena Cronin wrote that there was a wealth of evidence that men and women differed in this way, 'even at one day old, girls prefer a human face, boys a mechanical mobile'.[16] In her book *The Sexual Paradox*, Susan Pinker argued that the differences we see in working patterns among men and women arise partly because women are more empathetic, and that this is seen from early infancy, well before any cultural expectations about women as nurturers can be absorbed. 'Just a few days after birth, the majority of newborn girls show more interest in looking at a human face than at a mechanical mobile,' she said.[17]

If a single study is given this much weight, we might expect that it would be taken seriously by the scientists' peers. Yet some of these peers are much less than respectful. They are scathing. When I talked to Elizabeth Spelke, this is what she had to say about this famous experiment. 'This is one single isolated experiment. Its findings fly in the face of dozens of studies on similar aspects of cognition carried out on young babies over decades. It is astonishing how much this one study has been cited, when the many studies that show no difference between the sexes, or a difference in the other direction, are ignored.' In a published article, Spelke pulled the experiment to pieces, arguing that it was unsatisfactory in three respects.[18] First, because it stands alone. It is usual, in infant research, to replicate key findings and assemble multiple experiments in support of any claim, in order to ensure that the result wasn't down to pure chance – chance will always produce a few rogue results. Yet no replication of this particular experiment has been published. This lack of replication is particularly telling because the other, numerous studies in this field, 'provide no evidence that male infants are more focused on objects and female infants are more focused on people from birth onwards'.[19] Second, because no attempt was made to break down the raw finding into something more precise – what was it that the male infants preferred about the mobile? Would their preference for an inanimate object remain if it was something other than this particular object that was chosen? And lastly, she feels that the study was not protected against experimenter's bias; it is rare for one person to devise and also carry out a study of this nature, as it is too easy in those situations for the researcher to bring her expectations to bear on the material.

Of all these criticisms, it is obviously the first, that this is an isolated result and that the other numerous studies in this field have failed to find similar results, that stands out. The history of such experiments, as Elizabeth Spelke states, goes back a long way. No one else has done a study identical to that carried out by Connellan, but other scientists have carried out studies that should, if the grand claims for innate gender differences are correct, show similar results. For instance, way back in 1966 five researchers – Jerome Kagan, Barbara Henker, Amy Hen-Tov,

Janet Levine and Michael Lewis – chose to study four-month-old infants and see how they reacted to four different three-dimensional objects: a regular face, a face in which the eyes, nose and mouth were rearranged, a face with no eyes, and a blank face (a face shape with the features removed). It seemed pretty clear that infants preferred the regular face – they smiled more at it. The only difference to emerge between the boys and girls was that the boys looked more at all the faces and smiled more at all the faces than the girls did; a difference that goes in the opposite direction to the observations of Connellan and Baron-Cohen.[20]

Reading through the article that describes this experiment, I was struck by another distinct difference. Connellan and Baron-Cohen took as given that longer gaze from babies on a particular object showed 'preference' for that object. So when the boy babies looked longer at what they called a mechanical mobile (though it was less a machine than a piece of abstract art), they called it 'mobile preference', and proof of 'stronger interest in mechanical objects', while female gaze at the face shows 'a stronger interest in the face'.[21] But the earlier researchers, Kagan, Henker, Hen-Tov, Levine and Lewis, have a much more intriguing view of what a longer gaze on the part of a pre-verbal baby might mean. It might mean liking, but it might mean being disconcerted. A baby does not have the luxury of speech to explain why it is gazing. We should be careful how we interpret their glances. As the earlier researchers stated, 'Adults gaze at colourful, graceful birds out of preference' but 'they stare at wingless flying objects because they wish to categorize them and reduce the uncertainty created by violation of a familiar schema. A long fixation, without additional information from other response modes, does not allow one to determine which of these two incentives is eliciting the sustained attention'.[22] In other words, if a baby looked longer at a scrambled face, one could have said that he or she was disconcerted that it didn't look as they expected and hoped a face should look, and was gazing at it out of anxiety. The greater subtlety and nuance expressed by researchers forty years ago when looking at infants' behaviour is telling.

Other researchers tell similar stories about the similarities among boys and girls and the ways they respond to faces. In 1968, two researchers called Howard Moss and Kenneth Robson set up an experiment which investigated how much boy and girl infants at one and three months of age looked at their mothers, how much they looked at geometric patterns, and how much they looked at regular and scrambled images of faces.[23] The study was primarily concerned to test the correlation between maternal anxiety and the behaviour of the infant, so it is coming from a rather different angle. Yet again, unlike Connellan and Baron-Cohen, they found no preference for the geometric over the picture of the face among the boys. It's particularly striking to note that the amount of time the babies spent gazing at their mothers' faces was similar for males and for females.

If boys were more drawn to objects than girls are, then it would follow that baby boys would be better than girls at assessing objects' properties and behaviour. This is where there is even more available research, none of which shows any such differences among infants.[24] Some find that girls were better 'systemisers' than boys. For instance, psychologists have found that babies look for longer when shown impossible physical events, such as boxes being suspended in mid-air, than at possible events, such as the box falling, but girls sometimes show this awareness of the difference between certain impossible and possible events at a younger age than boys do.[25] Given this long history of study of boy and girl infants over the years, Elizabeth Spelke has said this with confidence: 'Hundreds of well-controlled experiments reveal no male advantage for perceiving objects or learning about mechanical systems.'[26] The male and female babies in the three decades of research before Jennifer

Connellan and Simon Baron-Cohen's experiment have engaged equally with objects and people. When I spoke to Spelke by telephone, she was damning about the way that the one study that did show a difference in the hoped-for direction between male and female babies had been allowed, by the media, to drown out this long history of research on infants' development. 'Thirty to forty years of experiments in the field of cognitive development in young children have shown no consistent evidence for cognitive sex differences favouring males. If anything, young girls often seem to outperform boys in tests of early spatial awareness.'

Another popular writer who has promoted the theory that biology lies behind all observable differences between boys and girls is Louann Brizendine, whose book *The Female Brain* was published in 2006, and was covered numerous times in the British press, including extracts, interviews and commentaries in the *Daily Mail*, *Sunday Times* and *Daily Telegraph*. She believes that in contrast to boys, who have no interest in social interaction, girls are born with an automatic investment in relationships. 'Baby girls are born interested in emotional expression,' she writes. 'They take meaning about themselves from a look, a touch, every reaction from the people they come into contact with. . . . Little girls do not tolerate flat faces.'[27]

There are a series of studies that look directly at how baby girls and baby boys react to flat faces: the 'still face' studies. These studies have been carried out on infants between one and twelve months old, over the last thirty years. The classic experiment was simply to watch the interaction of baby and mother, both in a normal responsive interaction and then when the mother remained completely unresponsive, with a flat expressionless face, for three minutes. The baby's reactions, which seem to range from furious to flirtatious, are then assessed by psychologists, and shed interesting light on how babies seem to long for responsiveness and are deeply disconcerted by the lack of it. The long history of the still-face experiments shows that people have been wondering for many years whether baby boys and girls are primed to look for different things from the faces around them, and the results show only how impossible it is to get any clear answer. Although Brizendine would like us to believe that girls will not tolerate still faces, in fact similar reactions are observed in boys and girls. Lauren Adamson and Janet Frick, at Georgia University, carried out an overview of all the forty-three still-face studies that had been published from the late 1970s to 2001. They could say only this: 'Results related to gender effects have run the full gamut from none, to girls displaying more distress than boys, to girls appearing more positive than boys.'[28]

Those writers who believe that girls are born with a greater interest in people than boys also often say that from birth you can see easier relationships between baby girls and their carers than between baby boys and their carers. This is now a view that you often hear from parents in everyday life; I have lost count of the number of times that mothers of baby boys have told me that my easy relationship with my baby girl was down to her sex rather than her individual personality. Louann Brizendine sums up this view when she says, 'This superior brain wiring for communication and emotional tones plays out early in a baby girl's behaviour . . . The baby girl is able to resonate more easily with her mother and respond quickly to soothing behaviour, stopping her fussing and crying. Observations made during a study at Harvard Medical School found that baby girls do this better with their mothers than do boys.'[29] But when I went to look at Brizendine's reference for this statement, which is a study undertaken by Katherine Weinberg and colleagues at Harvard Medical School in 1999 I discovered that the picture these researchers found was more complicated than Brizendine suggested.

The male infants were indeed fussier and crosser, but they were more interested in emotional interactions with their mother than the girls were, who were more interested in their surroundings and less bothered by what their mother was up to. Although boys showed more negative expressive behaviour than girls, they surprisingly displayed significantly more positive expressions directed to the mother as well. Boys were also more likely than girls to display facial expressions of joy, to look at the mother and to vocalise to the mother. Girls, on the other hand, were more likely than boys to look at and explore objects. As these researchers put it: 'Boys were more socially oriented than girls. They were more likely than girls to look at their mother . . . Girls, in comparison with boys, spent substantially more time exploring objects.'[30]

When I read or listen to scientists such as these, whose work allows these nuanced pictures to emerge about babies' behaviour, it feels to me that they are much braver in the way they will accept the complexity of individual responses among infants. As Elizabeth Spelke said to me, 'I think there is now a tendency to focus on the finding that will reinforce a stereotype rather than the findings that challenge it.' As anyone who has brought up a baby will attest, the behaviour of infants is not always easy to predict and to summarise; as their individuality emerges they pass through many scudding moments of unexpected responses. Yet there is now a strand of thought that is becoming more and more powerful, which is so keen to fit babies of this generation into pink and blue boxes that it seems afraid to do justice to the full richness of their emerging humanity.

B: Words

For a long time there has been a general assumption that women talk more than men and are better at talking than men are. As Richard Madeley and Judy Finnigan joked on their popular daytime television show: 'Women may talk more than men,' Judy announced, 'but they've got twice as big a vocabulary.' Richard

retorted, 'I don't know what you, erm, what you, erm . . .'
'Mean, Richard?' cooed Judy.[31] John Gray rests much of his
case about the vast differences between men and women on the
apparent differences in the way that they talk. One chapter in his
classic book, *Men are from Mars, Women are from Venus*, is
called, 'Men go into their caves and women talk'. Here he puts
forward the example: 'When Tom comes home, he wants to
relax and unwind by quietly reading the news. He is stressed by
the unsolved problems of the day and finds relief through for-
getting them. His wife, Mary, also wants to relax from her
stressful day. She, however, wants to find relief by talking about
the problems of her day.'[32]

This assumption that femininity is based on a greater ease
with language is often presented as fact in the media, as when
the *Daily Mail* stated categorically in a headline, 'Women talk
three times as much as men, says study.'[33] This article was based
on statements made by Louann Brizendine in her book *The
Female Brain*. In this book, Brizendine stated that girls speak
two to three times more words per day than boys, and that on
average girls speak twice as fast as boys.[34] One expert in particular was nonplussed by her claims. Mark Liberman is a
professor of phonetics who contributes to a wry, witty blog (the
Language Log). When Brizendine's book was first published, he
saw a copy in a bookshop. 'The impressive list of bullet points
on the dust jacket caught my attention,' he told me. One of
these bullet points was: 'A woman uses about 20,000 words per
day while a man uses about 7,000.' Liberman was intrigued, as
he had never heard of such a figure. 'I figured that this must refer
to a new study that I hadn't heard about. I read the book and
checked the references. I was surprised – the book has copious
references to the scientific literature, and yet in the cases that I
checked, the cited references offered little or no support for the
controversial claims in the text.' The citation that she gave for
this claim for women speaking more than men was to a self-help

book,[35] rather than to any research evidence. In an article in the *Boston Globe*, Liberman commented, 'Unfortunately, this is just one of several cases in recent books on sex and neuroscience where striking numbers turn out to be without apparent empirical support.'[36]

Scientists at Arizona University then decided to try to prove or disprove the claim by studying the daily utterances of nearly four hundred people. Matthias Mehl, the lead researcher, commented that the claims that women speak three times as much as men appeared to have achieved the status of a cultural myth, having been so widely reported in so many different media. Yet this study showed conclusively that there was no statistically significant difference between men and women in the amount they talked. Women used a little more than 16,000 words a day, on average, and men a little less, but the difference was insignificant.[37]

Mark Liberman also investigated Brizendine's claim that girls speak more quickly than boys. He found that the only evidence she cited in support of the claim that girls speak at 250 words per minute as against 125 words per minute for boys was a paper that had no findings in it at all about speech rates broken down by gender. The only research that has been carried out into different speech rates among men and women has found small differences in the opposite direction, finding that men speak slightly faster than women. One paper that Liberman and his colleagues presented in 2006 found that: 'Males tend to speak faster than females . . . The difference between them is, however, very small, only about 4 to 5 words or characters per minute (2%), though it is statistically significant.'[38]

The idea has also taken hold that the typical woman does not only talk more, and more quickly, than men do, but she is simply better at talking than the men around her. This assumption is seen throughout our culture, particularly tellingly among those involved in children's education and upbringing. For instance, the Girls' Schools Association explains the importance of single-sex education because of: 'The tendencies of girls to be more contemplative, collaborative, intuitive and verbal, and boys to be more physically active, aggressive, and independent in their learning style.'[39] On the Supernanny website, which is a spinoff from an extremely popular television programme both in the UK and the US, advice on how to discipline your child tells parents they will need to use different strategies for their boys, 'Because boys aren't as good at expressing themselves verbally.'[40]

Funnily enough, there is no solid evidence for the idea that women's verbal skills are so much better than men's, although it has become such a touchstone of our current culture. On average, girls do develop language skills slightly earlier than boys, and so differences can be seen within age cohorts at school, but boys can catch up. Even if boys do not, on average, now perform as well as girls in some exams in the UK, there is no evidence that this is a biological and unchanging difference rather than one produced by a particular culture at a particular time when many boys are encouraged to believe that reading and homework are not cool.

Dr Janet Shibley Hyde is a psychologist who has specialised in meta-analysis – a way of combining results from many published studies – of gender differences in cognition. She started doing massive meta-analyses of studies of language skills in the 1980s and has consistently found that the differences are far smaller than are usually believed. In 1988 Dr Hyde carried out a meta-analysis of 165 studies that assessed differences in verbal abilities between girls and boys, including abilities in vocabulary, analogies, reading comprehension, essay writing, anagrams and general verbal ability. All the differences did favour girls – boys did a little better on analogies, but otherwise the girls came out better. But the telling point of her analyses is the size of the differences. They were tiny. There is a huge range in the verbal abilities within each sex, but hardly any difference between each sex.[41] Overall, she concluded that 'gender differences accounted for only about one per cent of the variance in verbal ability'. So you are just as likely, as a woman, to bump into a woman who is very different from you in verbal skills as you are to find a man who is very different from you. This means that to talk of a 'female brain' that is 'wired for communication', as some writers do, is nonsense, since male brains seem to be working in exactly the same way.[42]

Why is it, then, that we seem to return so frequently to the idea that women are better at talking than men are? In an interview with the *Guardian*, Liberman said that Louann Brizendine's claim about women speaking more than men was simply an urban myth, and commented that: 'Urban legends come about because they concern things that resonate with people's experiences in some way. They are factually untrue but mythically resonant.'[43] It is hard not to agree with Liberman's assessment here, and although this legend is often characterised by a nod towards female superiority – as with the Richard and Judy joke at the beginning of this section – it can also feel very constraining. The idea that women talk so much more than men seems to grow from the idea that women talk too much, that their words are surplus to requirements. Even when this myth is voiced positively, it can be restrictive. It has long been a tradition of Western culture that women like to gossip with friends at home, while men are out working, often in a solitary and single-minded way. Although men and women are now beginning to cross into each other's roles at work and at home, it is clearly highly reassuring for many people to believe that there is one sex-based division of labour, the work that women do to preserve relationships through their greater verbal skills, which will continue. And so even when this assumption is clothed in rhetoric about women's superiority, it still reinforces traditional stereotypes about a woman's place in society.

Even if we could shrug off the myths that women talk better

than men or talk more than men, we are likely to be left with the persistent view that women talk differently from men. This is the most recalcitrant belief of all when it comes to words: that women are good at cooperative, supportive talk, while men are good at point-scoring and logical argument. For instance, Deborah Tannen, a professor of linguistics, writes bestselling books that promote this view of how men and women differ. In her world, a typical man engages with the world, 'as an individual in a hierarchical social order in which he was either one-up or one-down. In this world, conversations are negotiations in which people try to achieve and maintain the upper hand if they can.' A typical woman, on the other hand, approaches the world 'as an individual in a network of connections. In this world, conversations are negotiations for closeness in which people try to seek and give confirmation and support, and to reach consensus.'[44]

This view of the differences between men and women does not just assume that women have a superior ability to talk, it also assumes a superior ability to empathise, and these skills are commonly seen as inextricably linked. 'The safest conclusion at this point is that females are *both* better empathisers and better in many aspects of language use,' says Simon Baron-Cohen in *The Essential Difference*.[45] When the new supporters of biological explanations for sex differences have argued that women are characteristically 'empathisers', they have received powerful support from the media. The questionnaires developed by Simon Baron-Cohen and his team at Cambridge University, which are supposed to test whether you have an empathetic or systemising brain, can be found on the *Guardian's*[46] website, and a related version is on the BBC's website.[47]

Most people could probably agree that anecdotally we can all call to mind situations that back up the observation that women are more empathetic communicators than men, situations in which women do the work of preserving and extending relationships through their words, while men don't bother to talk unless they want something specific communicated or discovered. Most of us have experienced these situations, both at work and at home, in our friendships and professional relationships.

However, it is a big step from observing a difference to assuming that it is rooted in biological factors that are necessarily resistant to change. The arguments of the biological determinists take the observed differences between men and women and link them to genetic and hormonal differences which were laid down for us aeons ago by evolutionary pressures, and which cannot be wiped away by social change. If you are sceptical about the narrative of biological determinism, you need not disregard the differences you can often see in the ways that men and women communicate in our society. But you could look at the way these current differences may be produced not just by innate drives but by the expectations around us. Some fascinating research has shown that our expectations about the way men and women differ will even influence our apparent ability to empathise. So women do tend to score more highly than men in many studies of adults' empathy, whether those entail judging how people are feeling from looking at photographs of their eyes, or simply reporting how much they care about those close to them. Yet two psychologists who reviewed these studies found this striking truth: that this apparent superiority in empathising was clearly linked to the expectations that individuals knew they should be living up to. They found, looking at a number of studies, that it was only when women and men were aware of what was being assessed that significant differences were found between male and female responses. They concluded: 'There was a large sex difference favouring women when the measure of empathy was self-report scales; moderate differences (favouring females) were found for reflexive crying and self-report measures in laboratory situations; and no sex differences were evident when the measure of empathy was either physiological or unobtrusive observations of nonverbal reactions to another's emotional state.' In other words, when people are aware of what they are being asked to do and can control their responses, they live up to the stereotypes about how men and women should behave. But when reactions are being observed that are less controllable or when the subjects are not sure what is being assessed, men and women are much more variable.[48] This suggests that much so-called research on this subject is not actually testing innate differences, because it fails to screen out the way we try, maybe without even consciously knowing we are doing so, to conform to social norms.

If the way we communicate is not just influenced by our innate aptitudes but also by the situation around us, it is absolutely vital to remember that when we look at men and women talking, we are still not always looking at communica-tion between equals. The effects of an imbalance of power on the way we communicate have been revealed in some telling research. For instance, Sara Snodgrass of Florida Atlantic University created studies in which she put thirty-six pairs of people together and gave one a dominant, teacher-like role and one a subordinate role for their first task, before giving them games to play. Their responsiveness to the other's emotions and feelings was then assessed. It became clear that those given the subordinate role were more sensitive to the other person than those given the leader's role – whatever their sex. '"Women's intuition" would perhaps more accurately be referred to as "sub-ordinate's intuition",' Snodgrass concluded.[49]

This study and others like it suggest that the empathy and sen-sitivity that are celebrated as feminine traits in our society may be less down to our innate aptitudes and more down to the sit-uations in which we find ourselves and the expectations that have been formed by the culture around us. In fact, we may all have much more potential to cross these pink and blue bound-aries than the biological narrative would suggest. I think we can see this flexibility constantly in everyday life. We have all met women who are utterly chilly communicators, and men who are able to encourage others to feel immediately at ease. The simplistic view of male and female communication peddled by some writers who believe our behaviour is determined by biology denies the true complexity of how we really communicate with one another. At times most of us are capable of being empathetic, at other times authoritative, at times loving, at other times heartless. To point out that women may have no natural superiority in empathising is not to say that the association between femininity and empathy is a negative aspect of being female: on the contrary, to respond to another's needs, to be sensitive to another's emotions – this is an essential part of being fully human. Rather than asking women to sweep this 'subordinate's intuition' out of their lives, it may be time to insist that more men learn these responses themselves. But this change will be slowed, or even blocked, if we keep telling men that ordinary empathy and sensitivity to others relies on an innate gift that only women are likely to have.

If it is wrong to believe that men and women communicate so differently, then why do so many people buy into this myth? Why do millions of people buy *Men are from Mars, Women are from Venus*, and so (relatively) few a debunking book like Deborah Cameron's excellent *The Myth of Mars and Venus*? I think that the resilience of the myth of men and women's differing communication rests on the fact that it foregrounds something we all feel to be true: that we are often misunderstood. Many of us long for the perfect partner, who can understand everything without being told; many of us are disappointed by reality. Many of us find that we are blocked, whether in our working life or our home life, from achieving the transparent communication we desire. It is easy, therefore, to look at the communication problems described by writers such as John Gray or Deborah Tannen and to nod in agreement. If we are honest, however, we would acknowledge that the problems men and women face when they talk to one another do not always run along the lines of the grunting male and the chattering female. We are more individual, more variable, more subtle, than that narrative will ever allow.

C: Maths

Another key theme of the new biological determinism when it comes to differences between the sexes is that while women may excel at empathising, they are deficient in systemising skills, or in logic as against intuition, or reasoning as against feeling. Above all, one key theme that emerges in this new biological determinism is that despite our decades of equal opportunity, men are still so much better at certain areas of maths. The theory that men have a biological superiority at maths is now often used to explain why many fewer women go into careers that require mathematical ability. In *The Blank Slate*, the eminent psychologist Steven Pinker says, 'The fact that more men than women have exceptional abilities in mathematical reasoning and in mentally manipulating 3-D objects is enough to explain a departure from a fifty-fifty sex ratio among engineers, physicists, organic chemists, and professors in some branches of mathematics.'[50] And it was this argument that the then president of Harvard, Lawrence Summers, picked up on when he said that 'issues of intrinsic aptitude' would be one of the factors that produced female under-representation on the science and engineering faculty at Harvard.

This view has been generally accepted by much of the mainstream media. As one science journalist put it in the *Sunday Telegraph* in 2004: 'The highest ranks of mathematicians throng with male minds that are more comfortable with its abstract concepts of space, geometry and number . . . In recent years, various studies have concluded that sex differences are more than skin deep: the brains of men and women handle language and emotion in different ways, with differences in brain structure. This, in turn, may reflect our evolutionary past, and how men's brains were optimised to hunt and women's to gather.'[51] Or as a commentator put it in the *Sunday Times* in 2008, 'We are also recognising that across a population women's and men's abilities vary; you would expect women to be underrepresented in quantum mechanics or navigation; though individual women may excel in these fields, women in general are unlikely to do so, for innate reasons.'[52]

For all the categorical certainty that some writers bring to the discussion of this difference between men and women, many scientists question whether it is true that there are differences in aptitude for maths or science among men and women. Janet Shibley Hyde, the psychologist who has spent years on meta-analysis of studies that investigate gender differences in cognition, has found that even for maths, 'the findings were quite surprising, given the long-held belief in a male superiority in mathematics,'[53] since the differences found were all small except in a couple of narrow areas. The only area of maths that consistently throws up a moderate or large difference in favour of men is their ability for spatial visualisation. This is particularly shown in a standard test used to diagnose the ability to rotate three-dimensional objects mentally. This test involves looking at line drawings of 3-D shapes consisting of blocks in different positions, and deciding which of the shapes is identical. This does not mean that in all tests of 3-D skills men score more highly; if people are asked to pick out shapes in complex patterns or to visualise what a folded paper would look like unfolded, men and women score similarly. In fact, if you look at this one test that shows a large difference in aptitude it is extraordinary what a narrow area of intellectual ability it is testing, and many scientists question how significant it is. Melissa Hines's book *Brain Gender* discusses the full panoply of

sex differences in cognition, and as she says sharply, 'Most scientific fields require numerous skills in addition to (and
probably even more than) the ability to rotate a three-dimensional shape in the mind.'[54]

What's more, there is a growing and fascinating literature
which suggests that differences between men and women on
basic tests of spatial awareness can be reduced or wiped out by
practice. Not practice over years, but practice over just hours.
For instance, in one study published in 2000, forty-four men and
women were asked to do the standard mental rotations test.
Half of the subjects were first of all given a similar test, a 'familiarisation task', that did not involve mental rotation, instead
involving colour matching, but did involve pressing similar but-
tons on the computer and following similar instructions. In the
group who were not given any familiarisation with the task sex
differences were found, but in the group who performed the
mental rotation task after the colour-matching task, sex differences were not found.[55] The researchers ponder whether this is
because women are more anxious and need to be warmed up to
the task, or whether they simply are less used to using computers to play games and take tests. Other studies have found
similar results.[56] When men and women were asked to do about
ten hours of playing a 'first-person shooter action game' called
Medal of Honor: Pacific Assault, it had a measurable effect on
their spatial abilities. Before and after playing the game, they
took two tests, one involving spatial attention and the other the
standard mental rotations test. After practice, women no longer
did worse than the men at the test of spatial attention, and their
performance in the mental rotation test was also improved. The
researchers concluded – maybe tongue in cheek – 'we can only
imagine the benefits that might be realised after weeks, months,
or even years of action-video-gaming experience.'[57]

When men and women are enrolled on identical maths
courses, it is hard to see any differences in the way the sexes per-

form. For instance, although fewer girls than boys do maths A level in the UK, the girls now get higher grades. Similarly, in the US a recent study looked at the results from seven million students in ten states, and found that: 'Now that enrollment in advanced math courses is equalized, we don't see gender differences in test performance.'[58] Since the expected gaps in many tests are closing, those writers who would still prefer to believe that sex differences in mathematical ability are innate and unchanging tend to cite one test that still tends to show boys outperforming girls, the mathematics section of the SAT that is taken by students in the US prior to college entry. Even British writers such as Simon Baron-Cohen cite the results from the American mathematics SAT rather than results from British exams.[59] Yet the results even of this test are showing a shrinking gap. Steven Pinker said in *The Blank Slate*, published in 2002, that the ratio of boys to girls getting the highest scores was thirteen to one.[60] This figure was drawn from tests administered in the 1980s. But by the 1990s this ratio had dropped substantially, to just 2.8 to one.[61] The continued gap in the SAT-M results can in fact be explained by the reality that many more girls take it than boys do, since more girls now try for college, and therefore the pool of girl entrants is less highly selected than the pool of boys.[62]

Melissa Hines is American, a graduate of Princeton and UCLA, and she now works at the University of Cambridge in the UK. She has seen the way the debate on boys' and girls' maths performance is handled differently in the US and the UK, so that two different situations can be interpreted in a way that still backs up the fatalistic view that girls should do worse than boys. As Hines said to me when we met in London: 'In the US where the girls are doing not as well as boys in some tests, the information seems to be interpreted as showing that girls just aren't as good at these things so we can't expect them to be mathematicians. But here in the UK people are reacting to boys not doing as well as girls in maths exams by saying, what can we do about that, we need to fix that . . . This difference is telling.' It is indeed.

Evidence that the gap is closing between men and women in many maths tests has begun to make some writers rather wary about citing 'intrinsic aptitude' when explaining the lack of women in certain occupations. We have therefore seen a shift in the argument, from the idea that there are innate differences in aptitudes, to the idea that there are innate differences in aspirations. To put it most simply, the argument goes, men are born to like maths, and women are not. To put it more subtly, as Susan Pinker does in *The Sexual Paradox*: 'Biological differences may underlie aspects of women's occupational choices – the type of work they find appealing and how many hours they want to commit to it. Even with dramatic changes in customs, laws and social expectations . . . there are aspects of women's work preferences that are likely to stay the same.'[63]

In this narrative, it doesn't matter how much you encourage women to do maths, they will never choose to be scientists or engineers or computer programmers in the same numbers as men. And it's true that at the moment more men than women clearly do aspire to these fields: women do not go into higher level maths courses, do science degrees or take up work in science, engineering and maths at the same rate as men, and this is not just about raw ability. Women who do well in the mathematics section of the SATs are only half as likely to pursue such careers as men who have the same test scores as they do.[64] So there is something else that pushes women away from such careers, other than pure ability.

But it is way too early for commentators to go from there to the conclusion that men's greater preference for and performance in careers involving maths and science is innate and unchanging. We still live in a society in which women are not being encouraged into these areas in the same way that boys are;

not just by school and university teachers, but by peer and parental expectations, and by the culture around them. For instance, studies have shown that mothers overestimate the maths abilities of their sons and underestimate the maths abilities of their daughters, and that male high-school students in the US are aware that their teachers, mothers and fathers have more favourable views of their maths abilities than those of female high-school students. Psychologists have also found that mothers' perceptions of their children's abilities influence those children's beliefs about their abilities even more than the children's own grades, and that parents' low expectations for their daughters are related both to the girls' lower expectations of their own performance, and to their intentions not to do so much maths at school.[65]

Although some of this research was carried out in the 1980s and 1990s, I think we should not underestimate the fact that in some ways things are moving backwards, and this is a culture in which women are now frequently told, by bestselling writers and the media that often follow them uncritically, that women who have typical feminine brains and normal levels of feminine hormones may be naturally unsuited to mathematical and scientific careers. When we assume that our sons will be more interested in systems, from chess to mathematics, and that our daughters will be more interested in relationships, are we letting their choices lead us, or are we moulding their choices? The next chapter will look in much more detail at the way that stereotypes influence even women's performance in supposedly objective tests and even their choices in apparently unconstrained situations.

It seems far too early, to me, to make assumptions about what girls on average and boys on average would be interested in if they were growing up free from these expectations. Far from being in a position yet to judge whether men and women would have equal aspirations to work involving maths and science in an equal world, we are still living with attitudes that make it surprising women are making the strides that we can see. In the US, women were 8 per cent of the science and engineering workforce in 1973; in 1999 they were 24 per cent.[66] So it is clear that those who would see our working patterns as biologically determined have their work cut out in stating that women's minds are unsuited to working in scientific careers. In order not to trammel the dreams of the next generation, perhaps it is better not to peddle ideas of what women are naturally suited for before they have shown us what they can actually do.

D: Hormones

Writers who look to biological explanations for all sex differences tend to see hormones as having an irresistible power to mould our behaviour. Hormones are indeed what make us male or female. Information encoded in the genes begins the process of physical sex differentiation, but it is the production of testosterone and the response of cells to testosterone that turns a foetus fully male. For instance, if a boy foetus has a rare condition that means his cells do not respond to testosterone (Complete Androgen Insensitivity Syndrome), he will look exactly like a girl when he is born even though he is genetically male; testosterone is essential to make a boy a boy.

The promoters of biological explanations for sex differences are keen to establish direct links not only between hormones and physical sex differences, but also between hormones and those differences in intelligence and behaviour that they believe are innate to men and women. If those links didn't exist, or were tenuous, then we might have to look again at the influence of society and parents and friends. I would have thought that nobody would want to deny that our personalities and our moods, as well as our physical being, are affected by the hormone environment in the womb or the levels of our sex hormones during our lifetimes. But current theories of how sex hormones act tend to gloss over all complexities. While many scientists suggest that we are only at the beginning of understanding how hormones can interact with one another and with other physical experiences, we often hear from the media and some popular writers that certain hormones simply pull the strings of our personalities. For instance, a television programme called *Battle of the Sexes* that aired on ABC in Australia in 2002 laid out its agenda from the start. 'Program one presents men and women as two separate species with radically different evolutionary agendas. . . . The film then takes the hormone-fuelled rocket journey to puberty to show that many of the differences between the sexes are pre-programmed.'[67]

More than one hormone has been implicated in the creation of feminine behaviour. For a long time the spotlight was on oestrogen, and it was suggested that men who were exposed to elevated levels of oestrogens would have no choice but to fall in with feminine patterns of behaviour. There was a time when women were prescribed a synthetic oestrogen (diethylstilbestrol) in an attempt to prevent repeated spontaneous miscarriages, so studies were then carried out to find out whether this had any effect on the behaviour of the babies after birth. According to some writers, the observed effects were clearcut, as Simon Baron-Cohen explains: 'Boys born to such women are likely to show more female-typical behaviours – enacting social themes in their play as toddlers, for example, or caring for dolls.'[68]

Yet such a categorical claim is not supported by much of the evidence, as Melissa Hines shows in her book *Brain Gender*: 'Information on boys exposed to DES or other estrogens prenatally . . . suggests a general lack of influences on childhood behaviour,' she states.[69] For instance, one large study confounded the expectations of the researchers. They tested 140 adult subjects whose mothers had taken female hormones during pregnancy, asking them about their childhood play behaviour and running various cognitive and psychological tests on them. One key finding was that, 'The DES [diethylstilbestrol] exposed subjects had the most conventionally "masculine" childhood behaviours.'[70]

More recently the idea has taken hold that the hormone responsible for femininity is oxytocin. Many scientists and media commentators have turned to this hormone for the explanation for women's apparently innate abilities to empathise and nurture. For instance, both the ABC series *Battle of the Sexes* and a very similar BBC series *Secrets of the Sexes* showcased the same 'experiment', in which a little girl was left alone on a street to see who would stop to offer help, men or women. Women stopped far more often; which is what one would expect in a society in which to be suspected of interest in pre-pubescent girls is likely to lay men open to intense criticism. But only one explanation was offered – as the Australian series put it: 'There is a chemical reason for empathic behaviour in women,' the narrator told the viewers. 'Women produce more oxytocin, which is a brain chemical stimulated by childbirth. Oxytocin is designed to help mothers nurture their offspring, and it also gives women a greater ability to empathise with others. Why do men not share this natural ability?'[71] The writer John Gray has also embraced oxytocin as a catch-all explanation for feminine behaviour. As he puts it, oxytocin creates the need in women to invest a great deal of energy in loving and being loved: 'Oxytocin creates a feeling of attachment. Levels increase when women connect with someone through friendship, sharing, caring and nurturing and decrease when a woman misses someone or experiences a loss or breakup or feels alone, ignored, rejected, unsupported, and insignificant. To feel good in a relationship, a woman needs to trust that her partner cares for her as much as she cares for him. This kind of support directly affects her oxtyocin levels, which in turn will lower her stress. Messages from him of caring, under-standing, and respect can build trust and nourish her soul while stimulating higher levels of oxytocin.'[72]

Oxytocin is indeed released during childbirth and during breastfeeding, when it stimulates the contractions of the womb and the let-down reflex of breasts, and for both sexes it seems to be released at orgasm. At these times it certainly does correlate to the moving sense of being connected and in love with another being. There has also been interesting research carried out which suggests that if individuals' levels of oxytocin are artificially raised they may be more ready to behave in a trusting manner. But if you search for the evidence to prove that higher levels of oxytocin are behind women's greater investment in their social and family lives, you will be a long time looking. Most research on oxytocin has been carried out on other animals, especially rodents, and one recent review of all the human and animal stud-ies on the effects of oxytocin could only conclude that the evidence for the influence of oxytocin on human behaviour seemed 'contradictory' and open to 'competing' interpretations.[73]

At times elevated levels of this hormone correlate with loving and unstressed behaviour in humans, but at times they correlate with the opposite. For instance, when scientists at the University of California investigated the relationship between older women's social networks and their oxytocin levels, they found the opposite result to the one that the popular narrative would predict. Oxytocin was actually higher in women experiencing chronic problems in their social relationships, including 'decreased contact with friends and family and an unrewarding partner relationship'.[74] These researchers had to conclude that far from being John Gray's straightforward hormone of love and understanding, 'Oxytocin levels may be a marker of rela-tionship stress.'[75] Similarly confusing for the idea that oxytocin is behind women's feminine, empathetic behaviour was a recent study which found that when couples kissed, oxytocin levels went up for men, but down for women; which was in the opposite direction to that predicted by the theory that women look for love in order to boost their oxytocin levels.[76]

It is often assumed that typical femininity is created not just by the presence of some magical pink elixir, but also by the absence of a magical blue elixir. As we all know, the hormone testosterone is thought to create the mythical masculinity of aggression and competitiveness, and women's low levels of testosterone are often assumed to lie behind their poor showing in masculine traits. That BBC1 series *Secrets of the Sexes* presented the idea that men are innately better at logical thinking and competing because of their testosterone, and in a driving competition in which men did better than women the voiceover intoned: 'Women can be competitive, but they don't have the edge that testosterone gives men.'[77] There is nothing new about the reliance on testosterone as the explanation for everything we associate with masculinity. Connections have been made between testosterone and all kinds of power-hungry, aggressive, competing behaviour everywhere in the media, in fiction, non-fiction, journalism and broadcasting. As one typical commentator in *The Times* put it, 'My sons charging around, competing, building, climbing and fighting, are run on that human rocket fuel, testosterone.'[78] Testosterone has been implicated in men's greater reliance on logic, on their supposedly greater sense of humour,[79] apparently greater artistic abilities, and perceived advantage in systemising and spatial skills.[80]

To find evidence for this picture of the effects of testosterone, scientists over the years have been particularly interested in those people who were exposed to high levels of testosterone as foetuses. In the rare condition called Congenital Adrenal Hyperplasia, foetuses, male or female, are exposed to excessive levels of testosterone in the womb. We know what many writers would assume would be the results of this deluge of testosterone for girls: they will lose their femininity and become more aggressive, less empathetic, and better at systemising. Many writers would also assume that it means they would have better spatial skills, so Simon Baron-Cohen tells us: 'As one would predict, girls with CAH have *enhanced spatial systemising*, compared with their sisters or other close female relatives without CAH . . . Girls with CAH *score as well as normal boys*, and *dramatically better than normal girls*.'[81] Helena Cronin, the Darwinian philosopher, writes in the *Guardian*: 'females exposed to "male" hormones in the womb are typically "tomboyish" and *surpass the female average in spatial skills* – and vice versa for males'.[82] Steven Pinker in *The Blank Slate* says that girls with CAH 'grow into tomboys, with more rough and tumble play, a greater interest in trucks than dolls, *better spatial abilities*.'[83] Susan Pinker, in *The Sexual Paradox*, says, 'They have *better spatial skills* and are more competitive, aggressive, and self-confident than other girls.'[84] [My italics all through.] However, if you look at the evidence, this has simply not been proved. Melissa Hines analysed all the available studies in her book *Brain Gender*, and found that of seven studies assessing spatial abilities in females with CAH, only three found evidence that females with CAH perform better than unaffected females, and the largest studies showed no such result – indeed, the study with the second largest sample found that females with CAH performed worse than matched female controls.[85]

Similarly unpredictable results are seen throughout the literature on the effects of testosterone. Far from bringing us a clearcut story of how testosterone sets up stereotypical masculinity, we find a very muddled picture about how this hormone affects behaviour. Some studies go in the right direction for the biological narrative. For instance, Simon Baron-Cohen's team at Cambridge University tested samples of amniotic fluid from women who had given birth at Addenbrooke's Hospital and then observed their babies as toddlers. They found that toddlers who had been identified as having been exposed to less testosterone in the womb had 'higher levels of eye contact and a larger vocabulary'.[86] Other studies have also shown a relationship between pre-natal testosterone and whether children will fall in with stereotypical masculine behaviour. For instance, one large recent study has suggested that high levels of testosterone in the womb correlate with masculine play behaviour for girls.[87]

These are two studies that do show a role for testosterone in creating masculinity along the expected lines, and you can find others.[88] But as I trawled through some of the literature I found there is also a lot of research that has failed to reinforce the expected narrative, and that gives us a much more complicated picture of the effects of testosterone in the womb.

For instance, a Canadian psychologist, Jo-Anne Finegan, measured testosterone in amniotic fluid and outcomes in children at the age of four years. She found that for the girls in the study, the more testosterone they were exposed to, the worse they were at counting and sorting, number questions, and block building. That result is in the opposite direction to the one you would expect if you assumed a link between testosterone and systemising skills. She also found that there was a relationship between higher levels of testosterone in girls and higher language comprehension, which was also against the direction predicted. For the boys in the study, no relationships were found.[89] When four Dutch psychologists set out to test whether higher prenatal testosterone was associated with more masculine play behaviour in toddlers, they found no significant relationship between maternal sex-hormone levels and masculine or feminine play behaviour in either boys or girls. The only correlation those psychologists found was between progesterone and masculine play for boys, which was hardly predicted.[90]

There is much other evidence on the record that shows how the predicted relationships between testosterone and masculinity have been hard to find.[91] When I looked through the studies that fall on one side and those that fall on the other I could not judge which of them were right, as obviously I am not qualified to do that, but I could see, very clearly indeed, that the consensus some commentators assume is there does not, in fact, exist. Where consensus does exist in the academy about testosterone, it often works against the traditional narrative. One of the links that is always made most strongly in the popular imagination is, of course, the link between testosterone and aggression. The reason why women are so much more cooperative and gentler than men, it is thought, is simply because they don't get the necessary injection of testosterone. In animals, the relationship is very clear. Melissa Hines, who started her career more than thirty years ago by looking at aggression and the correlation with testosterone, laughs when she says how simple it is in rats. 'If you give rats more testosterone they become more aggressive; take it away and they become less aggressive. But in humans? People have been trying to find the same pattern in humans for years. But it's much, much harder to find. We do have to ask if it's really there.'

What we may think is evidence of the effects of testosterone may in fact be evidence of the effects of social expectations. Take this famous Californian experiment as an example. It was a double-blind experiment – an experiment in which neither the subjects nor the administrators know who is receiving the real drug – in which forty-three healthy men were given either a high dose of testosterone or a placebo for ten weeks. Those who received testosterone, but did not know it, did not experience increased anger, according to self-reports, and ratings by observers including parents and spouses suggested no changes in angry or aggressive moods or behaviour. On the other hand, in a second study those men given a placebo and told it was testosterone did report greater anger, irritation and impulsivity. This shows that when we are talking about what we think are the results of men's higher testosterone we may be talking about something else altogether.[92]

Our belief that there must be a direct, one-way link between hormones and typically masculine behaviour may blind us to the part that social expectations play in keeping women and men within stereotyped roles. I was very taken by the description of one intriguing study, which seemed to dramatise the way that women mask their own aggressiveness – even from themselves. Two Princeton psychologists asked eighty-four men and women to play a video game in which they would be bombed by an opponent and then would have the chance to bomb that opponent. Half the study participants were told that their identities were known to the researchers; the other half were told they were anonymous. What was so interesting was that women became as aggressive as men when they thought they were anonymous, but held back when they thought they were being watched. What's more, when, after the game, participants were asked to describe their own aggressiveness and the number of bombs they dropped, the men accurately described themselves as aggressive. But the women reported that they had behaved less aggressively than they really had. The failure of women's self-reports to reflect their own high levels of aggression in the anonymous condition was striking, given the evidence that they were at least as aggressive as males. The researchers concluded, 'We consider the findings to be evidence that people do not accurately perceive their own behaviour, but instead assume it to be in accordance with established norms and expectations.'[93]

Such research alerts us to the possibility that even though we are so eager to look for biological reasons behind masculine and feminine behaviour, other factors could be equally, if not more, important.

E: Brains

Alongside the theory that the differences in feminine and masculine behaviour are produced by the action of certain hormones, is the theory that the proof that we are destined for such different roles can be seen in physical differences in men's and women's brains. This theory has really taken off in this generation, since recently developed techniques such as positron emission tomography and functional magnetic resonance imaging make it possible to look into the workings of the living brain, and these techniques have spawned much research that shows differences between male and female brains. Month after month, broadcast media and broadsheet and tabloid newspapers make excited statements such as: 'Do men really listen with just half a brain? Research sheds some light'[94] or 'Men may as well be from Mars and women from Venus for all the sexes have in common emotionally; brain scans showed major differences in the ways in which men and women responded to emotional stimuli.'[95]

One of the most commonly expressed ideas about men's and women's brains is that women use the left brain more, and men use the right brain more, and that the right hemisphere processes space and systems while the left processes words and emotions. As one commentator in *The Times* put it when writing about her sons, 'With their greater muscle bulk and *right-brain development*, they are less likely to sit around threading beads, making subtle, nuanced, *left-brainy* conversation [my italics].'[96] Neuroscientists over the years have examined whether this difference can be seen in a physically larger right hemisphere in men's brains. And much of the media have now assumed that this is the case, so a recent study of the relative sizes of brain hemispheres among gay and straight men and women was reported as though there was a simple consensus that straight men's brains show greater rightward asymmetry. 'Scans reveal homosexual men and heterosexual women have symmetrical brains, with the right and left hemispheres almost exactly the same size. Conversely, lesbians and straight men have asymmetrical brains, with the right hemisphere significantly larger than the left,' was how this study was reported in the *Guardian* in a huge and lavishly illustrated article.[97]

Funnily enough, there is dissent even about the basic proposition that rightward asymmetry exists in the physical structure of the male brain. When the results of this particular study were scrutinised by Mark Liberman, he found that not only was the sample studied extremely small, there was also a great overlap between the men and the women.[98] Other studies, what's more, have found different patterns. While some studies of the human brain have found that 'cerebral volume for males was larger on the right than on the left',[99] others have found that 'leftward asymmetry was more pronounced' in males,[100] or that 'males exhibited a leftward and females a rightward asymmetry for grey matter and females exhibited greater rightward asymmetry than males for total matter',[101] or that 'In human male foetuses a larger right hemisphere volume has been identified, but so far no equivalent pattern has been reported in adults.'[102]

This is one example of the current gap between what is seen as a consensus about men's and women's brains, and the range of evidence that actually exists. Although so many differences between the male and female brain have been found in recent research, many of these findings have come under intense questioning, either for their reliability or for their significance. The reality is that there is no proof that femininity is laid down for women in the structure of their brains. Another example of the gap between a purported consensus and the range of evidence which I found very intriguing is the debate about the size of the corpus callosum, which is the area of the brain that contains millions of nerve fibres connecting the two hemispheres. The fashionable idea is that this area is bigger in women than in men. This idea first gained prominence in 1982, when an article was published in *Science* which claimed to be the first report of a reliable sex difference in the arrangement of the human brain, noting that the splenium of the corpus callosum was larger and more bulbous in women's brains.[103]

Since then, it has been constantly repeated that this larger corpus callosum is linked to women's greater empathy, or intuition, or ability to multi-task. One American journalist wrote in 2005: 'Women's brains have a larger corpus callosum – the connective tissue between the right and left sides of the brain – whose job it is to transfer data back and forth. Consequently, women integrate incoming data faster than men do. Women's intuitive "sixth sense" about when the baby in the nursery is going to start squawking, or the boss is about to blow a gasket, or what someone else's response will be before it's stated probably has its origins not in the netherworld, but right there in the highly active corpus callosum of the female brain.'[104] This journalist was along the same lines as the scientific writers who lean towards biological determinism. As Susan Pinker puts it: 'Previous studies had shown that women have a thicker corpus callosum, the bundle of nerves that connects the two hemispheres . . . Scientists infer that this allows women to process emotions with dispatch.'[105, 106] This theme has also filtered into self-help books in a highly exaggerated way, as we see in John Gray's *Why Mars and Venus Collide*: 'A woman's brain has a larger corpus callosum, the bundle of nerves that connects the right and left hemispheres of the brain. This link, which produces cross-talk between the hemispheres, is 25 per cent smaller in men.'[107, 108]

Yet there is no solid evidence for these sweeping claims. That first article in 1982 which found that the corpus callosum is larger in women was followed by many more studies, some of which backed it up, and some of which found the opposite. In 1997 two scientists conducted a thorough review of the forty-nine studies of the subject that were published between 1982 and 1994. These scientists, Katherine Bishop and Douglas Wahlsten, had already noted the poor methodology

and shaky conclusions of the famous 1982 study, noting that
this article did not meet 'conventional scientific standards' for
demonstrating a sex difference in the size of the splenium of the
corpus callosum. They were concerned to see that it had been
so uncritically taken up and promoted by the popular press as
the source of supposed sex differences in cognition. It was
because of the stark contrast, as they saw it, between opinion
among popular writers and opinion among most neuroscientists, that they undertook their review, and their results were
conclusive. 'Our review of a substantial literature on the
human corpus callosum does not support any sex-related difference in the size or shape of the splenium, whether or not
adjustments are made for whole brain or cortex size.'[109]

The gulf between the evidence that is available and the way
the story has been generally told clearly yawns widely here, but
the corpus callosum is hardly the only area in which one can
see this gulf. The popular view of the differences between men's
and women's brains is that women's brains are not only more
symmetrical in structure, but that they also work in a more balanced way than men's brains when processing certain tasks,
particularly those to do with language.[110] This is then tied into
the stereotype of feminine superiority in language skills. Some
research by neuroscientists has backed up this point of view;
for instance, in 2000, men and women were asked to lie down
in a room and listen to a John Grisham story being read. The
men showed more activity on their left side, the women
showed activity spread across their brains.[111] The BBC chose
to put it in this way: 'Why men don't listen: there may be a ring
of truth in the female complaint that men never seem to listen
to a word they say.'[112] The *Daily Mail* stated: 'It's the news
Sybil Fawlty knew all along. New research suggests men really
do listen with only half their brains. In a study of men and
women, brain scans showed that, when listening, men mostly
used the left sides of their brains, the region long associated

with understanding language. Women in the study, however, used both sides.'[113]

This particular study tested ten men and ten women. Its conclusions have not been replicated in many other tests of such tasks. In 2004 when four neuroscientists carried out a meta-analysis of fourteen studies providing data on 377 men and 442 women, no significant difference showed up in language lateralisation between men and women. In other words, men and women showed a similar balance of brain activity when doing tasks related to language such as listening or talking.[114] I have not been able to find any report in any mainstream media of this analysis, compared to the widespread report of the one study that seemed to suggest the opposite.

The preference for research on the brain that seems to back up traditional sex differences over research that does not is not only seen in the media; some scientists have suggested that it occurs earlier on in the research food-chain, in the very decisions about which studies actually get published. Some have pointed out that, while a vast number of studies of brain activation are currently being carried out, those that show sex differences are much more likely to be published than those which fail to prove sex differences. This is the file-drawer problem; that the studies we have on record are a small proportion of the studies carried out, most of which show no publicity-friendly gender differences and are therefore languishing in academics' file drawers.[115]

What's more, although differences in activation and structure in women's brains and men's brains can be picked up in certain studies, and some of these studies may prove to be significant in the long run, there is nothing to prove as yet that these must be put down to innate differences rather than differently learned behaviours. When these differences are reported in the media or by writers who rely on biological explanations for sex differences, the assumption is often made that if you can see a difference in the brain, this suggests the difference is innate and unchangeable, that it is 'hardwired'. Yet as we grow and change, our brains change with us. What we learn doesn't take place in an ethereal, immortal soul with no physical being, it takes place in the connections of our living brain.[116]

If you want to see the way that experience can even change the size of the anatomical structures of the human brain, take a look at one clever study that compared London cab drivers to other men. For once, it wasn't the sexes under a spotlight, but men who had chosen different paths through life. As all Londoners know, taxi drivers in London are required to learn The Knowledge, a thorough mental map of the city. The cab drivers in this test had spent an average of two years doing The Knowledge, and so had spent significant time building up their spatial memory. And when the structures of their brains were compared to those of a control group, it was seen that part of the brain, the posterior hippocampus, was larger among the cab drivers than among the other men. The researchers therefore concluded that the posterior hippocampus was the area of the brain they relied on to store this encyclopaedic spatial under-standing of London's streets. Those who support theories of biological determinism might have jumped in to argue that it was the greater size of this part of the brain that had decided the men in favour of this career, but the researchers also found that the longer these men had been cab drivers, the bigger the poste-rior hippocampus, so that as they went on adding detail to their knowledge of the city, their grey matter grew. Since the volume of grey matter in this part of the brain correlated with the amount of time spent as a taxi driver, this suggested that the human brain can change physically in response to its environ-ment, even during adulthood.[117, 118]

So if neuroscientists look at the brains of men and of women and see differences between them, we shouldn't assume that these are present at birth and will be there till death. As the neuroscientist Melissa Hines says, 'Sex differences in brain structure cannot be assumed to imply innate or immutable processes.'[119] The complicated story of how the brain we are born with develops in response to our life's experiences cannot be summed up by a narrative that seeks to reduce it to a rigid stereotype laid down at birth.

The narrative of biological determinism does not, of course, just rest on describing the differences between men and women. It speculates that these differences were laid down in our genes because it was evolutionarily advantageous for men and women to have specialised in different skills, aeons ago, way back in the prehistory of humanity. This prehistoric scenario has been described by many writers, from anthropologists to self-help gurus. For instance, the anthropologist Sherwood Washburn argued, in the seminal book *Man the Hunter* in 1968, that it was man's specific role as the hunter of big game and the 'sexual division of labour' this entailed that lay behind the evolution of modern humans.[120] To this day, a similar view of our past is used to prop up the argument that traditional gender differences are hardwired into our genetic heritage. So, to take a popular example, Allan and Barbara Pease, in their book *Why Men Don't Listen and Women Can't Read Maps*, talk about this ancestral paradise: 'Once upon a time, a long, long time ago, men and women lived happily together and worked in harmony. The man would venture out each day into a hostile and dangerous world to risk his life as a hunter to bring food back to his woman and their children, and he would defend them against savage animals or enemies. He developed long-distance navigational skills so he could locate food and bring it home, and excellent marksmanship skills so that he could hit a moving target. ... The woman's role was equally clear ... Being appointed the child-bearer directed the way she would evolve and how her skills would become specialised to meet that role.

She needed to be able to monitor her immediate surroundings for signs of danger and have a highly tuned ability to sense small changes in the behaviour and appearance of children and adults.'[121]

Many of the writers I have quoted who support biological explanations for sex differences tend to return to a similar vision of our ancestral past in order to back up their view of why it is that men and women are so different in cognition and behaviour. This theory that men and women specialised for such different traits makes sense if our evolutionary past was one in which men and women were placed in such different situations and never needed to cross into the other's world. We could indeed have evolved in this Stepford Wives scenario. But over the last few decades anthropologists have provided an alternative narrative of what our evolutionary past might have looked like, and suggested that it would not necessarily have been one in which men and women occupied such utterly different niches. This narrative has reassessed the evidence from modern hunter-gatherer societies and the archaeological evidence of previous societies, and questioned whether the females were solely carers who were so reliant on the achievements of the male hunters for food and protection. The consensus has arisen that the hunting of big game was not the most significant source of protein for such societies, which were more reliant on the work of the female foragers than previously supposed. Some anthropologists have suggested that it was the work of grandmothers as foragers rather than fathers as hunters which could be vital to the survival of the children in these societies.[122] Others have suggested that rather than relying on the aggressive, clever men, in some hunter-gatherer societies women kill much of the hunted game, carrying their babies in slings or leaving them with other women.[123] Others have suggested that fathers in such societies did more caring than was popularly supposed, without any loss of status.[124] These writers have broken through what one writer has called the 'Paleolithic glass ceiling'[125] by suggesting that the gulf between man the provider and woman the carer in the societies in which humans evolved may never have been quite as rigid as some modern writers would like to think. We might have evolved in societies in which, rather than gentle, chatty women in the cave being dependent on solitary, aggressive men in the bush, everyone – male and female – had to be able to cooperate with others in their community and everyone – male and female – had to be able to meet the need to work hard and bravely to find food.

I like reading these descriptions of traditional societies and of our possible evolutionary past as much as the next person. But whether we are reading of sexist societies that seem to be the direct precursor of modern Saudi Arabia, in which the aggressive leader keeps his women in the cave to gossip and get bored and wait for his return, or of societies which sound more like modern Sweden, in which men and women go out hunting for rabbits and come back to share the childcare with each other and with the grandparents, we will never be given a kind of telescope back into the past through which we can gaze at the precise scenario that shaped our own genetic heritage. When you read those writers who seem to think that our responses to the contemporary world were decided for all of us millions of years ago, a creeping fatalism often takes over which makes it impossible for us even to imagine the possibility of creating further social change. In this fatalistic world view, the desires we have to create a better and more equal society will founder.

But surely those writers are most compelling who argue that the reason humans have managed to spread over the entire planet in so many different physical and social environments is that we adapted to be adaptable. As the eminent anthropologist Barbara Smuts said in Natalie Angier's book *Woman: An Intimate Geography*: 'Flexibility itself is the adaptation.'[126] This is not to say that we are blank slates; the dynamic between biology and culture must be a mutual dynamic. But it can also be a very variable dynamic – while there are different things that each individual brings to the table in terms of innate talents, desires and visions, there are also ways in which changing situations create changing responses. Rather than getting hung up on what might have happened in the Pleistocene era, we can still discuss whether we feel there is a better society that we can work towards today.

This is not as simple as saying there is a nature–nurture divide in this debate, and that we have to choose one side or the other. The nature–nurture divide is a false one, since the experiences we have in our lives will change the physical structures of our brains or our production of hormones. There is no unchanging biological reality, free from history, just as there is no blank slate on which the finger of experience writes. Our genetic inheritance helps to determine how we filter and respond to experience, and our experience modifies how our genetic inheritance expresses itself. If we have the will and the desire to create social change, we should not be held back by the false belief that such change will necessarily founder on the rock of innate differences. There is a way beyond this fatalism.

9: Stereotypes

I remember, when I first started thinking about some of these issues, idly asking a friend of mine who has three children, two girls and a boy, 'Do you think boys and girls are innately different?' At the time I dismissed her answer: 'I think boys and boys are different, and so are girls and girls.' But the more time I have spent with this subject, the more I have seen how vital is this apparently obvious point. The constant threat posed by the promotion of biological determinism is that it blinds us to the true variability among women and men. Instead of the unpredictable men and women we meet every day, who might be aggressive or nurturing, who might be solitary or gregarious, we are being asked to believe that all men and all women should fit templates modelled more on a pink doll or a blue robot than a real man or a real woman.

As we see in the work of those writers, academic and popular, who support biological explanations for all sex differences, their constant refrain is: 'Girls do . . . Boys do . . . Women are . . . Men are . . .' We hear from them these unqualified statements: 'Girls prefer a human face . . . Women talk three times as much as

men . . . Females are better empathisers . . . Men really do listen
with only half their brains.' They may nod to the possibility of
variability by conceding that some, anomalous women will be
engineers and some, anomalous men will be carers. The concession will be made briefly and then the writer will return to his or
her sweeping statements.

This is typical of the way that many of us tend to generalise
about male and female differences in everyday life. When boys
or girls act out of their pink or blue moulds, it's easy for parents
and others to skim over those moments, which are seen as
untypical and easily forgettable. Yet when girls and boys fall in
with expectations, the stereotypes are reinforced and strength-
ened. Every aggressive boy feeds the stereotypes that are given to
us by traditions and by the new biological determinism; every
aggressive girl is a forgettable anomaly. Even if many aspects of
the new narrative of biological determinism are shaky, they resonate with such deeply held myths about boys and girls that it is
hard for us not to be influenced by them.

But even where average differences can be observed between
men and women in cognition and emotional aptitudes, these
average differences are tiny compared with the vast differences
among individuals of the same sex. As we saw in the analysis of
verbal skills, it appears that gender accounts for only 1 per cent
of the differences between boys and girls. This means that, far
from being able to make any generalisations about boys and
girls, if all you know about someone is their sex you can make
no predictions about their verbal ability. The truth is that the
graphs for all these supposed intellectual differences tend to
show great overlap between men and women and great variability for both men and women.

Although there may be small average differences in the intellectual and emotional capabilities of men and women, to express
these as truths about all – or even almost all – men and women
is nonsense. But in so much of the work done on sex differences

today, instead of a recognition of the true variability of men and women, we are presented simply with stereotypes.

This is partly the fault of some scientists. As Melissa Hines said to me, ruefully: 'There are a lot of pressures that result in scientists looking for a simple picture. That's kind of what science is meant to be about; we're meant to be able to discover some rules that let us predict things, so there's a tendency to want to simplify things in order to discover rules and predict things, and in most fields that works fine. But it doesn't work well in fields where people already have stereotypes, because the stereotypes become the rules.' But this is not really a problem that can be blamed on individual scientists. As we have seen in the last chapter, there is a pervasive tendency in the wider culture to pick up these biological explanations for the differences we see around us without investigation.

This is partly because biological explanations for sex differences are now often assumed to be the freshest ideas, bravely argued against an old guard who have tried to shut down debate. So Simon Baron-Cohen said that he delayed publishing *The Essential Difference* for some years, because 'the topic was just too politically sensitive'.[1] Steven Pinker has also presented himself as the daring breaker of a taboo: 'At some point in the history of the modern women's movement, the belief that men and women are psychologically indistinguishable became sacred . . . The tragedy is that this mentality of taboo needlessly puts a laudable cause on a collision course with the findings of science and the spirit of free inquiry.'[2] Journalists often support this idea, that such theories must battle against some taboo. As one American journalist put it recently, 'We'll probably never know how great a role biology plays in gender differences, because feminists try to prevent anyone from researching it.'[3] However, to an objective observer, it is rather strange that writers can claim that it is difficult to debate this subject openly, when, as the linguist Mark Liberman said in response,

'Neuroscientists are by no means being prevented from researching the biology of sex differences. It's hard to think of any topic
that has been getting more study recently, at least among questions without direct pharmacological or clinical applications.'[4]

Even if journalists don't fall in with the idea that biological
explanations have to fight for space against a taboo, these explanations are still often seen as the freshest thinking, in contrast to
the outdated political correctness of an old-fashioned establishment. So one writer in the *Daily Mail* said that explanations from
biology blow 'a large hole in the feminist orthodoxy – and the
painfully politically correct line – that holds that men and women
possess interchangeable emotional, intellectual and psychological
traits.'[5] Or, we can read in the *Economist* that: 'Biological explanations of human behaviour are making a comeback as the
generation of academics that feared them as a covert way of
justifying eugenics, or of thwarting Marxist utopianism, is retir-
ing.'[6]

It's odd to see theories of biological determinism being promoted as the freshest thinking on the block, given that these
theories have such a long, and not very illustrious history. Ever
since the retreat of religion during the Enlightenment, explanations for sexual inequality have been sought in biology. There is
nothing new about the idea that masculinity and femininity are
not just seen in physical characteristics and the ability to bear
children, but also in intellectual and emotional capabilities.
Nineteenth-century scientists told women that they should not
read serious books because certain brain activities were incom-
patible with their fertility, and they studied the size and shape of
the human brain to explain the inferior intelligence of women.
So the president of the British Medical Association told its
annual meeting in 1886 that if girls studied too much,
'Amenorrhoea and chlorosis, and development of great nerv-
ousness, are frequent results of overpressure in education at or
near the important epoch – fifteen to twenty years of age.'[7]

While Sir Henry Maudsley, a leading Victorian psychiatrist, said in an influential article in 1874 that a woman 'does not easily regain the vital energy that was recklessly spent on learning . . . if a woman attempts to achieve the educational standards of men . . . she will lack the energy necessary for childbearing and rearing'.[8]

As Anne Fausto-Sterling documents in her classic book *Myths of Gender*, biological explanations for women's inferiority have come and gone like fashions in hem length. There was a long period when it was assumed the relatively smaller size of their brains proved that women were less intelligent than men; until people pointed out that in that case, elephants should be more intelligent even than human males. So others argued that intelligence did not rest on a larger brain overall but on the greater development of certain areas of the brain. In the mid-nineteenth century there was a fashion for believing that intelligence was linked to the size of the frontal lobe of the brain. Thus it was noted that men possessed larger frontal lobes than women, and woman was 'homo parietalis' after the parietal lobe, which lies towards the back of the head, while man was 'homo frontalis'. Yet after a while the relevant scientists began to think that the parietal lobe was actually the seat of the intellect, and so executed a deft turnaround. 'The frontal region is not, as has been supposed, smaller in woman, but rather larger relatively. But the parietal lobe is somewhat smaller.'[9] As Fausto-Sterling puts it, when it comes to biological explanations for sex differences: 'The popular press fanfares each entry with brilliant brass, bright ribbons, and lots of column space, but fails to note when each one in its turn falls into disrepute.'[10]

Even in the heyday of interest in social conditioning, there were many writers keen to promote the idea that human behaviour is determined as much by biology as by culture. The father of sociobiology, Edward O Wilson, was a key figure in these debates. In the 1970s he made statements such as, 'The evidence for a genetic difference in behaviour is varied and substantial. In general, girls are predisposed to be more intimately sociable and less physically venturesome.'[11] Such views have flourished ever since in the terrain called sociobiology or evolutionary psychology. However, in the 1970s and 1980s it is fair to say that the critics of sociobiology were heard as much as its followers.

When the controversy over race and IQ, in which some writers argued that certain races were intellectually inferior to others, erupted in the 1990s, the determinist point of view was thoroughly challenged in the mainstream media. What we can see now, however, is that biological explanations for human behaviour are often going unchallenged in the mainstream media. Far from having to plough a lonely furrow through a field characterised by unrelenting political correctness, we have seen in the last chapter how scientists and academics who put forward biological explanations for sex differences are enthusiastically praised and widely published.

The spread of biological determinism through the media during recent years has been linked to the rise of politically conservative views. This makes sense, since those who have lost faith with the possibility of creating egalitarian social change are obviously likely to be attracted by apparently scientific theories that back up their feelings that the unequal status quo is only natural. Researchers at Yale University have shown that American newspapers with a conservative political bent – as assessed by which presidential candidate they supported – use far more biological explanations for gender differences than the liberal newspapers, which use more explanations based on conditioning and expectations.[12] Right-wing media in the UK are also keen to publish theories of biological differences. But the spread of these ideas has now gone well beyond obviously conservative realms. In the UK, these ideas are now found frequently in, for instance, the *Guardian*, the *New Statesman* and the BBC, as well as, say, in the *Daily Mail* and the *Financial*

Times. These ideas have taken up residence throughout the political spectrum, and are promoted not just by people who would never call themselves feminists, but also by many people who do call themselves feminists, such as Rosie Boycott, who co-founded the feminist magazine *Spare Rib*,[13] or Helena Cronin, the Darwinian philosopher who says, 'in talents men are on average more mathematical, more technically minded, women more verbal; in tastes, men are more interested in things, women in people; in temperaments, men are more competitive, risk-taking, single-minded, status-conscious, women far less so.'[14]

The problem is that the unquestioning dissemination of such views can itself strengthen the persistence of stereotypes about how men and women should behave in everyday life. To state this is not to suggest that therefore we should shut down discussion of such theories, but it is to argue that we should be careful that the dissenting voices are heard as well. Because the strengthening of such stereotypes matters. There is a growing and fascinating literature on how the performance of individuals in certain fields may be heavily affected by their knowledge of what is expected of the group to which they belong. The effect of what is called 'stereotype threat' on the sexes has been revealed in groundbreaking and intriguing psychological research over the last few years.

One of the founding blocks of this research was published in 1999. Three psychologists, Claude Steele, Stephen Spencer and Diane Quinn, got together male and female undergraduates to take a difficult maths test in which women had previously been seen to do worse than equally qualified men. They wanted to find out if women's underperformance in such maths tests could really be said to be down to innate differences in aptitude, or whether other forces were at work. So they split the men and women into two groups. They told the men and women in one group that when this test had been administered in the past, there had been clear gender differences in performance. But the other group was told that men and women had performed equally on this test in the past. In the group who had been primed to believe that the sexes were unequal in their attainment, women did worse than the men. In the group told that women and men had performed equally in the past, the sex difference in attainment was eliminated.

This result was striking in and of itself, showing us that attainment in supposedly objective tests may not be a reflection of pure ability. The psychologists went further in the following test, and found that they did not even have to 'activate' the stereotype for women to do worse than men. If told nothing about sex differences in attainment on the test, women did worse than men; if they were told that gender differences had never been seen on the test, they performed as well as their male counterparts.[15] The fact that the researchers did not even have to activate a stereotype explicitly for it to hold women back from doing as well as they could shows us that stereotype threat may be all around us, not just in maths tests, affecting our behaviour even when we are not consciously aware of it.

Other research has suggested that this is the case. For instance, the moderate male advantage seen in some tests of spatial ability is also seen in everyday life, where certain tasks that rely on spatial awareness – such as parking and navigation – tend to be performed better by men. You can see this in the fact that men on average do better in some aspects of driving tests, and women are 40 per cent more likely to fail their driving test by fluffing their three-point turns than men are. Many writers who discuss this kind of phenomenon assume, in deference to the ideas of biological determinism, that the difference must be produced by hormones. So in one typical report about men's higher ability in such driving skills in *The Times*, the journalists quoted a psychologist claiming that this is because of higher testosterone exposure in the womb.[16] But the very existence of a stereotype can, it seems, affect some women's ability to drive well. Dr Courtney von Hippel, from the University of Queensland in Australia, showed that if women given a driving test were told that the test would investigate why women are worse at driving than men, they were twice as likely to have an accident in the test than were women who were not reminded of the stereotype.[17]

What's more, there is growing evidence to suggest that this kind of stereotype threat can affect not only our apparent abilities, but also our ambitions. Shelley Correll, a professor of sociology at Stanford University, set up a random ability test in which men could not possibly outperform women – the test consisted of judging the contrasts in black and white patterns, and in fact there were no right and wrong answers. She found how quickly even our aspirations are moulded by the activation of stereotypes about men and women. One group was told that men were better at this task, and the other group was told that men and women tended to do the same. All the subjects were given the same score – 13 out of 20. Yet in the group in which participants were told that men had more ability at this task, the men not only rated their performance more highly than the women did, but were more likely to say they would go into a career in which this kind of ability was required. Correll concluded that she had shown that individuals form their ambitions by assessing their own competence, and that men and women will assess their competence partly by drawing on different cultural beliefs about male and female abilities. Again, it is probably safe to assume that this holds good even outside sociology departments in universities, and that the operation of stereotypes in the wider culture can constrain the choices we make in our real lives.[18]

What effect does the popularity of false ideas of biological determinism have on the power of stereotypes in everyday life? The researchers at Yale who looked at links between political

conservatism and biological determinism in the media found
that when readers are exposed to biological narratives, they
became more inclined themselves to endorse stereotypes about
how men and women should behave. These researchers gave
participants articles which explained sex differences either by
reference to biology – evolutionary programming or brain structure – or by reference to society – socialisation and expectations.
The effect was striking. Those participants who read the article
with biological explanations went on to score more highly in a
questionnaire that asked them to endorse stereotypes such as
women being more nurturing and men more arrogant. It also led
them to answer more negatively when asked if they thought
people could change their behaviour. This was the case even if
the article was putting forward a sex difference in which women
were 'better' than men.[19] So even when we are told that girls
have, say, 'superior' language skills we may be encouraged into
a fatalistic view of sex differences that discourages us from
seeing individuals' – even our own – true flexibility and potential
for change.

Such research shows that poor use and reporting of science
matters more than we might think; it's not just that bad science
gets things wrong, but that it can affect our beliefs and therefore
our behaviour.[20] What is fashionably called stereotype threat
we might call social conditioning, or sexism, but whatever words
we use to describe this phenomenon, it is time to become more
alert to the impact the new fashion for biological determinism
might have on strengthening stereotypes in everyday life and
therefore on holding back the possibility of greater equality.

Because there is still an unfinished revolution in our society.
Inequality is still the reality. Men still have much more political
and economic power than women, and women still do much
more work that is unpaid and unrecognised at home. Although
in theory glass ceilings have been broken everywhere, and
women have flooded into jobs once seen as the preserve of men,

the upper echelons of businesses and professions and politics are still masculine. For instance, in the law, 49 per cent of the lowest rank of judges (deputy district judges and the like) are women; but only 10 per cent of high court judges.[21] In 2007, women made up just 11 per cent of directors at FTSE 100 companies, 12 per cent of senior police officers, 14 per cent of local authority council leaders, 14 per cent of editors of national newspapers and 20 per cent of MPs.[22] Meanwhile, women do the bulk of unpaid domestic work, even if they are working full-time. A woman who works full-time does an average of twenty-three hours of domestic work a week; a man who works full-time does an average of eight hours of domestic work each week.[23] This has a huge knock-on effect on their rewards in the work-place. When men and women become parents, the gap between their experiences looms particularly large. While childless women earn about 9 per cent less than men, women with children earn about 22 per cent less than their male colleagues, even if they work full-time.[24]

In the eyes of those who subscribe to biological determinism, there is a good fit between the world as it is today and the innate aptitudes of men and women. There is no dissatisfaction, there is no frustration, there is no misfiring between our desires and our situations. Every aspect of inequality that we see today can be explained by the different genetic and hormonal make-up of men and women; if women earn less, if men have more power, if women do more domestic work, if men have more status, then this is simply the way that things are meant to be. In this way the biological determinism of the twenty-first century works in the same way as the biological determinism of the nineteenth century, which told women who sought change that they were entirely unsuited to higher education or physical exertion. In Victorian Britain dissent was nevertheless voiced by a small but determined minority, which created real social change for women that proved the fatalists wrong. If we are to move

forward towards greater freedom and equality in this generation, we would need to overcome the influences of these
stereotypes, which currently affect our expectations of our children and our expectations of our partners and ourselves. We
would need to ask again why it is that we are allowing the
stereotypes of the nurturing, empathetic woman and the powerful, logical man to be seen as natural and inevitable and look
instead at how these assumptions have been constructed, how
they are maintained and how they can be challenged.

The stereotype of the male leader

As we saw in the first half of this book, the pervasive sexualisation of women in the public realm cuts away at their true
empowerment. It encourages many women to model themselves
on a sexy doll rather than seeking other kinds of success. But this
is not the only reason women may find that it is still hard for
them to reach for empowerment in many fields. The operation
of traditional stereotypes in public and private life also discourages women from taking on certain roles.

The continued influence of traditional stereotypes encourages
people to believe that women will lack the authority and competence of men in certain areas. In the eyes of some of those who
subscribe to biological explanations for sex differences, the pursuit of power is seen as peculiarly male. As a writer in the *New
York Times* said recently: 'It makes some sense that after almost
a century of electorates made up by as many women as men, the
number of female politicians remains pathetically small in most
Western democracies ... Those qualities associated with low
testosterone – patience, risk aversion, empathy ... are just lousy
qualities in the crapshoot of electoral politics ... It is foolish to
insist that numerical inequality is always a function of bias
rather than biology. . . We shouldn't be shocked if gender

inequality endures.'[25] Or, as an article in *Newsweek* had it: 'Alpha males are high on testosterone, the hormone that underlies almost all the typical traits of the politico-sexual animal: high levels of testosterone make for a high sex drive, a love of risks, aggressiveness and competitiveness. "These people have a strong need to win at games, which is obviously important in power politics".'[26]

One characteristic of the new biological determinism is that it promotes a zero-sum view of masculinity and femininity, in which the more masculine you are, the more you are assumed to be lacking in feminine traits, and vice versa. This was made particularly explicit in the BBC programme *Secrets of the Sexes*, where, in one telling scene, the men and women in the programme were placed on a ruler, where the middle was zero, the left-hand end said 100 per cent female and the right-hand end 100 per cent male. If an individual excelled in systemising or aggression, they were moved rightwards; if they excelled in empathy or language, they were moved leftwards.[27] There was no possibility, in this visual realisation of the new determinism, for a person to combine the strengths of a man and a woman. The way that masculinity and femininity are now so often seen as mutually exclusive, so that the more masculine you are the less feminine you are, operates against women who seek power. Because in the eyes of those influenced by traditional stereotypes, a man seeking power enhances his masculinity, but a woman seeking power reduces her femininity. And this can be extremely negative for a woman who goes into politics, as it makes her seem not quite human, as though she has given up something essential about herself.

We can see this unease with powerful women constantly in our culture. Every woman who seeks power runs the risk of becoming a figure such as Hillary Clinton, who was the failed candidate for the Democratic presidential nomination in the US in 2008, and who was constantly characterised as competent, but cold and inhuman, or a figure such as Ségolène Royal, who was the failed candidate for president of France in 2007, who was characterised as elegantly feminine, but therefore insufficiently competent and authoritative. What women who seek power gain in authority, they will lose in femininity, and vice versa. It takes a terrific balancing act, achieved by few women, to maintain both the necessary authority and the necessary femininity to be seen as fully human in politics. On the other hand, there will always be a man running alongside the would-be powerful woman, who will be benefiting from the operation of the stereotype of the masculine leader, and whose humanity will be enhanced rather than threatened by his bid for power.

The discomfort our society still feels about the woman who overtly seeks power means that thirty years after Margaret Thatcher managed to crack the stereotype temporarily, British politics has reverted to an aggressively masculine cabal; the leaders of all the major parties are men. Women who attempt to break through this wall of masculinity do not need to be substantively attacked, they can simply be mocked as unfeminine, and the operation of the stereotype will do the rest. A loss of femininity in style or appearance, in speech or manner, will be enough to discredit the woman who seeks power, who will immediately be seen as strident, chilly and even inhuman. This discomfort with her loss of femininity is often framed in terms of criticism of the unfeminine appearance of a powerful woman. So we hear about the 'prison warden haircut' and 'too tight on top mannish pinstripe' of Jacqui Smith, then the British home secretary,[28] and the German chancellor Angela Merkel's 'unstylish haircut, frumpish appearance'.[29] The way that powerful women are easily wrongfooted by their lack of femininity can be seen when you look at the reaction by the political press to the visit of the ex-model Carla Bruni to London with her husband, Nicolas Sarkozy, president of France. The silent beauty was held up as the perfect specimen of womanhood against the failings of the British politicians. While she 'looked chic in a simple one-shoulder purple gown', according to the *Daily Mail*, 'back on dowdy street' the MP Hazel Blears wore 'hideous boots, horrible bag, untidy and needs her roots retouching'.[30] The delight the press took in her presence threw into relief the unease they express towards all women who actually enter politics to seek power on their own terms, rather than marry politically powerful men, and the defeminisation this seems to entail.

To see how strongly the stereotype against power-hungry women still operates, look at the reactions to Hillary Clinton in her bid for the presidential candidacy in the US in 2008. Her very competence was recast not as a qualification for the job, as it would have been in a man, but as something cold and artificial. Much debate was generated about whether or not her laugh was a human sound or a sign of her lack of normal humanity. As the *New Yorker* described the reaction to her laughter in one debate: 'Sean Hannity played an audio clip seven times and described the candidate's laughter as "frightening." Bill O'Reilly trotted out a Fox News "body-language expert" to pronounce the laughter "evil." Dick Morris, the onetime Clinton adviser turned full-time Clinton trasher, described it as "loud, inappropriate, and mirthless." ... In the *Times*, Frank Rich wrote, "Now Mrs. Clinton is erupting in a laugh with all the spontaneity of an alarm clock buzzer." ... And *The Politico*, a new online political newspaper, identified the problem as "a laugh that sounded like it was programmed by computer."'[31] The idea that Clinton's laugh – which people who know her in real life tend to describe as warm and genuine – is fake, frightening and more like an alarm clock or a computer than a human being, suggests to everyone that a woman like Clinton, a woman seeking power, has lost her femininity to such a degree that she is almost unnatural.

Women in the UK experience similar reactions when they are

seen to be too powerful. When Baroness Vadera, an adviser to Gordon Brown, made some ill-advised comments to the press about the possibility of recovery from the recession in 2009, we heard a deluge of criticism from the media, much of which focused on how unfeminine she was. As a writer in the *Guardian* summed it up, this media coverage implied that Baroness Vadera 'is not exactly a woman. According to some fella in the *Spectator*, she is an "assassin . . . ass-kicker . . . axe-wielder"'. One presenter on the *Today* programme apparently said of her: 'Civil servants call her Shrieky Shriti. Others choose to leave.' As the writer rightly put it, 'Can you imagine that ever being said about a man, that he was such a big meanie, he had such a shouty voice, that people under him had to leave their jobs?'[32]

This prejudice against the authoritative female may have an influence on female advancement in other spheres of work. Recent research has suggested that women are still often rated more poorly than men in terms of professional standing and leadership qualities in many occupations, even when the evidence is on the side of the women, and though the evaluators always think they are being objective. For instance, researchers in Sweden have shown that in medicine – an area that women might see as pretty welcoming – women had to be far more qualified and productive than men to get postdoctoral fellowships. The supposedly objective process by which they were assessed was in fact a highly subjective process in which just being a woman was a severe handicap, since, 'The peer reviewers overestimated male achievements and underestimated female performance.' If they had previously worked with their assessors the women might be able to bring up their chances a bit, but: 'Being of the female gender and lacking personal connections was a double handicap of such severity that it could hardly be compensated for by scientific productivity alone.'[33] It is pretty certain that the men doing the assessments would have said – and probably believed – that they were being objective, but people are not always aware of how their judgements are affected by prejudice.[34]

The resurgence of biological determinism, with its traditionalist views of women's aptitudes, may be strengthening the operation of such stereotypes in certain fields. For instance, between 1997 and 2005 the proportion of women employed in technology industries fell from 27 per cent to 21 per cent.[35] In an article in *Management Today* about this phenomenon, the reporter found influential people willing to put at least some of the inequality down to innate aptitudes. Anthony Seldon, headmaster of a large school and father of two girls, was quoted saying, 'There are differences between boys and girls. Boys are more interested in computers than girls, and it often correlates with maths. It just so happens that girls are more interested in feelings and boys are more interested in things.' No wonder a Microsoft survey conducted among women in information technology in 2007 concluded that some of them found their careers affected by sexism: 'Some men discriminate against female colleagues by assuming they have less facility for deeply technical matters.'[36]

Although many people would like to believe that women do not face discrimination at work any longer, throughout the professional world stereotypes against female leaders can hold women back. The psychologist Virginia Valian has examined much research into the ways that people relate to colleagues, and how they hire and promote others, and has found that this stereotype operates in subtle ways in many different situations. For instance, researchers once asked more than 250 managers to describe the typical characteristics of certain individuals – men in general, male managers, successful male managers, or women in general, female managers and successful female managers. They discovered that when 'female' was attached to managers or successful managers, there was a higher likelihood that they would be expected to be bitter, quarrelsome and selfish and less likely that they would be expected to have leadership ability.[37]

And in a particularly intriguing piece of psychological research carried out in 1990, men and women who had been trained to act according to certain scripted patterns went into groups of participants who didn't know that these men and women had been trained. The groups were given ten minutes to reach a decision on a certain task – ranking the usefulness of nine items to a person who had crash-landed on the moon. When the trained women took on the role of leader, they received many more negative facial reactions from the participants than the trained men received. Although they acted in an identical fashion as leaders, for the women, the negative reactions outweighed the positive, but for the men, the positive reactions outweighed the negative.[38]

This imbalance, when played out in everyday life, may go to the heart of why some women may feel that seeking leadership roles in society is just too stressful, and why it is that women sometimes can't understand why men are drawn to those roles. Is it that women just don't receive the payoffs that men do in terms of positive reactions from colleagues and peers, however competent they are? After all, even if we were to get equal pay or equal promotion, this would be dust and ashes in our mouths if we weren't to get that great feeling that having peer approval gives you – that warm sense of being liked and admired, of being a valued part of a team. Successful men may be able to count on that in a way that successful women cannot. And why should anyone want to be a loner even if they are at the top?

Such research shows us that the persistence of stereotypes cannot simply be shattered by personal force of will; even if a woman trains herself to act just as a man would in her position, she may not be able to resist the force of expectations that consign her to a different role. For instance, women are often told that their low pay relative to men's is their own fault: they don't ask for higher pay often enough. It is true that women do not ask for higher pay as much as men do. As the researchers Linda Babcock and Sara Laschever explained in 2003, when they looked at a cohort of graduates from Carnegie Mellon University, they found that only 7 per cent of female students attempted to negotiate their initial salary offers compared to 57 per cent of men. Those who negotiated gained on average 7.4 per cent on their initial offers.[39] But this failure of women to negotiate successfully is not just about their own decisions, it is also about the expectations around them. In another striking study, Linda Babcock and her colleagues ran a number of tests in which groups of people were asked to evaluate – after viewing videotapes or transcripts of interviews – men and women who were applying for a fictitious job, half of whom tried to negotiate their salary and half of whom did not. Babcock found that: 'Men were always less willing to work with a woman who had attempted to negotiate than with a woman who did not. They always preferred to work with a woman who stayed mum.' So women's reluctance to negotiate is actually based on an accurate view of how they might be treated. 'This isn't about fixing the woman,' Babcock said. 'It isn't about telling women, you need self-confidence or training. They are responding to incentives within the social environment.'[40] The researchers theorised that the persistence of masculine and feminine stereotypes encourages people to assume that resources should be allocated asymmetrically. This means that women can appear inappropriately demanding if they attempt to negotiate for more money. So women enter a loop in which they fail to negotiate, and they fall behind in status.

If we are honest about the ways in which women may be held back from seeking power, status and money not because of their innate desires or abilities, but because of the expectations in the culture around them, we begin to see again why it is important for us to look at how social factors still create inequality. We will never challenge the ways that women's freedom is still constrained if we simply acquiesce in the idea that women are biologically programmed to fit in with the most limited stereotype of femininity.

The stereotype of the female carer

The search for greater equality does not just entail changes in women's lives, and the existence of the backlash is not only holding women back from change. The narrative of biological determinism not only includes sweeping rhetoric about women's lack of aptitude for high-intensity careers, but also moves into grand claims for men's lack of aptitude for empathy. This stereotype can be seen to operate at a very early age, when little boys are expected to be aggressive and uninterested in social interaction. In later life it operates against men's further movement into the domestic world, and is just as dangerous as the stereotype against authoritative women, because there can be no further progress towards equality unless men are prepared to do their fair share of home-making. A woman's attempts to take a greater part in the world of paid work can so easily founder if there is nobody who will work with her to create a full and rewarding homelife. And as long as employers can assume that the typical worker is prepared to work any hours at any intensity while his wife picks up the slack at home, there will not be sufficient pressure to reshape the workplace in the way that is essential not just for greater equality, but also for greater happiness. Many women have written recently about their disillusionment with the notion that one can 'have it all', both a demanding job and a good home life. I agree that we should not be in thrall to the idea that paid work is all that gives life value. But the joys of family life are not just the responsibility of women, and it is strange to see how our culture seems to be retreating into the idea that men will never play a full part in creating those joys.

The stereotype that men are deficient in nurturing and empathising skills has been reinforced by some of those writers who rely on biological explanations for sex differences. In the view of some writers, the autistic man – a man who has a brain development disorder which impairs social interaction and communication – is only an exaggerated example of a pattern characteristic of many men. 'Extreme men, to be sure,' says Susan Pinker, commenting on men with autism, 'their profiles still illustrate a pattern that has been documented in average males.'[41] This view of masculinity encourages us to forgive men their poor showing in family life and domestic work; it's not just that they prefer the rewards of paid work, but that they are handicapped in the everyday skills required to create a satisfactory domestic environment.

We see examples of this stereotypical man, whose bumbling lack of social skills is in extreme contrast to the poise and capability of his girlfriend, everywhere in our culture, from the grunting men seen as typical of their sex in self-help books, to the perpetual adolescents we meet in popular films from *Knocked Up* to *The Break Up*. And the rise of this stereotype encourages a fatalistic attitude towards men's underachievement at home. For instance, as one writer in the *Daily Mail* put it, while reviewing Louann Brizendine's book on the female brain: 'We blokes, struggling to live up to the template of "new men" who can be caring and empathetic, are apparently being forced to behave in a way for which we are simply not designed.'[42] Such commentary may not always be entirely serious, but even so it often encourages a lazy acquiescence in the status quo. It is reinforced by the use of bad science by the media, as we saw in the last chapter. For instance, the BBC series *Secrets of the Sexes* highlighted an 'experiment' that showed that men responded less well to babies' needs. They sent five women into a room with five babies, and asked them to change the babies' nappies, and then five men to do the same task. The voiceover concluded that because the women were more likely to pick the baby up: 'Men find emotional connection difficult.' When one man did pick up the baby, we were told that this was not a natural response: 'Lloyd is aware that he is not naturally empathic, so he has made more of an effort.'[43] There was no exploration of, for instance, what kind of experience any of the men and women had had with babies or whether they behaved the same way if they believed they were not being watched.

But other research has suggested that men can respond very much as women do to babies, especially if they are given the chance to spend time with children. As Adrienne Burgess has recorded in her study of men as parents, *Fatherhood Reclaimed*, when tapes of babies crying were played to boys and girls and their reactions were recorded, 'Their social responses – whether they smiled or frowned – were different, with the girls on the whole showing greater concern. But when their concealed responses – their heart-rates, blood pressure and so on – were measured, there were no differences. Both sexes were reacting with the same degree of disquiet.' Similarly, if new fathers are left alone with their babies, they are just as deft, just as responsive, and just as able, if blindfolded, to recognise their babies by the shape of their hands.[44]

The fact that the biological ability to bear children has been given only to one sex does not necessarily mean a biological gift for caring has been similarly unequally distributed. The narrative of biological determinism is often intensely idealistic about women's natural bond with their children. But let's be honest: although they are biologically fit for bearing children, not all women slip entirely easily into caring for them. Women learn to care, and for some of them that entails a real struggle. Although women often keep this struggle to themselves, sometimes their frustrations, and their desire to have their male partner alongside them in the struggle rather than pushed out to work, can be clearly heard. On one thread in 2008 on the parenting website Mumsnet, women remembered their feelings when their partners went back to work. 'I very clearly remember that in the early days, when he left the house I had an incredible urge to open the door and run up the street screaming "PLEASE DON'T LEAVE

ME WITH THE BABY!"'; 'I also had that horrible dread when he was leaving for work that "I just can't do it, don't go"'; 'I used to be so jealous of my husband swanning off to work with not a care in the world whilst I was stuck at home with a colicky, refluxy baby who wouldn't stop screaming'; 'I even used to watch neighbours pootling off in their cars and feel envious of them going about their day to day business'; 'I used to find that by 5pm I was at breaking point. I remember one night calling him on his bus journey home (15 min journey) several times, demanding "where is the bus now". And even meeting the bus so that I could hand my daughter over!'[45]

In the past feminists have often explored these struggles and frustrations – not in order to downgrade the work of caring, but in order to show that what looks natural may in fact be the product of a great effort. For instance, Naomi Wolf in *Misconceptions* laid bare the ways in which women may feel often unsuited to mothering, even when they are determined to be good mothers. There is a telling scene in this book, where a friend of hers remembers how she was playing with her baby son, sorting cubes, for 'what seemed to me to be a really long period of time. Ed came in, saw this scene and said, "Oh, you're just entranced." And I said, "Are you out of your mind? I'm bored silly." And he was stunned – he had no idea.'[46]

I see this 'Ed' over and over again in men who look at women behaving in a certain way and assume that the behaviour is utterly natural, without bothering to imagine the other desires or frustrations that may lie beneath that behaviour. Once I talked to a senior editor at a national newspaper about why there are so few women in senior editorial roles, and so many very young women in junior roles at newspapers. This successful, hugely confident, well-paid man, who also happened to be a divorced father who rarely saw his children, told me that most women simply didn't want to continue their careers in their thirties because what they really wanted was to stay home with their children. 'That's what they want!' he laughed. 'You see them come in, all fresh and keen, and then ten years later they are telling you they're off to look after their kids. But that's what they want – you can't stop it. It's nature.' I have talked to dozens of women over the years who have done exactly that – started a career with great verve and commitment, and then moved away from it once they have started a family – and what I have heard, alongside the pleasures of their changing lives, is also a great deal of frustration and anger, about the impossibility of setting up part-time work in the field they loved or the difficulties they had in getting their husbands to take on a fair share of the child-care. The new fashion for biological determinism encourages us to see as natural a division of labour between men and women that could otherwise be challenged.

To be honest about how mothering does not necessarily come naturally to all women is not to downgrade the bonds of family life and the happiness they bring. Home is the centre of a life well lived. Yet the insistence that this haven must be created and protected by women because of our unique aptitudes rests on a shaky assumption. A mother does have a special physical relationship to a baby during pregnancy and birth, but it's fatally easy to overstate the ongoing difference this will necessarily make to her parenting. For some women, the very exhaustion of pregnancy and childbirth makes the early days of parenting harder for them than for their partners. For some women, hormonal imbalances or the pressures of childcare cause depressions that take months to lift. For many men, the entry of children into family life is just as real a joy as it is for many women.

The fact that women are still, by and large, the keepers of the hearth, is not just about nature, but also about nurture. Girls are still training themselves in the work done at home from an early age, with their dolls and dolls' houses, their little pushchairs and their toy cookers. Women still find that they will be judged harshly if they do not create a good home for their families.

Despite the movement of many men into the home, there has recently arisen a tendency to emphasise the femininity of domestic work. I wouldn't judge any woman for wanting to spend time at home, cooking or doing housework or looking after her children. I know myself that the times I have spent purely in family life have been among the happiest hours of my life. But I have always assumed this would be true of my partner, too, and I have been surprised by the way that we have recently seen a resurgence in much of the media and in certain social circles of an almost 1950s image of a perfect stay-at-home mother who wants to create her domestic haven single-handedly. With her Cath Kidston aprons and home-made Christmas decorations, her cupcakes and her languorous Sunday lunches, this idealised mother is recreating the look of a world in which women had no choice but to embrace domesticity. Some young women who have fallen for this image wholeheartedly say that they feel this old-fashioned domestic ideal amounts to a new movement among younger women. Jazz D Holly, a woman in her twenties who has joined the Women's Institute and spends time baking cupcakes, told the *Guardian*, 'For my generation, girls in their 20s, all my friends, it's a cultural shift, almost a movement: many people are fascinated by retro ideas.'[47]

This investment in an almost kitsch domesticity runs alongside a new glorification of the image of the perfect wife, who enables the powerful man next to her to consolidate his status through her physical beauty or her domestic perfection, or, ideally, both. This glorified wife crosses all social groups, from the WAG whose glossy sexiness is as necessary for a successful sportsman as the latest model of a fast car, to the charming, smiling politician's wife who enhances her husband's power without trespassing in his realm. While the 1990s saw 'first wives' such as Hillary Clinton and Cherie Booth, who never made any secret of their desires to carry on their high-powered careers next to their husbands, the twenty-first century swoons over the reassuring first wives Sarah Brown and Michelle Obama, who have decided to give up paid work. They call themselves 'mom-in-chief' and receive admiration not for their incisive intelligence and active careers, but for their toned arms and great clothes. They have learned to smile sweetly when their husbands call them 'good-looking' or 'spectacular'. Perhaps they once felt anger at having to fill the role of the angel in the house. Indeed, we know from Barack Obama's memoirs that Michelle Obama was, at one point, furious. By the time their second child was born, he wrote, 'my wife's anger toward me seemed barely contained. "You only think about yourself," she would tell me. "I never thought I'd have to raise a family alone."'[48] But her anger disappeared, her career was put on hold, and the powerful man was enabled to carry on in his pursuit of power by the shining presence of his acquiescent wife.

I wouldn't judge any woman for deciding to spend time with her family. But the reception given to those wives in the media is highly revealing of our current expectations of women. The culture of domestic goddesses and yummy mummies is often presented as ironic and playful, not least by its leaders – the cooking guru Nigella Lawson often refers to her sense of irony. But, nevertheless, the recreation of this ideal of a devoted woman who, in Nigella's own words, doesn't 'want to feel like a post-modern, post-feminist, overstretched woman but, rather, a domestic goddess, trailing nutmeggy fumes of baking pie in our languorous wake,'[49] has created an image that can put greater stress on those women who try to live up to it. 'I never thought,' one mother said wryly to me at our regular school bake sale, 'that I'd see so many professional women competing over baking fairy cakes. Is this the new feminism?' I looked down at my own handiwork, the cupcakes decorated with icing hearts, and saw what she meant. It is as though we are fetishising the accessories of old-fashioned motherhood to prove that at heart we are all still perfect mothers, whatever we get up to in the world beyond the home.

The narrative of biological determinism fits this new wife culture very well, and by suggesting to us that nurturing and domestic work comes more naturally to women than to men, it obscures the fact that nurturing behaviour is learned and reinforced for women in our culture, and that in fact men can and do learn this too when the situation is right. When men do take on the care of their children, they often find, just as women do, that their priorities and their abilities are changed. As one journalist, Rafael Behr, put it on returning from paternity leave: 'When I first went back to work I felt agoraphobia for the first time. My reassuringly narrowed horizons were forced back open. The idea that you are expected, after a few hearty pats on the back, to get on with business as usual struck me as grotesque. I sat in meetings struggling to care. I now live in fear of missing some minuscule step my daughter might have taken down the road of infant development, a newly articulate gurgle or a very prolific poo. Fathering is addictive like that.'[50] Fathering is addictive, just like mothering; people learn to care by caring.

Far from feeling that they have done something unnatural, men tend to find increased happiness when they step up their contribution to domestic work. In Australia, two social policy researchers at the University of New South Wales found that fathers were more satisfied when they spent more time at home. 'The more fathers reported that they do more than their fair share of looking after the children, the *more* satisfaction they reported with their work–family balance. There was no variation by age of the child. . . . This suggests that allowing men opportunity to spend more time with children, through easier access to (for example) part time work, could be a welcome policy change.'[51] Another study found that men's involvement in infant care positively correlated with their satisfaction with family life and adjustment to fatherhood; and that 'when men do almost as much child care as their wives their psychological well-being soars'.[52]

The genuine, positive happiness men can find in family work does mean that despite the backlash visible in some areas of our culture, men are taking steps into doing more domestic work. The amount of time spent by men with young children on child-care activities has increased eight-fold since the 1970s, and in one recent survey seven out of ten fathers said they would like to spend more time with their children.[53] We can all see that change around us, from increasing numbers of men at the school gates to increasing numbers of men asking for flexible working patterns. Men often make these changes in the teeth of cultural and workplace opposition and a loss of status and pay; for instance, employers are more likely to turn down requests for flexible working from men than from women.[54] One analysis by the Equal Opportunities Commission found that one in five working men wanted to change their working patterns in order to spend more time with their children, but felt prevented from doing so due to workplace obstacles.[55]

Whatever changes have been made in men's lives, this is still far from the revolution; men still do by far the majority of paid work and women by far the majority of unpaid work. A necessary first step for challenging this unequal situation would be to equalise rights to spend time with one's children. At the moment, government policy locks fathers out of childcare by giving them the most unequal parental leave rights in Europe, with just two weeks' paternity leave compared to a potential fifty-two weeks for women. So even if a mother and father go into parenthood with the same ideas about childcare and the same aptitudes for it, once the mother has spent months at home with her child, while the father has to work his usual long hours outside the home, it is almost inevitable that she will feel she is more keyed into her child's needs, and is far more likely than the father to have discovered an identity beyond her working self. We need not mystify this shift in priorities by putting it down to the oxytocin surge or the way a woman's brain is wired. The difference in the time a mother currently spends with her child and the expectations laid upon her by everyone around her are bound to reinforce and exaggerate the difference between her behaviour and her partner's. The fact that parental leave rights in the UK have been made so unequal has disadvantaged women in the workplace as well as disadvantaging men in the home. This imbalance means that employers still assume that women will be less committed to work than men – and in our current situation they are often right to make this assumption. That creates a circle in which expectations of women's lesser attachment to paid work is perpetuated. It means that employers can continue to rely on many male workers who can shuffle off their responsibilities at home and force themselves into the all-hours commitment upon which so many workplaces rely.

Until we give men the same rights to care for their children that women have, we will never reach equality both at work and at home. Yet when such a reform is suggested in the UK, the language of biological determinism is immediately marshalled against it. 'They are up against the realities of human nature,' is how one typical commentator in the *Daily Mail* put it.[56] Or, as another writer put it in the *Sunday Times*: 'It flies in the face of human nature and it's deeply unfair on men. What if men don't want to spend their time changing nappies and nurturing their feminine side? Actually, there's no "if" about it: they don't ... modern men just aren't interested in the paternity leave which the government is preparing statutorily to impose on business. They are much happier working long hours, avoiding childcare as much as possible and generally being men.'[57] It is tragic that a narrative about men's biological inability to care has infected this debate, so that instead of looking clearly at the inequality of their situations once they become parents, we talk about men's natural lack of empathy. This means that the urgency regarding the need for changes in government policy and employment practice has lessened. The new fashion for biological determinism does not encourage us to look at the current situation clearly and seek to change it. On the contrary, it wraps an aura of inevitability around current inequality, giving it the status of enduring archetype rather than a social situation that could be changed.

Arguments against the continuing assumption that women should embrace the role of the nurturing wife while men should concentrate their energy on paid work are often answered by recourse to the same rhetoric of individual choice that is also trotted out to defend the hypersexual culture. In reaction to any criticism of continuing inequalities, traditionalists mutter, 'I thought feminism was meant to be all about choice.' Feminism is all about choice, but at the moment the language of choice is used almost always in relation to those women and those men who choose to follow traditional patterns of behaviour. 'If given *the choice* between staying at home with the newborn bairn or pottering off to work, the modern British dad comes to the same conclusion as his forebears have since caveman days, [my italics]' says one male commentator in the *Daily Mail*.[58] 'As a mother of three, I *chose* to stay at home instead of hanging on to a well-paid job, [my italics]' writes a female commentator in the same newspaper.[59]

When we hear these automatic responses about choices, we have to remember the situations in which those choices are made. Given our unequal society, it is much too early to make the assumption that the choices we see today are free. Although the imbalance of caring work and paid work can be put down to free choice, individuals are affected in these choices by the expectations and relationships around them. In so many ways women and men are not developing as parents in the same situation. If men were expected to take at least six months at home with the birth of each baby, and were frowned on if they worked full-time before their child was twelve, and were judged by other fathers if they didn't bring cakes to the school cake sale, and never opened a newspaper without finding that the decision to work and be a father was under question; if they had to hassle and negotiate for every hour they spent away from their newborn baby, if the childcare costs were seen as coming out of their salary not their wife's, if their partner was not prepared to take up all the slack; if they lived, in other words, in the same world that women do, then their choices might look different.

And women and men do not develop their working lives in similar situations, either. If women could rely on their partners to create a haven away from work; if they knew that when they were not at home their children still had a committed and loving parent with them; if their voices and views were taken as seriously as those of their male colleagues, then their choices might also be very different. But right now the operation of systems and stereotypes that are bigger than the individual create such unequal situations that men and women are still not making their choices in the same world. If we concentrate on what appears to be 'natural' in these choices, we are deflected from looking at these social pressures and trying to change them. Our culture has entered a time when an exaggerated femininity often goes unquestioned, in which, from the very start of girls' lives, a pink frilly girliness is being seen as purely natural rather than at least partly constructed, and in which as they grow into adults women are often assumed to have very different talents and skills from the men around them.

Writers who promote biological explanations for sex differences often caricature their critics as social engineers who would like everyone to conform to a tedious and unrelieved androgyny. This is nonsense. In order to challenge this culture in which feminine stereotypes remain so restrictive for women, there is no need to deny the pleasures of femininity, no need to retreat into a caricatured feminism of drab clothes, sexless pursuits and dour political correctness. All women can enjoy all the positive aspects of our femininity, whether those pleasures are physical or emotional, but we do need much greater vigilance and much greater solidarity to ensure that these pleasures do not become a trap for us. We have to ensure that we do not see femininity as our only strength and only our strength. There are aspects of traditional femininity, from home-making to empathy, that should belong to men too. If we move away from biological determinism we enter a world with more freedom, not less, because then those behaviours traditionally associated with masculinity and femininity could become real choices for each individual.

10: Changes

Our society is not monolithic: despite all the evidence of a back-lash, the gains of the past have not yet been lost. Feminists in the West have already set in motion the greatest peaceful revolution the world has ever known, by achieving political representation for women, rights to equal education and working opportunities, and rights over contraception and reproduction. There are women who are still achieving their own dreams in a range of different realms, whether they are creating art or literature, succeeding in business or politics, or finding intimate relationships that answer their own emotional and sexual desires.

This means that successful women in many areas are as full of optimism as they ever were. For instance, I discussed women's current situation with Harriet Harman, just before she won the deputy leadership of the Labour party. 'Young women now have good role models, they are forging ahead,' she said. 'Why do you think things are bad for them?' I discussed it with Anne McElvoy, the deputy editor of the *London Evening Standard*, at a party to celebrate Doris Lessing's Nobel Prize. 'Are you feeling pessimistic?' she said incredulously, looking around a room full of female writers and publishers and editors. 'With all these women in powerful positions?'

Given the changes in our society that have already been achieved by feminism, and given the successes that have been achieved by many individual women, it's not surprising if we often feel complacent even when confronted by the reality of renewed sexism. After all, even if you feel irritated by the sale of irons labelled 'Mummy and Me' in a high-street store, or angered by the opening of a lap-dancing club in your town centre, you may feel that it would be a little extreme to complain. You may feel that the joke on a late-night comedy show is degrading to female participants, but then again you might wonder if you are overreacting. Even when you hear about or experience an example of outrageous sexism, from discrimination to violence, you may wonder if it is just one isolated and unfortunate incident.

But rather than being lulled by the idea that such incidents are just the side effects of our freedoms and our choices, it is time to wake up to the fact that the resurgence of such sexism is reducing the choices available to young women. If we are to create a future which genuinely values women for their full human potential, it is time for more people to put their complacency aside. I think that this is already beginning to happen; while writing this book I have been aware that more people are now communicating and acting upon their anger. Many of the women I interviewed for this book felt fatalistic about the possibility of challenging the culture around them, but other women are now beginning to question the resurgence of old-fashioned stereotypes. These individuals are looking at the current situation and, rather than feeling silenced, are trying to challenge it.

Here are ten initiatives among so many that have started in the last ten years which have broken through the complacency around us. Some are small, some are large. Some focus on a single issue, such as the need for more support for women survivors of rape or girls dealing with sexual bullying, others seek to revive understanding of the impact of inequality throughout women's lives. Some focus on affecting the decisions of politicians in order to create changes in legislation or funding, others look at shifting the attitudes of ordinary people. Of course there are many, many more than these ten that I could have chosen, but each of these has the potential to have significant impact even in areas where many people have lost hope of seeing change.

- In 2003 a group of women who were concerned about the sexual objectification of women created the organisation OBJECT. Recently they joined up with a long-established feminist organisation, the Fawcett Society, to campaign for changes in the law regarding the licensing of lap-dancing clubs. Although they have not achieved all their goals, in 2009 this campaign succeeded in getting the government to propose changes to the licensing regulations that would make it harder for new lap-dancing clubs to open.

- In 2007 some women began to take direct action against lads' magazines and advertisements for plastic-surgery firms by defacing them with stickers. Their witty stickers were placed on many advertisements and magazines, with lines such as: 'You are normal, this is not', and 'Beachball baps; so much more exciting than equal pay'. This stickering campaign then moved on into a Facebook group, 'Somewhat strident but who cares', where they could debate issues from these advertisements for plastic surgery to pornography. Mainstream media outlets from the *Daily Mail* to *Woman's Hour* have covered the actions of the group.

- In 2004 some women decided to revive the Reclaim the Night marches that had been a feature of the second-wave women's

to draw his attention to the issue, which was signed by women from the editor of *Cosmopolitan* to the chair of the Women's Institutes. In 2009 a group of women ambushed the London mayor, Boris Johnson, to ask him why he had failed to keep his promise to fund four rape crisis centres in London. They filmed his reaction and uploaded it on to YouTube.

• In 2008 two sisters, Emma and Abi Moore, decided to take action against the culture of pink which they believe is restricting their children's freedoms. They set up an online campaign, Pink Stinks, which seeks to raise awareness and focus dissent. In the 'name and shame' section of their website they draw attention to products such as the pink globe marketed to girls by the Early Learning Centre or the launch of a pink Monopoly game for girls. 'We want to raise awareness about the way that girls are being really restricted by the whole culture of pink,' Emma Moore told me. 'We aren't killjoys, but we don't think that there should be this monoculture that tells girls that there is only one acceptable way to be, and it's all about sparkles and make-up and princesses.'

These initiatives have touched many thousands of women. If you want to add your strength to any of them, you can go to page 264 to find the contact details for these organisations and give them your support.

Many other women who might not identify with any particular organisation are still being moved to take action when they see something that has an impact on their lives. For instance, they might complain to the ASA about an advertisement for a lap-dancing club placed opposite a school, or to the BBC about the removal of a respected female broadcaster. Often, this kind of unplanned swell of anger can produce real changes. For instance, in 2006 Tesco removed a pole-dancing kit, with fake money and a pole to dance around, from the toy section of its website, after customers decided to complain in large numbers. In online parenting forums such as Mumsnet, women and men discuss the rise of sexism in children's culture and support one another in complaining to outlets from W H Smith to Marks and Spencer. And of course it is not only women who are seeking greater equality and freedom, there are men working in all these campaigns and on all these issues, both publicly and privately.

Alongside this swell of campaigning, there are women who are not necessarily conscious activists, but who seek full respect as human beings and try to live their private and public lives without being pressed into one mould by the sexism around them. When these women make free choices – whether those are choices about what magazines or books they are going to read, what toys they are going to buy for their children or what behaviour they are going to challenge at work – they too have the potential to change the status quo.

Yet, as many women pointed out to me in the research for this book, while dissent both planned and unplanned, political and artistic, private and public, may be forceful and growing, it is not yet moving far enough into the mainstream. Many young women are not seeing their dissatisfactions reflected, and feel alone in their sense that the culture does not fully value them as human beings. But it feels to me as though we are at a crossroads. We can now see a groundswell in anger and solidarity that may, if enough people join, lead to real cultural and political changes.

What we can remember when we look at the past is that social change is always possible, and when an idea grips sufficient numbers of people, then it is inevitable. Despite all the disappointments of the last few years, there is no reason to give up hope or to stop believing that one day the future we desire could become the present we inhabit. There is no need to think we must start from scratch; the feminist foundations in our society are strong. We can be aware of and grateful for previous feminist successes while building upon them towards a better future. Because the dream that feminists first spoke about over two hundred years ago is still urging us on, the dream that one day women and men will be able to work and love side by side, freely, without the constraints of restrictive traditions. This dream tells us that rather than modelling themselves on the plastic charm of a pink and smiling doll, women can aim to realise their full human potential.

Notes

Dolls

1   MTV news report, 19 October 2006, retrieved 10 October 2008 from www.mtv.com/news/articles/1543510/20061019/duff_hilary.jhtml
2   The huge success of Bratz can be seen in the fact that they were selling 45 per cent of the fashion dolls in the UK in 2004 – the biggest market share for a single brand; Graham Hiscott, 'Bratz the new queen of the fashion-doll world', *Independent*, 10 September 2004
3   Retrieved 16 November 2008 from http://www.henheaven.co.uk/pole-dancing-hen-weekends/
4   Josephine Moulds, 'Lap dancing, the daily grind', *The Times*, 19 June 2008
5   Viv Hardwick, 'More cow than call-girl', *Northern Echo*, 11 September 2008
6   Kate Taylor, 'Today's ultimate feminists are the chicks in crop tops', *Guardian*, 23 March 2006
7   Naomi Wolf, *Fire With Fire* (London: Chatto & Windus, 1993), p6
8   Natasha Walter, 'Whoever wins, the suits will lose their majority', *Observer*, 27 April 1997
9   For instance, when Patricia Hewitt was secretary of state for trade and industry in 2001 she brought in new rights for workers to demand flexible working, saying, 'We want people to be able to balance their responsibilities as parents and their responsibilities as employees instead of having a struggle between being a good parent and a good employee.' 'Flexible hours boost for working parents', BBC News, 28 June 2001
10 George Lucas, 'Go on Tony, take paternity leave', *New Statesman*, 13 March 2000
11 Scottish Parliament debate, 5 March 2009, http://www.theywork-foryou.com/sp/?id=2009-03-05.15588.0

12 Caroline Flint's resignation letter, 5 June 2009

13 Marie Woolf, 'Paternity leave scheme shelved by Lord Mandelson', *Sunday Times,* 31 May 2009

14 Brendan Burchell, Colette Fagan, Catherine O'Brien and Mark Smith, *Working Conditions in the European Union: The Gender Perspective* (Luxembourg: Office for Official Publications of the European Communities, 2007), retrieved 24 January 2009 from http://www.euro-found.europa.eu/pubdocs/2007/108/en/1/ef07108en.pdf; statistics for the UK discussed in Sarah Womack, 'Career women work longer hours than men', *Daily Telegraph*, 2 December 2007

15 Pay statistics from the Equality and Human Rights Commission's analysis of data from the *Annual Survey of Hours and Earnings* (Office of National Statistics, 2008) and *Labour Market Statistics Bulletin* (Office of National Statistics, 2008), based on mean hourly earnings, retrieved 1 September 2009 from www.equalityhumanrights.com

16 From 2007 to 2008 the pay gap widened by 0.1 per cent. Based on mean earnings, from the *Annual Survey of Hours and Earnings* (Office of National Statistics, 2008), retrieved 26 May 2009 from http://www.statistics.gov.uk/cci/nugget.asp?id=167. In 2007 the pay gap for women and men in senior professional positions also widened for the first time in more than a decade, according to the *National Management Salary Survey* (Chartered Management Institute, September 2007). 'In real terms female managers earned an average of £43,571, last year – £6,076 less than the male equivalent of £49,647. The difference (12.2 per cent) is up from 11.8 per cent, last year. At director level the gap is £49,233 or 23 per cent, up from 20 per cent, last year.' Press release retrieved 24 January 2009 from http://www.managers.org.uk/listing_media_1.aspx?id=10:347&id=10:138&id=10:11&doc=10:3364

17 Jill Treanor, 'Women quit before hitting glass ceiling', *Guardian*, 8 March 2007

18 Anya C Hurlbert and Yazhu Ling, 'Biological components of sex differences in colour preference', *Current Biology*, 17, 16 (2007), 623–5

19 Steve Connor, 'Boys like blue, girls like pink, it's in our genes', *Independent*, 21 August 2007

20 Martin Wainwright, 'Pink for a girl and blue for a boy – and it's all down to evolution', *Guardian*, 21 August 2007

21 Girls' Schools Association website, 'Answers to frequently asked questions', retrieved 13 October 2008 from http://www.gsa.uk.com/default.aspx?id=135

22 Quoted in Melissa Fletcher Stoeltje, 'Little girls carried away on a pink wave of princess products', *San Antonio Express*, 3 October 2007

23 Simon Baron-Cohen, *The Essential Difference* (London: Allen Lane, 2003), p20

24 Simon Baron-Cohen, *The Essential Difference*, op cit, p185

1: Babes

1   Sales of *Zoo* slipped 13.6 per cent from 2007 to 2008, sales of *Nuts* slipped 9.8 per cent over the same period. Statistics from the Audit Bureau of Circulation (ABC), quoted in Owen Gibson, 'Lads' mags cocktail of booze, birds and banter loses its fizz', *Guardian*, 15 August 2008

2   Traffic to the *Nuts* website increased sharply in 2008, with over 1 million unique users in June 2008, a 121 per cent year-on-year increase. Figures from IPC press release, retrieved 26 May 2009 from http://www.ipcmedia.com/press/article.php?id=270943

3   Survey carried out by the Lab, 6 June 2005, retrieved 10 October 2008 from http://www.manchestereveningnews.co.uk/news/s/161/161338_naked_ambition_rubs_off_on_teen_girls.htm

4   *Martlet*, newsletter of Pembroke College Cambridge, 9 (September 2005)

5   Telegraph reporter, 'Cambridge University magazine prints topless page three picture of student', *Daily Telegraph*, 20 November 2008

6   Quoted in Janice Turner, 'Is the misogyny of lads' mags good clean fun?' *Guardian*, 22 October 2005

7   Ariel Levy, *Female Chauvinist Pigs: Women and the Rise of Raunch Culture* (London: Simon & Schuster, 2006)

2: Pole-dancers and prostitutes

1   Estimate from OBJECT and Fawcett Society's briefing on lap dancing, retrieved 1 September 2009 from www.object.org.uk.

2   Retrieved 29 June 2009 from http://www.thestagcompany.com/lapdancing-stag-weekends/

3   Retrieved 15 October 2008 from http://www.clubmuse.co.uk/club-muse.htm

4   Gordon Stuart, 'Spice Girls learn to pole dance', *Sun*, 24 October 2007

5   Gordon Stuart, 'Sugas are sweet on pole-dancing', *Sun*, 3 April 2008

6   Louise Gannon, 'Emilia Fox on the noble art of pole-dancing and how she learned to undress for her husband', *Daily Mail*, 12 April 2008

7   *Stranger* magazine, August 2006, retrieved 1 June 2009 from http://www.stranger-mag.com/features/life/the-importance-of-being-immodest.html

8   Kelly DiNardo, 'Burlesque comeback tries to dance with feminism', Womens ENews, 12 July 2004, retrieved 1 June 2009 from http://www.womensenews.org/article.cfm/dyn/aid/2099

9   'Take a peep at Mel B', *Sun*, 3 April 2009

10   See for instance, Conrad Astley, 'Lap dance girls pay for naked ambition', *Manchester Evening News*, 13 June 2003; Lee Sykes, 'Lap dancing club has fallen foul of the law', *Oldham Advertiser*, 22 March 2006; 'Call for curbs on lapdancing clubs', BBC News 17 August 2004, http://news.bbc.co.uk/1/hi/scotland/3572112.stm; Julie Bindel, *Profitable exploits:*

lap dancing in the UK (Child and Women Abuse Studies Unit, London Metropolitan University, 2004), retrieved 1 June 2009 from http://www.rapecrisisscotland.org.uk/documents/profitable%20 exploits.pdf

11   Lilith report on lap dancing and striptease in the London Borough of Camden (2003) p10, retrieved 15 October 2008 from http://www. eaves4women.co.uk/Lilith_Project/Documents/Reports/Lilith_report_lap _dancing_striptease_camden.pdf

12   Catherine Bennett, 'Why can't we stop the spread of degrading adverts for sex?', *Observer*, 1 June 2008

13   Belle de Jour, *The Intimate Adventures of a London Call Girl* (London: Weidenfeld & Nicolson, 2005); Miss S, *Confessions of a Working Girl* (London: Penguin, 2007); Tracy Quan, *Diary of a Manhattan Call Girl* ((2001), London: HarperCollins, 2005)

14   Emile Zola, *Nana* ((1880), Harmondsworth: Penguin, 1972), p452

15   Charles Dickens, *Oliver Twist* ((1839), Harmondsworth: Penguin, 1988), p364

16   Miss S, *Confessions of a Working Girl*, op cit, p89

17   Russell Brand, *My Booky Wook* (London: Hodder & Stoughton, 2007), pp126–7

18   Caroline Crowe, 'Meet the men who pay for sex', *Sun*, 30 October 2007

19   Maddy Coy, Miranda Horvath and Liz Kelly, *It's Just Like Going to the Supermarket: Men Buying Sex in East London,* report for Safe Exit at Toynbee Hall (Child & Woman Abuse Studies Unit, London Metropolitan University, 2007), p20

20   Helen Ward et al, 'Who pays for sex? An analysis of the increasing prevalence of female commercial sex contacts among men in Britain', *Sexually Transmitted Infections*, 81 (2005), 467–71

21   Peter Baker, of the Men's Health Forum, commented that: 'Many people will be surprised by the relatively large numbers of men who are willing to pay for sex. But it's not so surprising in the context of social trends – women are increasingly sexualised in the media.' Quotations from BBC report, 'Twice as many men pay for sex', 1 December 2005, retrieved 18 October 2008 from http://news.bbc.co.uk/1/hi/health/4482970.stm

22   The coverage of this report on the *Guardian* website linked to an internet soft porn site on 10 November 2007 – the link no longer exists. www.guardian.co.uk/uk_news/story/0,,1654880,00.html

23   K Elliott, H Eland, and J McGaw, *Kerb Crawling in Middlesbrough: An Analysis of Kerbcrawlers' Opinions* (Safer Middlesbrough Partnership, 2002) unpublished, cited in Coy, Horvath and Kelly, op cit, p3

24   Retrieved November 2007 from www.punternet.com, spelling and punctuation corrected

25   M A Barnard, G Hurt, C Benson and S Church, *Client Violence Against Prostitutes Working from Street and Off-street Locations: A three-city comparison* (Swindon: ESRC Violence Research Programme, 2002), cited in Coy, Horvath and Kelly, op cit, p3

26 *Paying the Price: A Consultation Paper on Prostitution* (Home Office, 2004), p11, retrieved 18 October 2008 from http://www.homeoffice.gov.uk/documents/paying_the_price.pdf?view=Binary

27 J Pearce, *It's Someone Taking a Part of You: A Study of Young Women and Sexual Exploitation* (National Children's Bureau for the Joseph Rowntree Foundation, 2002), cited in *Paying the price*, op cit, p95

28 H Kinnell, correspondence, 1993, cited in *Paying the price*, op cit, p95

29 J J Pearce, M Williams and C Galvin, *Research Findings: the Choice and Opportunity Project, Young Women and Sexual Exploitation* (Joseph Rowntree Foundation, 2003), cited in M Hester and N Westmarland, *Tackling Street Prostitution: Towards an Holistic Approach* (Home Office research, development and statistics directorate, July 2004), p60

30 R Campbell, *Working on the Street, an Evaluation of the Linx Project 1998–2001* (Liverpool Hope University, 2002), cited in Hester and Westmarland, op cit, p78

31 I Peate, 'Paying the price: health care and prostitution', *British Journal of Nursing*, 15 (2006), 246–7, cited in M Goodyear and L Cusick, 'Protection of sex workers', *BMJ*, 334, 7584 (13 January 2007), 52–3

32 Miss S, *Confessions of a Working Girl*, op cit, pp4–6

3: Girls

1 Quoted in Tanya Gold, 'The queen is dead', *Guardian*, 6 October 2004

2 'Express Yourself', Black Eyed Peas featuring Apl de Ap, Geffen/Universal 2007

3 Joan Jacobs Brumberg, *The Body Project: An Intimate History of American Girls* (New York: Random House, 1997), pxxi

4 Retrieved 15 August 2009 from http://www.trinnyandsusannah.com/

5 Esther Blum, author of *Eat, Drink and Be Gorgeous*, in *Daily Mail*, 12 January 2009

6 Sally Jeffrie, *The Girls Book of Glamour* (London: Buster Books, 2007)

7 Susie Orbach, *Bodies* (London: Profile, 2009), p136

8 'Girls diet for pop star bodies', BBC News, 20 July 2005

9 Beth Neil, 'The diet generation', *Daily Mirror*, 27 April 2009

10 Richard Garner, 'Girls aged six "unhappy with weight"', *Independent*, 8 March 2005

11 Dr Jan Stanek, quoted in Bel Mooney, 'On vanity', *Daily Telegraph*, 22 July 2000

12 Survey carried out by Dove in 2006, reported in 'Quarter of teens considering plastic surgery', *Daily Mail*, 10 March 2006

13 J Kelly and S L Smith, *Where the Girls Aren't: Gender Disparity Saturates G-rated Films*, 2006, www.thriveoncreative.com/clients/seejane/pdfs/where.the.girls.arent.pdf, cited in American Psychological Association, *Report of the APA Task Force on the Sexualization of Girls*, American

Psychological Association (Washington DC, 2007), retrieved 16 October 2008 from http://www.apa.org/pi/wpo/sexualizationrep.pdf

14 Kate Figes, 'Hello boys', *Guardian*, 20 January 2006

15 K E Dill and K P Thill, 'Video game characters and the socialization of gender roles: young people's perceptions mirror sexist media depictions', *Sex Roles*, 57, 11–12 (December 2007) 851–64

16 Jess McCabe, 'Sexual harassment is rife online', *Guardian*, 6 March 2008

17 L M Ward and R Rivadeneyra, 'Dancing, strutting and bouncing in cars, the women of music videos', paper presented at the annual meeting of the American Psychological Association (Chicago, August 2002), cited in *Report of the APA Task Force on the Sexualization of Girls*, American Psychological Association (Washington DC, 2007), retrieved 16 October 2008 from http://www.apa.org/pi/wpo/sexualizationrep.pdf

18 Retrieved 10 August 2007 from http://www.lookagain.co.uk/web/main/productdisplay.asp?An=0&A=26K742%5F15&N=428+583+4294967092&Au=P%5FMasterItem&Nu=P%5FMasterItem&Ns=P%5FColour%7C0%7C%7CP%5FSize%7C0

19 Rachel Bell, 'It's porn, innit?' *Guardian*, 15 August 2005

20 Colin Fernandez, 'Tesco condemned for selling pole-dancing toy', *Daily Mail*, 24 October 2006

21 BHS withdrew the underwear after criticism – 'Sexy children's underwear withdrawn', BBC, 26 March 2003

22 Next was criticised for selling these T-shirts to young girls – Judith Woods, 'Girls just need to be young', *Daily Telegraph*, 20 February 2007

23 Annie Leibovitz's photographs of Miley Cyrus were widely criticised – Sheila Marikar, 'Leibovitz defends provocative Miley Cyrus photos', ABC News, 26 April 2008

24 Survey conducted by the NSPCC and *Sugar* in 2006 among 674 *Sugar* website visitors. Retrieved 16 October 2008 from http://www.nspcc.org.uk/whatwedo/mediacentre/pressreleases/22_may_2006_unwanted_sexual_experiences_wdn33559.html

25 *Panorama: Kids Behaving Badly*, BBC1, 5 January 2009

26 BBC *Newsbeat*, 4 August 2009

27 Christine Barter, Melanie McCarry, David Berridge and Kathy Evans, 'Partner exploitation and violence in teenage intimate relationships', executive summary retrieved 10 September 2009 from www.nspcc.org.uk

28 '"Gang-raped girl was glad of the attention," says barrister', *Daily Mail*, 18 May 2007.

29 Statistics from the National Survey of Sexual Attitudes and Lifestyles, quoted in BBC report, Education 'prevents underage sex', 30 November 2001, http://news.bbc.co.uk/1/hi/health/1683271.stm and in Kaye Wellings et al, 'Sexual Behaviour in Britain: early heterosexual experience', *Lancet*, 358, 9296 (December 2001), 1851–4

4: Lovers

1   Quoted in Judith Weintraub, 'Germaine Greer – opinions that may shock the faithful', *New York Times*, 22 March 1971
2   Germaine Greer, *The Female Eunuch* ((1970), London: Harper Perennial, 2006), p275
3   Quoted in Judith Weintraub, op cit
4   Similarly, in her 1973 novel *Fear of Flying* the American writer Erica Jong described how essential the pursuit of the 'zipless fuck' was to the narrator as a married woman: 'Five years of marriage had made me itchy ... my response was to evolve my fantasy of the Zipless Fuck. The zipless fuck was more than a fuck ... For the true, ultimate zipless A-1 fuck, it was necessary that you never get to know the man very well.' Even though the zipless fuck turns out to be a chimera, the pursuit itself is worthwhile, as it leads her out of the stalemate of her claustrophobic marriage. Erica Jong, *Fear of Flying* ((1973), London: Minerva, 1974), p11
5   Doris Lessing, *The Golden Notebook* ((1962), London: Flamingo, 1993), p36
6   Statistics from the National Survey of Sexual Attitudes and Lifestyles 2000, quoted in Anne M Johnson et al, 'Sexual behaviour in Britain: partnerships, practices and HIV risk behaviours', *Lancet*, 358, 9296 (December 2001), 1835–42
7   Abby Lee, *Girl with a One-track Mind* (London: Ebury, 2006), pp110–13
8   Abby Lee, op cit, p103
9   Catherine Townsend, *Sleeping Around* (London: John Murray, 2007), pp207 and 222
10   Zoe Williams, 'I don't write to titillate', *Guardian*, 11 August 2006
11   Mary Wollstonecraft, Letter to William Godwin, 4 October 1796, in *The Collected Letters*, Janet Todd ed (London: Penguin, 2003), p371
12   Emma Goldman, *Living My Life*, Volume 1 (New York: Alfred Knopf, 1931), p441
13   Michèle Roberts, *Paper Houses* (London: Virago, 2007), p67
14   Michèle Roberts, *Paper Houses*, op cit, p295
15   Michèle Roberts, *Paper Houses*, op cit, p67
16   Anaïs Nin, *Henry and June* (San Diego: Harcourt Brace Jovanovich, 1986), p66
17   Abby Lee, op cit, p113

5: Pornography

1   Leo Benedictus, 'Extreme close up', *Guardian*, 12 May 2007
2   Adam Thirlwell, *Politics* (London: Jonathan Cape, 2003), p216
3   Robin Morgan, 'Theory and practice, pornography and rape', (1974) in *The Word of a Woman* (London: Virago, 1993), p88

4   Andrea Dworkin, 'Why pornography matters to feminists', *Sojourner*, 7, 2 (1981)

5   At one protest in 1978 in Soho, sixteen feminists were arrested. 'Women in porn demo acquitted', *Guardian*, 3 May 1979

6   For a good discussion on the lack of evidence to link pornography and sexual violence, either through laboratory studies or through observational research, see Nadine Strossen, *Defending Pornography: Free Speech, Sex and the Fight for Women's Rights* (London: Abacus, 1996), Chapter 12; and Lynne Segal and Mary McIntosh (eds), *Sex Exposed: Sexuality and the Pornography Debate* (London: Virago 1992)

7   For a good discussion of the range of feminist reaction to pornography, see Nadine Strossen, op cit, Chapter 7

8   Nina Power, 'The dirty girl: Charlotte Roche brings Wetlands to the English-speaking world', *Der Spiegel* (online English version), 6 April 2009

9   Zoe Margolis, 'Something for the Ladies', *Guardian*, 29 November 2007

10 Survey carried out by Nielsen NetRatings for the *Independent on Sunday*, 28 May 2006

11 Janis Wolak, Kimberly Mitchell and David Finkelhor, 'Unwanted and wanted exposure to online pornography in a national sample of youth internet users', *Pediatrics*, 119, 2 (February 2007), 247–57

12 Sonya Thompson, 'One in three boys heavy porn users, study shows', University of Alberta, 23 February 2007. Report retrieved 22 October 2008 from http://www.eurekalert.org/pub_releases/2007-02/uoa-oit 022307.php; full unpublished study supplied by Sonya Thompson in personal correspondence

13 In 2004–5 eight hundred labial reductions were carried out on the NHS, double the number of six years earlier. One private cosmetic surgery business, Surgicare, reported in 2009 that labia reduction procedures increased 300 per cent in the last year. Retrieved 20 September 2009 from www.surgicare.co.uk

14 Retrieved 18 February 2009 from http://www.channel4embarrassingill-nesses.com/about/episodes/teen-bodies/teens-below-the-belt/

15 Retrieved 23 March 2009 from the website of the Laser Vaginal Rejuvenation Institute, http://www.cosmeticgyn.net/dlv.htm

16 Zadie Smith, *On Beauty* (London: Hamish Hamilton, 2005), p316

17 Zadie Smith, op cit, p397

6: Choices

1   Rod Liddle, 'Harriet Harman is either thick or criminally disingenuous', *Spectator*, 5 August 2009

2   Comment retrieved 12 August 2009 from http://www.spectator.co.uk/ the-magazine/features/5244693/harriet-harman-is-either-thick-or-crimi-nally-disingenuous.thtml

3   Retrieved 24 October 2008 from http://www.herobuilders.com/

4   India Knight, 'Aah, what a relief', *Sunday Times*, 7 September 2008

5   *The Graham Norton Show*, 23 October 2008, described in 'The BBC fills our living rooms with more smutty and degrading obscenities', *Daily Mail*, 31 October 2008

6   'The best of Breastminster', *Sun*, 12 October 2007

7   India Knight, 'Pity the women who come within range of Brand and Ross', *Sunday Times*, 2 November 2008

8   For instance, one intriguing study showed how women's over-preoccupation with their appearance may 'drain their mental energy'. Barbara Fredrickson, a psychology professor at the University of Michigan, asked 40 male and 42 female undergraduates to put on a sweater or swimsuit, and then take a mathematics test. Each participant tried on the swimsuit or sweater and completed the surveys and tests alone in a changing room. What concerned Fredrickson was the women's tendency to score lower than men on the maths tests when wearing bathing suits, which she believed was because baring their bodies made them think more about how they looked than what they were doing. Men who were asked to bare their bodies did not find that their maths performance was impaired. 'It appears that asking themselves the question, "How do I look?" becomes disruptive to women's math performance. By comparison, men have an easier time ridding their minds of that sort of cultural baggage.' B L Fredrickson et al, 'That swimsuit becomes you: sex differences in self-objectification, restrained eating and math performance', *Journal of Personality and Social Psychology*, 75, 1 (1998), 269–84; quotation retrieved 18 February 2009 from APA online, http://www.apa.org/monitor/nov98/looks.html

9   In one study published in 2005, psychologists asked groups of young men and young women to view television commercials before putting themselves forward for a leadership role or a subordinate role in a psychological test. One group viewed gender-neutral commercials, in which objects were sold impersonally, with no humans in the frame. Another saw two commercials that showed women in more stereotypically feminine and sexy roles, such as a female college student who dreams of being a homecoming queen. When the students went on to do the test in which they were asked to put themselves forward for a leadership or 'problem solver' role in a test, the women who had viewed the stereotypic commercial were more likely to avoid the leadership role, while the men were as likely in either group to think themselves fitted for leadership. The women who had seen only the impersonal commercials were as likely as the men to put themselves forward to be leaders. Paul G Davies, Steven J Spencer and Claude M Steele, 'Clearing the air: identity safety moderates the effects of stereotype threat on women's leadership aspirations', *Journal of Personality and Social Psychology*, 88, 2 (2005), 276–87

7: Princesses

1   Retrieved 22 October 2008 from www.marksandspencer.com
2   Retrieved 21 January 2009 from www.boots.com
3   Retrieved 22 October 2008 from www.hiya4kids.co.uk
4   Retrieved 10 March 2009 from http://www.amazon.co.uk/Magnetic-Words-complement-National-Literacy/dp/B000CDFTHE/ref=pd_bxgy_k_h_b_cs_img_b
5   Hamleys catalogue, autumn/winter 2006
6   Retrieved 15 August 2007 from www.hamleys.com
7   Simone de Beauvoir, *The Second Sex* ((1949), London: Vintage, 1997), p306
8   Sales of Disney Princess brand retrieved 22 October 2008 from http://www.laughingplace.com/News-ID506950.asp and 14 October 2008 from https://licensing.disney.com/Home/display.jsp?contentId=dcp_home_ourfranchises_disney_princess_uk&forPrint=false&language=en&preview=false&imageShow=0&pressRoom=UK&translationOf=null&region=0
9   Retrieved 10 October 2008 from http://www.shareholder.com/mattel/news/20021022-93103.cfm
10 Gwyneth Rees, *Fairy Dreams* (London: Macmillan, 2005), p137
11 Leapfrog leaflet for parents about children's reading habits, retrieved 18 December 2008 from http://www.welovetoread.co.uk/PDF/Booklet%20-%20whole/Love%20to%20Read%20Booklet.pdf
12 Mia Kellmer Pringle, *The Needs of Children* (London: Hutchinson Educational, 1974), p16
13 Playgroup Pamphlet Group, *Out of the Pumpkin Shell: Running a Women's Liberation Playgroup* (Birmingham Women's Liberation, 1975), cited by Glenda MacNaughton, 'Equal opportunities: unsettling myths', in Tricia David ed, *Promoting Evidence-Based Practice in Early Childhood Education* (Oxford: Elsevier, 2001), p212
14 Eg in A Elliot, 'Creating non-sexist daycare environments', *Australian Journal of Early Childhood*, 9, 2 (1984),18–23; K Aspinwall, *What are Little Girls Made of? What are Little Boys Made of?* (London: National Nursery Nurses Educational Board, 1984); H Cuffaro, 'Re-evaluating basic premises: curricula free of sexism', *Young Children* (Sept 1975) 469–78; M Guttenberg and H Bray, *Undoing Sex Stereotypes* (McGraw Hill, 1976), cited in Glenda MacNaughton, op cit, p212
15 Sally Koblinsky and Alan Sugawara, 'Nonsexist curricula, sex of teacher and children's sex-role learning', *Sex Roles*, 10, 5–6 (1984), pp357–67
16 Marianne Grabrucker, *There's A Good Girl: Gender Stereotyping in the First Three Years of Life: A Diary*, tr Wendy Philipson (London: The Women's Press, 1988)
17 Marianne Grabrucker, op cit, p93
18 Burkhard Strassmann, 'Woher haben Sie das?', *Die Zeit*, 28 June 2007, tr. Susan Morrissey

19 Naima Browne, *Gender Equity in the Early Years* (Maidenhead: Open University Press, 2004), p22
20 Steve Biddulph, *Raising Boys* (London: HarperCollins, 1998), p3
21 Steve Biddulph, op cit, p4
22 Anya C Hurlbert and Yazhu Ling, 'Biological components of sex differences in colour preference', *Current Biology*, 17, 16 (2007), 623–5
23 Fiona MacRae, 'Scientists uncover truth behind "pink for a girl, blue for a boy"', *Daily Mail*, 20 August 2007
24 Ben Goldacre, 'Out of the blue and in the pink', *Guardian*, 25 August 2007, and retrieved 21 November 2008 with full references and graphs from http://www.badscience.net/?p=518#more-518
25 Jo Paoletti, 'Gendering of infants and toddlers' clothing in America', in *The Material Culture of Gender: The Gender of Material Culture*, Katharine Martinez and Kenneth L Ames eds (Delaware: Henry Francis du Pont Wintherthur, 1997), p32
26 'A Mother', *Time*, 24 October 1927, Retrieved 10 October 2008 from http://www.time.com/time/magazine/article/0,9171,736917,00.html?promoid=googlep
27 See also: Jo Paoletti and Carol Kregloh, 'The children's department', in Claudia Brush Kidwell and Valerie Steele eds, *Men and Women: Dressing the Part* (Smithsonian Institution Press, 1989); Jo Paoletti 'Clothing and gender in America: Children's fashions 1890–1920', *Signs*, 13, 1 (Autumn 1987), 136–43.
28 Simon Baron-Cohen, *The Essential Difference: Men, Women and the Extreme Male Brain* (London: Allen Lane, 2003), pp53–4
29 Simon Baron-Cohen, op cit, p105
30 Simon Baron-Cohen, op cit, p1
31 Steven Pinker, *The Blank Slate: The Modern Denial of Human Nature* (London: Allen Lane, 2002)
32 Louann Brizendine, *The Female Brain* (London: Transworld, 2006)
33 Susan Pinker, *The Sexual Paradox* (London: Atlantic, 2008)
34 John Gray, *Why Mars and Venus Collide* (London: Harper Element, 2008), p90
35 Tracey Shors, 'The mismeasure of woman', *Economist*, 3 August 2006
36 Rosie Boycott, 'Why women don't want top jobs, by a feminist', *Daily Mail*, 22 April 2008

8: Myths

1 Lawrence H Summers, Remarks at NBER Conference on Diversifying the Science & Engineering Workforce, 14 January 2005, retrieved 10 October 2008 from http://www.president.harvard.edu/speeches/2005/nber.html
2 Christopher Caldwell, 'The battle lines at Harvard', *Financial Times*, 25 February 2005

3   Christopher Caldwell, 'Taboos that undid Summers', *Financial Times*, 24 February 2006

4   Andrew Sullivan, 'The truth about men and women is too hot to handle', *Sunday Times*, 23 January 2005

5   Sarah Baxter, 'Harvard's head hit by new war of non-PC words', *Sunday Times*, 20 February 2005

6   Alan Dershowitz, 'After Larry, who dares speak out?', *Sunday Times*, 27 February 2005

7   Margaret Talbot, 'The baby lab: how Elizabeth Spelke peers into the infant mind', *New Yorker*, 4 September 2006

8   The entire debate between Pinker and Spelke can be read online; retrieved 10 October 2008 from http://www.edge.org/3rd_culture/debate05/debate05_index.html

9   George F Will, 'Harvard hysterics', *Washington Post*, 27 January 2005

10   Deborah Cameron, *The Myth of Mars and Venus: Do men and women really speak different languages?* (Oxford University Press, 2007)

11   Melissa Hines, *Brain Gender* (Oxford University Press, 2004)

12   Jennifer Connellan, Simon Baron-Cohen, Sally Wheelwright, Anna Batki and Jag Ahluwalia, 'Sex differences in human neonatal social perception', *Infant Behaviour and Development*, 23, 1 (January 2000), pp113–18

13   Simon Baron-Cohen, *The Essential Difference*, op cit, p58

14   Simon Baron-Cohen, 'The male condition', *New York Times*, 8 August 2005; 'They just can't help it', *Guardian*, 17 April 2003

15   'Time out with Nick Cohen', *New Statesman*, 26 February 2007

16   Helena Cronin, 'The vital statistics', *Guardian*, 12 March 2005

17   Susan Pinker, *The Sexual Paradox*, op cit, p104

18   Elizabeth Spelke, 'Sex differences in intrinsic aptitude for mathematics and science? A critical review', *American Psychologist*, 60, 9 (December 2005), 950–8

19   Elizabeth Spelke, ibid, p951

20   Jerome Kagan, Barbara A Henker, Amy Hen-Tov, Janet Levine, Michael Lewis, 'Infants' differential reactions to familiar and distorted faces', *Child Development*, 37, 3 (Sep 1966), 519–32. See also: Peggy Koopman and Elinor Ames, 'Infants' preferences for facial arrangements, a failure to replicate', *Child Development*, 39, 2 (June 1968), 481–7, which suggests that there is no preference among two-and-a-half-month-old infants for regular as opposed to scrambled faces.

21   Jennifer Connellan et al, op cit, p116

22   Jerome Kagan et al, op cit, p520

23   H A Moss and K S Robson, 'Maternal influences in early social visual behaviour', *Child Development*, 39, 2 (June 1968), 401–8

24   Renée Baillargeon, 'Infants' reasoning about hidden objects: evidence for event-general and event-specific expectations', *Developmental Science*, 7 (2004), 391–424; Hespos and Spelke, 'Precursors to spatial language', *Nature*, 430 (2004), 453–6; Quinn and Eimas, 'Perceptual organisation

and categorisation in young infants', in Rovee-Collier and Lipsitt eds, *Advances in Infancy Research* (Norwoord NJ, 1996), pp1–36, all cited by Elizabeth Spelke, 'Sex differences in intrinsic aptitude for mathematics and science? A critical review', *American Psychologist,* 60, 9 (2005), 950–8

25   As one study found, 'Female infants looked reliably longer at the impossible than at the possible event suggesting that they . . . expected the box to fall in the impossible event and were surprised that it did not . . . In contrast with the female infants, the male infants . . . tended to look equally at the impossible and possible events . . .' Renée Baillargeon, Laura Kotovsky, and Amy Needham, 'The acquisition of physical knowledge in infancy', in *Causal Cognition: A Multidisciplinary Debate* (Oxford University Press, 1995), pp84–5

26   Elizabeth Spelke's response to 'The assortative mating theory', a talk with Simon Baron-Cohen, retrieved 10 February 2008 from www.edge.org/3rd_culture/baron-cohen05/baron-cohen05_index.html

27   Louann Brizendine, *The Female Brain*, op cit, p15

28   Lauren Adamson and Janet Frick, 'The still face: a history of a shared experimental paradigm', *Infancy*, 4, 4 (2003), 451–73, p465

29   Louann Brizendine, *The Female Brain*, op cit, p18

30   Katherine Weinberg, Edward Tronick, Jeffrey Cohn, Karen Olson, 'Gender differences in emotional expressivity and self-regulation during early infancy', *Developmental Psychology*, 35, 1 (1999), 175–88, p185. Weinberg and her colleagues used other studies to suggest that: 'Mothers and sons more carefully tracked each other's behaviour and facial expressions than mothers and daughters' (p185). And these researchers do not necessarily put any differences they see down to biology alone: 'It remains unclear whether the gender differences in self-regulation and expressivity observed in this study are attributable to biological factors or socialisation forces or, as is most likely, a combination of these factors.' (p186)

31   *Richard and Judy*, Channel 4, 1 October 2002, description by Ian Jones retrieved 30 October 2008 from http://www.offthetelly.co.uk/reviews/2002/richardandjudy.htm

32   John Gray, *Men are from Mars, Women are from Venus* ((1992), London: HarperCollins, 2002), p31

33   Fiona MacRae, 'Women talk three times as much as men, says study', *Daily Mail*, 28 November 2006

34   Louann Brizendine, *The Female Brain*, op cit, p36

35   Brizendine cited *Talk Language: How to Use Conversation for Profit and Pleasure* by Allan Pease and Alan Garner, 1991. Allan Pease's views about biological determinism can be understood from the title of his most successful book – *Why Men Don't Listen and Women Can't Read Maps*

36   Mark Liberman, 'Sex on the Brain', *Boston Globe*, 24 September 2006

37   Matthias R Mehl, Simine Vazire, Nairán Ramírez-Esparza, Richard B Slatcher, James W Pennebaker, 'Are women really more talkative than men?', *Science*, 317, 5834 (6 July 2007), 82. Mehl said that he hoped the

research would lead to a fresh, less hidebound way of thinking about the ways men and women behave. He said, 'The stereotype puts unfortunate constraints on men and women – the idea that you can only happily be a woman if you're talkative and you can only be happy as a man if you're reticent. The study relieves those gender constraints.' Richard Knox, 'Study: men talk just as much as women', NPR, 5 July 2007, retrieved 24 October 2008 from http://www.npr.org/templates/story/story.php?storyId=11762186

38 Mark Liberman, 'Sex and speaking rate', Language Log, 7 August 2006, retrieved 10 October 2008 from http://158.130.17.5/~myl/languagelog/archives/003423.html

39 Girls' Schools Association website, 'Answers to frequently asked questions', retrieved 13 October 2008 from http://www.gsa.uk.com/default.aspx?id=135

40 Supernanny advice on discipline for boys and girls, retrieved 30 October 2008 from http://www.supernanny.co.uk/Advice/-/Parenting-Skills/-/Discipline-and-Reward/Boy-oh-boy-or-girl-oh-girl-~-different-ways-of-teaching-discipline.aspx

41 Janet Shibley Hyde and Nita McKinley, 'Gender differences in cognition: results from meta-analyses', in Paula Caplan, Mary Crawford, Janet Shibley Hyde, John T E Richardson eds, *Gender Differences in Human Cognition* (Oxford University Press, 1997), 30–51; see also Janet Shibley Hyde, 'The gender similarities hypothesis', *American Psychologist* 60, 6 (September 2005) 581–592

42 See also Robert Plomin and Terry T Foch, 'Sex differences and individual differences', *Child Development*, 52, 1 (March 1981), 383–5

43 Stephen Moss, 'Do women really talk more?', *Guardian,* 27 November 2006

44 Deborah Tannen, *You Just Don't Understand: Women and Men in Conversation* (London: Virago, 1991), pp24–5

45 Simon Baron-Cohen, *The Essential Difference*, op cit, p62

46 How male or female is your brain?, retrieved 2 November 2008 from http://www.guardian.co.uk/life/news/page/0,12983,937443,00.html; questionnaire retrieved 2 November 2008 from http://www.guardian.co.uk/life/table/0,,937442,00.html

47 The Sex ID test, retrieved 2 November 2008 from http://www.bbc.co.uk/science/humanbody/sex/index_cookie.shtml

48 Nancy Eisenberg and Randy Lennon, 'Sex differences in empathy and related capacities', *Psychological Bulletin,* 94, 1 (1983), 100–31; see also Richard Fabes and Nancy Eisenberg, 'Meta analyses of age and sex differences in children's and adolescents' prosocial behaviour', Arizona State University (1998), retrieved 15 July 2007 from http://www.public.asu.edu/~rafabes/meta.pdf

49 Sara Snodgrass, 'Women's intuition: the effect of subordinate role on interpersonal sensitivity', *Journal of Personality and Social Psychology,* 49 (1985), 146–55, p152; see also Sara Snodgrass, 'Further effects of role

versus gender on interpersonal sensitivity', *Journal of Personality and Social Pscyhology*, 61 (1992), 154–8

50 Steven Pinker, *The Blank Slate*, op cit, p356
51 Roger Highfield, 'QED', *Sunday Telegraph*, 18 April 2004
52 Minette Marrin, 'This equality for women is an injustice for men', *Sunday Times*, 29 June 2008
53 Janet Shibley Hyde and Nita M McKinley, 'Gender differences in cognition: results from meta-analysis', in Paula Caplan, Mary Crawford, Janet Shibley Hyde, John T E Richardson eds, *Gender Differences in Human Cognition* (Oxford University Press, 1997), p35. See also Janet Shibley Hyde, 'The gender similarities hypothesis', *American Psychologist*, 60, 6 (Sept 2005), pp581–92
54 Melissa Hines, op cit, p222
55 Jonathan E Roberts and Martha Ann Bell, 'Sex differences on a computerised mental rotation task disappear with computer familiarisation', *Perceptual and Motor Skills*, 91 (2000), 1027–34
56 For instance, a test carried out in 2002 in which boys and girls were given their mental rotations tests after and before being given computer games to play found that boys outperformed girls before the groups had played the games, but their scores were the same after the girls and the boys had had the chance to play the computer games. R De Lisi and J L Wolford, 'Improving children's mental rotation accuracy with computer game playing', *Genetic Psychology*, 163, 3 (September 2002), 272–82. One review of evidence to 2002 concluded 'the evidence provides little reason to support nativist claims': Nora Newcombe, 'The nativist-empiricist controversy in the context of recent research on spatial and quantitative development', *Psychological Science*, 13, 5 (September 2002), 395–401. What's more, our very expectations can change people's performance in such tests. When a test of mental image rotation was run with two groups of students, one group was told that success in these tests correlated well with achievement in jobs such as 'in-flight and carrier-based aviation engineering, in-flight fighter weapons and attack/approach tactics' while the other group was told that it correlated with success in 'clothing and dress design, interior decoration and interior design'. In the first group, men significantly outperformed the women. M J Sharps, J L Price and J K Williams, 'Spatial cognition and gender: instructional and stimulus influences on mental image rotation performance', *Psychology of Women Quarterly*, 18 (1994), 413–25, cited in Virginia Valian, *Why So Slow? The Advancement of Women* (Cambridge, MA: MIT Press, 1998), p157
57 Jing Feng, Ian Spence and Jay Pratt, 'Playing an action video game reduces gender differences in spatial cognition', *Psychological Science*, 18, 10 (October 2007) 850–5, p854
58 Quoted in Tamar Lewin, 'Math scores show no gap for girls, study finds', *New York Times*, 25 July 2008
59 Simon Baron-Cohen, *The Essential Difference*, op cit, pp74–5
60 Steven Pinker, *The Blank Slate*, op cit, p345

61   D Goldstein and V B Stocking, 'TIP studies of gender differences in tal-
     ented adolescents', in K A Heller and E A Hany eds, *Competence and
     Responsibility* 2 (Ashland, OH: Hofgreve, 1994), pp190–203, cited in
     Elizabeth Spelke, 'Sex differences in intrinsic aptitude for mathematics
     and science?', op cit
62   Elizabeth Spelke, 'Sex differences in intrinsic aptitude for mathematics
     and science?' op cit, p954; Lewin, 'Math scores show no gap for girls,' op
     cit
63   Susan Pinker, *The Sexual Paradox*, op cit, p124
64   Catherine Weinberger, 'Is the science and engineering workforce drawn
     from the far upper tail of the math ability distribution?' September 2005,
     retrieved 10 July 2008 from http://econ.ucsb.edu/~weinberg/uppertail.pdf
65   P M Frome and J S Eccles, 'Parents' influence on children's achievement-
     related perceptions', *Journal of Personality and Social Psychology*, 74, 2
     (1998), 183–201; J S Hyde, E Fennema, M Ryan, L A Frost and C Hopp,
     'Gender comparisons of mathematics attitudes and affect: a meta-
     analysis', *Psychology of Women Quarterly*, 14, 3 (September 1990),
     299–324; J S Eccles and J E Jacobs, 'Social forces shape math attitudes
     and performance', *Signs: Journal of Women in Culture and Society*, 11,
     2 (Winter 1986), 367–80. For a good discussion of these studies and
     others see Diane Quinn, S J Spencer, 'The interference of stereotype threat
     with women's generation of mathematical problem-solving strategies',
     Journal of Social Issues, 57, 1 (2002), 55–71
66   Statistics compiled by the Association of Women in Science (US), from
     National Science Foundation statistics, retrieved 25 October 2008 from
     http://www.serve.com/awis/statistics/Rep_of_Women_in_S&E.pdf
67   *Battle of the Sexes*, part 1, 19 September 2002, retrieved 18 October
     2008 from http://www.abc.net.au/catalyst/stories/s686728.htm
68   Simon Baron-Cohen, *The Essential Difference*, op cit, p100
69   'Two studies of estrogen-exposed males found no consistent effects on
     sex-typed play. Although one study suggested possible enhancement of
     some male-typical activities following prenatal estrogen exposure, the
     effects were inconsistent.' Melissa Hines, *Brain Gender*, op cit, p120
70   Patricia Kester, Richard Green, Stephen J Finch and Katherine Williams,
     'Prenatal female hormone administration and psychosexual development
     in human males', *Psychoneuroendocrinology*, 5, 4 (1980), 269–85
71   *Battle of the Sexes*, part 1, 19 September 2002, retrieved 18 October
     2008 from http://www.abc.net.au/catalyst/stories/s686728.htm#contacts
72   John Gray, *Why Mars and Venus Collide*, op cit, p64
73   Anne Campbell, 'Attachment, aggression and affiliation, the role of oxy-
     tocin in female social behaviour', *Biological Psychology*, 77, 1 (January
     2008), 1–10
74   S E Taylor, G Gonzaga, L C Klein, P Hu, G A Greendale and T E Seeman,
     'Relation of oxytocin to psychological stress responses and hypothalamic-
     pituitary-adrenocortical axis activity in older women', *Psychosomatic
     Medicine*, 68 (2006), 238–45, p243

75   Another study of young women suggested that higher basal levels of oxytocin 'were associated with greater interpersonal distress'. R A Turner, M Altemus, T Enos, B Cooper, T McGuinness, 'Preliminary research on plasma oxytocin in normal cycling women: investigating emotion and interpersonal distress', *Psychiatry*, 62, 2 (1999), 97–113, p99. See also K M Kendrick, 'Oxytocin, motherhood and bonding', *Experimental Physiology*, 85, 1 (2000), 111–24; which stated, 'The role of brain oxytocin release in humans is still a matter for some speculation.'

76   Jonathan Leake, 'Science finds the secret of a hot kiss', *Sunday Times*, 8 February 2009; unpublished research presented at the American Association for the Advancement of Science conference on 14 February 2009, confirmed through personal correspondence with Professor Wendy Hill

77   BBC, *Secrets of the Sexes*, broadcast, 17 July 2005

78   Janice Turner, 'Planet Boy, where mum fades from the picture', *The Times*, 21 April 2003

79   'Humour comes from testosterone', BBC News, 21 December 2007

80   Satoshi Kanazawa, 'Why productivity fades with age: the crime–genius connection', *Journal of Research in Personality*, 37 (2003), 257–72

81   Simon Baron-Cohen, *The Essential Difference*, op cit, p104

82   Helena Cronin, 'The vital statistics', *Guardian*, 12 March 2005

83   Steven Pinker, *The Blank State*, op cit, p348

84   Susan Pinker, *The Sexual Paradox*, op cit, p217

85   Melissa Hines, *Brain Gender*, op cit, pp165–7, citing S M Perlman, 'Cognitive abilities of children with hormone abnormalities', *Journal of Learning Disabilities*, 6 (1973), 21–9; S W Baker and A A Ehrhardt 'Prenatal androgen, intelligence and cognitive sex differences', in R C Friedman et al, *Sex Differences in Behaviour* (New York: Wiley, 1974); L S McGuire et al, 'Congenital Adrenal Hyperplasia II: cognitive and behavioural studies', *Behaviour Genetics*, 5 (1975), 175–88; A A Ehrhardt and S W Baker, 'Males and females with congenital adrenal hyperplasia: A family study of intelligence and gender-related behaviour', in P A Lee et al eds, *Congenital Adrenal Hyperplasia* (Baltimore MD: University Park Press, 1977); R Nass and S Baker, 'Learning disabilities in children with congenital adrenal hyperplasia', *Journal of Child Neurology*, 6 (1991) 306–12

86   Simon Baron-Cohen, *The Essential Difference*, op cit, p101

87   Melissa Hines, Susan Golombok, John Rust, Katie Johnston, Jean Golding and the Avon Longitudinal Study of Parents and Children Study Team, 'Testosterone during pregnancy and gender role behaviour of pre-school children: a longitudinal population study', *Child Development*, 73, 6 (Nov/Dec 2002), 1678–87

88   See for instance Bonnie Auyeung et al, 'Fetal testosterone predicts sexually differentiated childhood behaviour in girls and boys', *Psychological Science*, 20, 2 (2009) 144–8

89   Jo-Anne Finegan, 'Relations between prenatal testosterone levels and cognitive abilities at 4 years', *Developmental Psychology*, 28, 6 (November 1992), 1075–89

90 Cornelieke van de Beek et al, 'Prenatal sex hormones (maternal and amniotic fluid) and gender-related play behaviour in 13-month-old infants', *Archives of Sexual Behaviour*, 38, 6 (2009), 6–15

91 Other studies that appear to disprove a clear link between exposure to testosterone in the womb and cognitive traits include a 2001 study that looked at the relationship between finger-digit ratio (associated with levels of prenatal testosterone) and various cognitive and personality tests. It found that 'no significant associations were found for the cognitive tests'. Elizabeth Austin et al, 'A preliminary investigation of the associations between personality, cognitive ability and digit ratio', *Personality and Individual Differences*, 33 (2002), 1115–24, p1121. In another study, Mark Brosnan at the University of Bath studied finger-digit ratio among academics. He found that academics in the science faculty had digit ratios 'consistent with the female norm' and that academics in the social sciences had digit ratios 'consistent with the male norm', whatever sex they were. This implied that male scientists were exposed to less testosterone than were social scientists. As Mark Brosnan commented: 'Those in faculties requiring higher systemising abilities . . . have an index of low prenatal exposure to testosterone. This contrasts with Baron-Cohen's findings.' Mark Brosnan, 'Digit ratio and faculty membership: implications for the relationship between prenatal testosterone and academia', *British Journal of Psychology*, 97, 4 (2006), 455–66. Another study that did not find the predicted relationship between foetal testosterone and later masculine behaviour was carried out by Simon Baron-Cohen's team after the publication of *The Essential Difference*. In 2005 his team found that variations in testosterone in the amniotic fluid did not contribute to individual differences in game participation as reported by the mother among fifty-three children aged four and five. R Knickmeyer et al, 'Gender-typed play and amniotic testosterone', *Developmental Psychology*, 41, 3 (May 2005), 517–28

92 Melissa Hines, *Brain Gender*, op cit, p136, citing R Tricker et al, 'The effects of supraphysiological doses of testosterone on anger behaviour in healthy eugonadal men', *Journal of Clinical Endocrinology and Metabolism*, 81 (1996), 3754–8 and K Bjorkquist et al, 'Testosterone intake and aggressiveness – real effect or anticipation', *Aggressive Behavior*, 20 (1994) 17–26

93 J R Lightdale and D A Prentice, 'Rethinking sex differences in aggression: aggressive behaviour in the absence of social roles', *Personality and Social Psychology Bulletin*, 20, 1 (February 1994), 34–44, p43

94 'Do men really listen with just half a brain? Research sheds some light', 28 November 2000, CNN; retrieved 18 October 2008 from http://archives.cnn.com/2000/HEALTH/11/28/brain.listening/index.html

95 James Chapman, 'Why men find it harder to show their emotions', *Daily Mail*, 23 July 2002

96 Janice Turner, 'Planet Boy', *The Times*, 21 April 2003

97 Ian Sample, 'Gay men and heterosexual women have similarly shaped

brains, research shows', *Guardian*, 16 June 2008, describing findings from Ivanka Savic and Per Lindstrom, 'PET and MRI show differences in cerebral asymmetry and functional connectivity between homo- and heterosexual subjects', *Proceedings of the National Academy of Sciences*, 16 June 2008, retrieved 18 June 2008 from http://www.pnas.org/content/early/2008/06/13/0801566105.abstract

98   Mark Liberman, 'Annals of essentialism: sexual orientation and rhetorical asymmetry', Language Log, 18 June 2008, retrieved 20 June 2008 from http://languagelog.ldc.upenn.edu/nll/?p=256

99   Murat Yucel et al, 'Hemispheric and gender-related differences in the gross morphology of the anterior cingulate/paracingulate cortex in normal volunteers: an MRI morphometric study', *Cerebral Cortex*, 11, 1 (January 2001), 17–25, p17

100 C D Good et al, 'Cerebral asymmetry and the effects of sex and handedness on brain structure: a voxel-based morphometric analysis of 465 normal adult human brains', *NeuroImage*, 14, 3 (September 2001), 685–700, p692

101 Thomas Barrick et al, 'Automatic analysis of cerebral asymmetry: an exploratory study of the relationship between brain torque and planum temporale asymmetry', *NeuroImage*, 24, 3 (February 2005), 678–91, p692

102 Arthur Toga and Paul Thompson, 'Mapping Brain Asymmetry', *Neuroscience*, 4, 1 (January 2003), 37–48, p43

103 Christine de Lacoste-Utamsing and Ralph L Holloway, 'Sexual dimorphism in the human corpus callosum', *Science*, 216 (1982), 1431–2

104 Lorraine Dusky, 'Just like a woman', 2 March 2005, Salon.com, retrieved 30 October 2008 from http://dir.salon.com/story/opinion/feature/2005/03/02/gender_differences/index1.html

105 Susan Pinker, *The Sexual Paradox*, op cit, p116

106 Other writers have joined this debate: for instance, Steven Pinker says, 'The brains of men differ visibly from the brains of women in several ways ... Portions of the cerebral commissures, which link the left and right hemispheres, appear to be larger in women, and their brains may function in a less lopsided manner than men's.' Steven Pinker, *The Blank Slate*, op cit, p347; Simon Baron-Cohen says, 'Women's brains, interestingly, have a thicker corpus callosum (the connective tissue between the two hemispheres, which allows for better communication between them)', Simon Baron-Cohen, 'Scientists have sex on the brain', *Guardian Weekly*, 4 February 2005

107 John Gray, *Why Mars and Venus Collide*, op cit, p38

108 Other commentators have popularised the same idea, for instance, the talk show host Phil Donahue commented that this original study showed that females had a corpus callosum 'as much as 40 per cent larger', and that this was the basis for 'women's intuition'. Quoted in Katherine M Bishop and Douglas Wahlsten, 'Sex differences in the human corpus callosum: myth or reality?', *Neuroscience and Biobehavioral Reviews*, 21, 5 (1997), 581–601

109 Katherine M Bishop and Douglas Wahlsten, ibid, p590

110 As Susan Pinker puts it in *The Sexual Paradox*: 'MRI studies show that males have most language functions localised in the left hemisphere. Meanwhile, most females use both hemispheres for language.' Susan Pinker, op cit, p45

111 Micheal D Phillips et al, 'Temporal lobe activation demonstrates sex-based differences during passive listening', *Radiology*, 220 (July 2001), 202–7

112 'Why men don't listen', BBC, 28 November 2000, retrieved 10 July 2008 from http://news.bbc.co.uk/1/hi/health/1044805.stm

113 'Why men don't listen', *Daily Mail*, 29 December 2000

114 Iris E C Sommer, André Aleman, Anke Bouma and René S Kahn, 'Do women really have more bilateral language representation than men? A meta-analysis of functional imaging studies', *Brain*, 127, 8 (August 2004), 1845–52. It's interesting that this meta-analysis was carried out by scientists who did agree with the idea that there are significant sex differences in cognitive abilities, but they couldn't see any evidence for them in the physical brain, concluding: 'It is therefore not likely that differences in language lateralization underlie the general sex differences in cognitive performance, and the neuronal basis for these cognitive sex differences remains elusive.' p1845

115 For discussion of the 'file-drawer' problem see for instance: John T E Richardson, *Gender Differences in Human Cognition* (Oxford University Press, 1997), p9; Caplan and Caplan, 'The perseverative search for sex differences in mathematics ability' in Gallagher and Kaufman eds, *Gender Differences in Mathematics* (Cambridge University Press, 2005), 25–47; Mark Liberman, 'Innate sex differences: science and public opinion', Language Log, 20 June 2008, retrieved 22 June 2008 from http://languagelog.ldc.upenn.edu/nll/?p=261; Erin McClure, 'A meta-analytic review of sex differences in facial expression processing and their development in infants, children, and adolescents', *Psychological Bulletin*, 126 (May 2000), 424–53

116 For instance, if you look at studies on rodents' brains, which can be experimented on in ways that we cannot with humans', changes to their environment have been shown to increase the size or density of particular brain regions. Melissa Hines, *Brain Gender,* op cit, p196

117 Eleanor A Maguire, David G Gadian, Ingrid S Johnsrude, Catriona D Good, John Ashburner, Richard S J Frackowiak and Christopher D Firth, 'Navigation-related structural change in the hippocampi of taxi drivers', *Proceedings of the National Academy of Sciences of the United States of America*, 97, 8 (11 April 2000), 4398–403

118 Similarly, when subjects in a test were given a three-month period of juggling practice, that led to an increase in grey-matter density in the area of the temporal cortex that was assumed to process that sort of task. After the practice stopped, the brain area changed back. Draganski, Gaser, Busch, Schuierer, Bogdahn and May, 'Changes in grey matter induced by training', *Nature*, 427 (22 January 2004), 311–12

119 Melissa Hines, *Brain Gender,* op cit, p196
120 Sherwood Washburn and Chet Lancaster, 'The Evolution of Hunting,' in Richard B Lee ed, *Man the Hunter* (Chicago: Aldine Publishing Company, 1968), p296
121 Allan and Barbara Pease, *Why Men Don't Listen and Women Can't Read Maps* (London: Orion, 1999), p13
122 Kristen Hawkes, 'Grandmothers and the evolution of human longevity', *American Journal of Human Biology*, 15 (2003), 380–400
123 Description of life among the Agta people of the Sierra Madre, Melvin Konner, 'Hunter-gatherer infancy and childhood, the !Kung and others', in Hewlett and Lamb eds, *Hunter-Gatherer Childhoods* (London: Transaction, 2005), 19–64, p55. See also Rayna Reiter ed, *Toward an Anthropology of Women* (London: Monthly Review Press, 1975); Frances Dahlberg ed, *Woman the Gatherer* (Yale University Press, 1981)
124 Barry Hewlett, quoted in Joanna Moorhead, 'Are the men of the African Aka tribe the best fathers in the world?', *Guardian,* 15 June 2005
125 Craig B Stanford, 'The ape's gift: meat-eating, meat-sharing and human evolution', in Frans B M De Waal, *Tree of Origin* (Harvard University Press, 2001), 97–117, p115
126 Natalie Angier, *Woman: An Intimate Geography* (London: Virago, 1999), p347

9: Stereotypes

1 Simon Baron-Cohen, *The Essential Difference,* op cit, p11
2 Steven Pinker, 'The science of sex difference', *The New Republic*, 14 February 2005
3 Ashley Herzog, 'Will feminists again attempt to censor science?', *Town Hall*, 13 March 2008, retrieved 31 October 2008 from http://town-hall.com/columnists/AshleyHerzog/2008/03/13/will_feminists_again_atte mpt_to_censor_science
4 Mark Liberman, 'More functional neuroanatomy of science journalism', Language Log, 18 March 2008, retrieved 30 October 2008 from http://itre.cis.upenn.edu/~myl/languagelog/archives/005472.html
5 Martin Newland, 'Why women prefer talking to sex', *Daily Mail*, 13 September 2006
6 Tracey Shors, 'The mismeasure of woman', *Economist*, 3 August 2006
7 Dr Matthews Duncan, quoted by William Withers Moore, president, at the fifty-fourth annual meeting of the British Medical Association, Brighton 1886, as reported in *Lancet*, 2 (1886), 315, cited in Joan N Burstyn, 'Education and sex: the medical case against higher education for women in England', *Proceedings of the American Philosophical Society*, 117, 2 (April 1973), 79–89, p84
8 Henry Maudsley, 'Sex in mind and education', *Fortnightly Review,* 15 (1874), 466–83, cited in Joan N Burstyn, op cit

9   G T W Patrick, 'The Psychology of Women', *Popular Science Monthly* 47 (1895) 209–225, cited in Stephanie A Shields, 'Functionalism, Darwinism and the psychology of women: a study in social myth', *American Psychologist*, 30 (1975), 739–54

10 Anne Fausto-Sterling, *Myths of Gender* (New York: Basic Books, 1985) pp38–9

11 Edward O Wilson, *On Human Nature* ((1978), London: Penguin, 1995), p129. See also Edward O Wilson, *Sociobiology: The New Synthesis* (Harvard University Press, 1975)

12 Victoria Brescoll, Marianne LaFrance, 'The correlates and consequences of newspaper reports of research on sex differences', *Psychological Science,* 15, 8 (August 2004), 515–20

13 See Rosie Boycott, 'Why women don't want top jobs, by a feminist', *Daily Mail*, 22 April 2008

14 Helena Cronin, 'Scientists reveal what changed their minds', *Daily Telegraph*, 31 December 2007

15 S J Spencer, C M Steele and D M Quinn, 'Stereotype threat and women's math performance', *Journal of Experimental Social Psychology*, 35, 1 (1999), 4–28

16 Zoe Brennan and Emma Smith, 'Driving tests: collision of the sexes: is the chief tester right about women drivers?', *The Times*, 13 February 2005

17 N C Jonathan Yeung and C von Hippel, 'Stereotype threat increases the likelihood that female drivers in a simulator run over jaywalkers', *Accident Analysis and Prevention*, 40, 2 (March 2008), 667–74

18 Shelley J Correll, 'Constraints into preferences: gender, status and emerging career aspirations', *American Sociological Review*, 69, 1 (February 2004), 93–113

19 'Conservatives may begin with a preference for biological explanations for sex differences and also read conservative newspapers containing more biological explanations for sex differences. Such reading may further justify and reinforce pre-existing opinions about the causes of sex differences.' Victoria Brescoll and Marianne LaFrance, 'The correlates and consequences of newspaper reports of research on sex differences', op cit, p520

20 See also: Shelley J Correll, 'Gender and the career choice process: the role of biased self-assessments', *American Journal of Sociology*, 106, 6 (May 2001), 1691–730. Studies carried out by Correll suggested here that 'Boys do not pursue mathematical activities at a higher rate than girls do because they are better at mathematics. They do so, at least partially, because they think they are better.' p1724

21 Statistics from the Judiciary of England and Wales, 1 April 2008, retrieved 10 October 2008 from http://www.judiciary.gov.uk/keyfacts/statistics/women.htm

22 *Sex and Power 2008* (Equality and Human Rights Commission, 2008), retrieved 2 November 2008 from http://www.equalityhumanrights.com/Documents/EHRC/SexandPower/Sex_and_Power_2008.pdf

23 Brendan Burchell, Colette Fagan, Catherine O'Brien and Mark Smith, *Working Conditions in the European Union: The Gender Perspective* (Luxembourg: Office for Official Publications of the European Communities, 2007), retrieved 24 January 2009 from http://www.euro-found.europa.eu/pubdocs/2007/108/en/1/ef07108en.pdf; statistics for the UK discussed in Sarah Womack, 'Career women work longer hours than men', *Daily Telegraph*, 2 December 2007

24 *Not Having It All: How Motherhood Reduces Women's Pay and Employment Prospects* (Fawcett Society, 2009), retrieved 25 July 2009 from http://www.fawcettsociety.org.uk/documents/NotHavingItAll.pdf

25 Andrew Sullivan, 'The he hormone', *New York Times*, 2 April 2000

26 Mary Carmichael, 'The cheating man's brain', *Newsweek*, 12 March 2008; quoting Marvin Zuckerman, psychologist and author of a 2006 book called *Sensation Seeking and Risky Behavior.*

27 BBC, *Secrets of the Sexes*, broadcast 17 July 2005

28 Liz Jones, 'Sarkozy's Sirens: why are French politicians so much more glamorous than ours?', *Daily Mail*, 12 March 2008

29 Kristina Cooke, 'Analysis: Germans focus on TV debate', 2 August 2005, CNN, retrieved 2 November 2008 from http://edition.cnn.com/2005/WORLD/europe/08/02/germany.cooke2/index.html

30 Liz Jones, 'Sarkozy's Sirens', op cit

31 Hendrik Hertzberg, 'Brouhaha', *New Yorker*, 15 October 2007

32 Zoe Williams, 'It wouldn't happen to a man', *Guardian*, 16 January 2009

33 Christine Wenneras and Agnes Wold, 'Nepotism and sexism in peer-review', *Nature*, 387, (22 May 1997), 341–3

34 For more evidence of continuing underrating of female academics, see this study which showed that a gender disparity remained for male and female scientists who had obtained prestigious fellowships: G Sonnert, G Holton, 'Career patterns of women and men in the sciences: women encounter social obstacles and may pay penalties for a careful research style', *American Scientist*, 84, 1 (1996), 63–71; another study showed that in economics women were 'underplaced' and women published more than men at the same academic level: Van W Kolpin and Larry D Singell, 'The gender composition and scholarly performance of economics departments: a test for employment discrimination', *Industrial and Labor Relations Review*, 49, 3 (April 1996), 408–23

35 Figures from the Office of National Statistics, quoted in 'Women are "put off" hi-tech jobs', BBC News, 8 September 2005

36 Emma de Vita, 'Where have all the IT girls gone?', *Management Today*, 1 February 2008, retrieved 1 April 2008 from http://www.management-today.co.uk/news/781020/where-girls-gone/

37 Heilman, Block, Martell and Simon, 'Has anything changed? Current characterisations of men, women and managers', *Journal of Applied Psychology*, 74 (1989), 935–42, cited in Virginia Valian, *Why So Slow? The Advancement of Women* (Cambridge USA: MIT Press, 1998), p126

38 Butler, Doré, Geis, 'Nonverbal affect responses to male and female

leaders: implications for leadership evaluations', *Journal of Personality and Social Psychology*, 58, 1 (1990), 48–59 cited in Virgina Valian, *Why So Slow?* op cit, pp130–1

39   Linda Babcock and Sara Laschever, *Women Don't Ask: Negotiation and the Gender Divide* (Princeton University Press, 2003), pp1–2

40   Quoted in Shankar Vedantam, 'The truth about why women are paid less – even if they ask for more', *Guardian,* 21 August 2007; citing Hannah Riley Bowles, Linda Babcock and Lei Lai: 'Social incentives for gender differences in the propensity to initiate negotiations: sometimes it does hurt to ask', *Organisational Behaviour and Human Decision Processes*, 103, 1 (May 2007), 84–103

41   Susan Pinker, *The Sexual Paradox*, op cit, p35

42   Martin Newland, 'Why women prefer talking to sex', *Daily Mail*, 13 September 2006

43   BBC, *Secrets of the Sexes*, broadcast 17 July 2005

44   M E Lamb, *The Role of the Father in Child Development* (NY: Wiley, 1981), cited in Adrienne Burgess, *Fatherhood Reclaimed* (London: Random House, 1997), p94

45   Mumsnet conversations, 'Do you ever feel frustrated at being left to hold baby?' (edited for ease of reading), retrieved 2 November 2008 from http://www.mumsnet.com/Talk?topicid=relationships&threadid= 612947-do-you-ever-feel-frustrated-at-being-left-to-hold#12489852

46   Naomi Wolf, *Misconceptions* (London: Chatto and Windus, 2001), p204

47   Viv Groskop, 'Do good feminists bake cupcakes?', *Guardian*, 22 August 2008

48   Barack Obama, *The Audacity of Hope* ((2006), Edinburgh: Canongate, 2007), p340

49   Nigella Lawson, *How to be a Domestic Goddess* (London: Chatto & Windus, 2000), pvii

50   Rafael Behr, 'Is being a good Dad ruining your career?', *Observer*, 11 June 2006

51   Lyn Craig and Pooja Sawrikar, 'Work and family: how does the (gender) balance change as children grow?', *Gender, Work and Organisation* 16, 6 (2009), 684–709

52   L Barclay and D Lupton, 'The experiences of new fatherhood: a socio-cultural analysis', *Journal of Advanced Nursing*, 29, 4 (1999), cited in Rosalind Barnett and Caryl Rivers, *Same Difference: How Gender Myths are Hurting Our Relationships, Our Children, and Our Jobs* (New York: Basic Books, 2004), p43

53   M Thompson, L Vinter and V Young, *Dads and their Babies: Leave Arrangements in the First Year* (Equal Opportunities Commission, 2005); M O'Brien, *Shared Caring: Bringing Fathers into the Frame* (Equal Opportunities Commission, 2005), cited in *Twenty-first Century Dad* (Equal Opportunities Commission, 2006), retrieved 14 November 2008 from www.equalityhumanrights.com/Documents/Gender/Employment/ 21st_century_dad.pdf

54 *More Time for Families* (Trades Union Congress, March 2006), p7, retrieved 1 November 2008 from www.workingfamilies.org.uk/asp/ main_downloads/Families%20Need%20Time%20Report.doc

55 D Smeaton, *Dads and their Babies, a Household Analysis* (Equal Opportunities Commission, 2006), cited in *21st Century Dad* (Equal Opportunities Commission, 2006), op cit

56 Harry Phibbs, 'As the father of a five-week-old daughter I say thanks but no thanks', *Daily Mail*, 31 March 2009

57 James Delingpole, 'At last I'm allowed to be a man', *Sunday Times*, 3 September 2006

58 Quentin Letts, 'Modern men are not interested in paternity leave', *Daily Mail*, 30 August 2006

59 Jill Parkin, 'Sorry Ms Harman, but your "family friendly" policies are no such thing', *Daily Mail*, 27 August 2006

Give your support

Birds Eye View Film Festival
Unit 306 Aberdeen Centre
22–24 Highbury Grove
London N5 2EA
020 7704 9435
www.birds-eye-view.co.uk

The Fawcett Society
1–3 Berry Street
London EC1V 0AA
020 7253 2598
www.fawcettsociety.org.uk

The F Word
www.thefword.org.uk

OBJECT
PO Box 50373
London W4 3ZP
www.object.org.uk

Pink Stinks
www.pinkstinks.co.uk

Reclaim the Night
www.reclaimthenight.org

Rosa
c/o WRC, Ground Floor East,
33–41 Dallington Street
London EC1V 0BB
020 7324 3044
www.rosauk.org

Womankind Worldwide
56–64 Leonard Street
London EC2A 4LT
020 7549 0360
www.womankind.org.uk

Women for Refugee Women
56–64 Leonard Street
London EC2A 4LT
020 7549 0360
www.refugeewomen.com

Women's Resource Centre
Ground Floor East,
33–41 Dallington Street
London EC1V 0BB
020 7324 3044
www.wrc.org.uk

Index

Adams-Short, Grace 30
Adamson, Lauren 164
Agent Provocateur 36
aggression 184, 187–8, 211
'Ali' 111–12, 114, 116
'Angela' 51–3, 61–2
Angier, Natalie 197; *Woman: An Intimate Geography* 197
'Anna' 88–9, 92
Anti-Bullying Alliance 235
Astrid, Princess 146

Babcock, Linda 216–17
babies, and sex differences 155, 158–65
Baldwin, Michelle 43
Barbie 2–3, 4
Baron-Cohen, Simon 13, 147–8, 149, 158, 159, 161, 163, 170, 177, 181, 185, 201; *Essential Difference, The* 13, 147–8, 159, 170, 201
Battle of the Sexes (TV) 150, 181, 182
Baxter, Maggie 235
Beauty Myth, The (Wolf) 3
de Beauvoir, Simone 3, 129, 132, 138, 140, 144; *Second Sex, The* 3
Beckham, Victoria 3, 68
Behr, Rafael 225
'Bella' 88–90, 92
Bennett, Catherine 47
Beyoncé 71

Biddulph, Steve 143
Big Brother (TV) 30–1, 123
biological determinism 11–14, 143–230; history of 202–3; in education 143, 167–8, 202–3, 209
Birds Eye View Film Festival 235
Bishop, Katherine 191–2
Blaize, Immodesty 43
Blank Slate, The (Pinker) 148, 174, 177, 185
Blears, Hazel 213
Blue Peter (TV) 70
'Bobbijo' 64
Bodies (Orbach) 66
Booth, Cherie 223
Boycott, Rosie 150, 205
Brain Gender (Hines) 156–7, 175–6, 181–2, 185
brains: and sex differences 12, 143, 149, 155, 156, 159, 175, 188–95, 203; asymmetry 189–90; corpus callosum 190–2; hippocampus 194
Brand, Russell 53–4, 122
Bratz: dolls 2, 4, 63–4, 70; *Bratz: The Movie* 64
Break Up, The (film) 219
Brett, Cara 23, 27–8, 34–5
Brizendine, Louann 148, 163–5, 166, 169, 219; *Female Brain, The* 148, 163, 166
Brown, Sarah 224
Brumberg, Joan Jacobs 65–6

Bruni, Carla 212–13
Buchanan, Keisha 42
Burgess, Adrienne 220; *Fatherhood Reclaimed* 220
burlesque 43–5
Bushnell, Candace 92

Caldwell, Christopher 153
Californication (TV) 51
Cameron, Deborah 156, 173; *Myth of Mars and Venus, The* 156, 173
Celebrity Big Brother (TV) 31
Chadha, Gurinder 235
Child Exploitation and Protection Centre 78
choice 13, 14, 28–38, 48–9, 56, 57, 68, 73, 75, 119–25, 142, 178, 179, 207, 228–30, 237
Class, Samantha 59
Clinton, Hillary 211–12, 213, 223
Clubb, Natalie 59
Cohen, Nick 159
Cole, Cheryl 71
Complete Androgen Insensitivity Syndrome 180
Confessions of a Working Girl ('Miss S') 49–50, 59–60
Congenital Adrenal Hyperplasia [CAH] 184–5
Connellan, Jennifer 158–9, 160–1, 163
Corner, Jennie 30
Correll, Shelley 207
'Courtney' 64
Crisis in Rape Crisis campaign 235–6
Cronin, Helena 159, 185, 205

Davies, Sheilagh 79
Deayton, Angus 54
'Demi' 64
Dershowitz, Alan 154
Diary of a Manhattan Call Girl (Quan) 49, 89

diethylstilbestrol [DES] 181–2
dieting 2, 33, 65, 66, 67, 124
Disney 1, 69, 130; Princess brand 2, 12, 132
Dixon, Alesha 36, 122
Duff, Hilary 3
Dworkin, Andrea 29, 104; *Pornography: Men Possessing Women* 29

Edgar-Jones, Phil 30–1, 123
education 10, 12, 15, 142; non-sexist 138–9; biological determinism in 143, 167–8, 202–3, 209
Elle (magazine) 67
'Ellie' 6–7, 39–40, 45–6, 48–9
Elliott, Michele 77–8
Embarrassing Teenage Bodies (TV) 108–9
empathy 147, 170–4, 191, 210, 211, 218–28
equality 7–10, 14, 33, 96, 119, 218, 227, 237
Essential Difference, The (Baron-Cohen) 13, 147–8, 159, 170, 201
'Esther' 98–9
evolution 11, 145–6, 148, 171, 175, 181, 195–8, 208

F-Word (website) 234
Fat is a Feminist Issue (Orbach) 66
fashion 66, 67, 124
fatherhood 218–30
Fatherhood Reclaimed (Burgess) 220
Fausto-Sterling, Anne 203; *Myths of Gender* 203
Fawcett Society 233
Female Brain, The (Brizendine) 148, 163, 166, 166
Female Chauvinist Pigs (Levy) 32
Female Eunuch, The (Greer) 3, 84–5
feminism, *passim*: and activism 28, 233–6; and Enlightenment 96;

and Romanticism 96; second
wave 5, 84–6, 97–9, 104–5,
129, 135, 134–41, 233
'Fenella' 135–7
FHM (magazine) 21, 22
Figes, Kate 70
file-drawer problem 193
Finegan, Jo-Anne 186
Finnigan, Judy 165–6
First Weekenders Club 235
Fox, Emilia 42
French, Marilyn 85; *Women's
Room, The* 85
Frick, Janet 164

Gardner, Rachel 76–7, 80, 82, 101
Girl with a One-track Mind ('Abby
Lee') 93–4, 95, 105
Girls Aloud 2, 71
Girls Book of Glamour, The 66
Girls' Schools Association 12, 168
glamour modelling 4, 5, 19–38, 48,
76, 90, 123
Godwin, William 97
Goldacre, Ben 145–6
Golden Notebook, The (Lessing) 85
Goldman, Emma 97
Grabrucker, Anne-Marie 140–3
Grabrucker, Marianne 139–43, 144;
There's a Good Girl 139
'Grace' 80–1
Grahame, Nikki 31
Gray, John 149, 166, 173, 182–3,
191; *Men are from Mars,
Women are from Venus* 166,
173; *Why Mars and Venus
Collide* 149, 191
Greer, Germaine 3, 44, 84–5; *Female
Eunuch, The* 3, 84–5; *Whole
Woman, The* 44
Gyllenhaal, Maggie 36

Hamleys 131–2
Harman, Harriet 121, 231

Have I Got News For You (TV) 120
High, Luke 107
Hilton, Paris 3
Hilton, Phil 29–30, 31, 35–6, 124
Hines, Melissa 156–8, 175–7,
181–2, 185, 187, 195, 201;
Brain Gender 156–7, 175–6,
181–2, 185
von Hippel, Courtney 207
Hiya Kids 131
Holly, Jazz D 223
Hopkins, Nancy 154–5, 155–6
Horgan-Wallace, Aisleyne 30
hormones 12, 14, 143, 148, 149,
150, 180–7, 198, 206;
diethylstilbestrol [DES] 181–2;
oestrogen 181–2; oxytocin 148,
149, 182–4, 226; testosterone
147, 148, 149, 180, 184–7,
206, 210, 211
Hurlbert, Anya 145
Hyde, Janet Shibley 168–9, 175
hypersexual culture 5, 8, 10, 37, 49,
61, 74, 75, 76, 82, 102, 120,
122, 123, 125, 228

Indigo Worldwide 131
inequality 11, 14, 33, 120, 142, 143,
152, 202, 208–9, 215, 217,
227–8
internet: and lads' magazines 22, 36;
and pornography 4, 102, 104,
105, 106–7, 111–16; and
prostitution 55–6, 61; and
social networking 26, 27, 52, 72
*Intimate Adventures of a London
Call Girl, The* ('Belle de Jour')
49, 51, 89, 94

'Jade' 64
Jackie (magazine) 67
'Jim' 110–16
'Joanne' 64
Jordan (Katie Price) 21, 22, 25, 68

de Jour, Belle (Brooke Magnanti) 49, 51, 56, 94; *Intimate Adventures of a London Call Girl, The* 49, 51, 89, 94
Juska, Jane 95

'Katie' 20–5
Kidscape 77–8
Knight, India 122
Knocked Up (film) 219

L-Word, The (TV) 51, 89
lap-dancing 4, 5, 6, 35, 39–49, 54, 62, 90, 102, 125, 232, 233, 236
'Lara' 112–14
Laschever, Sara 216–17
Lawson, Nigella 224
Leapfrog 133–4
Lee, Abby (Zoe Margolis) 93–4, 95; *Girl with a One-track Mind* 93–4, 95, 105
Lessing, Doris 85, 231; *Golden Notebook, The* 85
Levy, Ariel 32
Liberman, Mark 166–7, 169, 190, 201–2
Lilith Project 47
Lloyd, Gavin 22
Lopez, Jennifer 21
love 90–101
Loughborough University 26

Mackay, Finn 234
MacKinnon, Catharine 104
Madeley, Richard 165–6
magazines: lads' magazines 4, 5, 19–38, 55, 73, 90, 102, 107, 233, *see also Nuts, Zoo, FHM*; women's and girls' magazines 2, 66, 67, 80, *see also Vogue, Elle, Jackie*
Man the Hunter (Lee, ed) 195
Margolis, Zoe ('Abby Lee') 93–4, 95, 100, 105; *Girl with a One-track Mind* 93–4, 95, 105
Marsh, Jodie 22, 36, 123
maternity leave 8, 226
mathematics 148, 155, 158, 174–80
Mattel 3, 133
Maudsley, Sir Henry 203
Maxim (magazine) 32
Mayhem nightclub 19–25
McCabe, Jess 71, 234
McElvoy, Anne 231
Mehl, Matthias 167
'Melanie' 60–1
'Melissa P' 95
Men are from Mars, Women are from Venus (Gray) 166, 173
Merkel, Angela 212
Merrill, Paul 29
Messenger, Melinda 22
Millward, Rachel 235
Misconceptions (Wolf) 221
'Miss S' 49–50, 50–1, 59–60; *Confessions of a Working Girl* 49–50, 59–60
Moore, Emma and Abi 236
Moorhead, Joanna 134–5
Morgan, Hayley 59
Morgan, Robin 104
Moss, Howard 162
Moss, Kate 41
motherhood 220–30
Mumsnet 237
Myth of Mars and Venus, The (Cameron) 156, 173
Myths of Gender (Fausto-Sterling) 203

National Society for the Prevention of Cruelty to Children 77, 79
National Survey of Sexual Attitudes and Lifestyles 91
Needs of Children, The (Pringle) 138
Neon Management 40, 123
New Feminism, The (Walter) 8, 33
Nicol, Tania 58

'Nikki' 20–1
Nin, Anaïs 100
Nuts (magazine) 19–20, 21, 22,
    29–30, 31, 37, 73–4, 124

Obama, Michelle and Barack 224
OBJECT organisation 47, 233
oestrogen 181–2
On Beauty (Smith) 117–18
Orbach, Susie 66; *Bodies* 66; *Fat is a
    Feminist Issue* 66
oxytocin 148, 149, 182–4, 226

Palin, Sarah 121
Paoletti, Jo 146
Paper Houses (Roberts) 97
parental leave 9, 147, 226–7
Parliament 9, 119; Scottish
    Parliament 9
paternity leave 8, 9, 226–7
pay gap 10, 119, 216–17
Pease, Allan and Barbara 195; *Why
    Men Don't Listen and Women
    Can't Read Maps* 195–6
Pembroke College, Cambridge 26
Penn, Helen 78
Penny, Laurie 43–4
Phillips, Arlene 122
pink for girls 1–3, 12, 129–37; and
    biological determinism 11, 145–7
Pink Stinks 236
Pinker, Steven 148, 154, 155, 174,
    177, 185; *Blank Slate, The* 148,
    174, 177, 185;
Pinker, Susan 148, 159, 178, 185,
    191, 219; *Sexual Paradox, The*
    148, 159, 178, 185
Piper, Billie 5, 51, 61
plastic surgery 2, 22, 68, 108–9, 233
Playboy: bunny outfits 20; logo 72;
    nights 26
pole-dancing 3, 4, 5, 14, 26, 37, 41–2,
    46, 52, 72, 75, 119, 125, 237
Politics (Thirlwell) 104

pornography 4, 26, 29, 73, 76, 78,
    90, 102–18, 119, 123, 125, 233
*Pornography: Men Possessing
    Women* (Dworkin) 29
power 208–16; equation of
    hypersexual culture and power
    5–7, 25, 37, 43–5, 49, 52, 61,
    77, 96, 101, 122, 234
Price, Katie, *see* Jordan
Pringle, Mia Kellmer 138; *Needs of
    Children, The* 138
promiscuity 5, 52, 84–101
prostitution 4, 5, 35, 46, 49–62; and
    violence 57–62
Pussycat Dolls 76

Quan, Tracy 49; *Diary of a
    Manhattan Call Girl* 49, 89
Quinn, Diane 205

rape 8, 47, 61, 104, 114, 119, 235
Read, David 35, 40, 123
Reclaim the Night marches 233–4
Redfern, Catherine 234
Reynolds, Helen 28
Roberts, Michèle 97; *Paper Houses* 97
Robson, Kenneth 162
Roche, Charlotte 105; *Wetlands* 105
Rock, Daisy 103
Romance Academy 80–1
Rooney, Wayne 54
Rosa 235
Royal, Ségolène 212
'Ruby' 86, 88–90, 92

Salisbury, Wendy 95
Salmon, Zoe 70
scientific aptitude 152–3, 155, 159,
    174, 176–80
Second Sex, The (de Beauvoir) 3
second wave feminism 5, 84–6,
    97–9, 104–5, 129, 135, 134–41,
    233

Secrets of the Sexes (TV) 150, 182, 184, 211, 219
Seldon, Anthony 215
serial killers 58–9
Sex and the City (TV) 51, 89, 90, 92–3, 103–4
sex industry 3, 4, 6, 33, 36, 125; *see also* lap-dancing, pornography, prostitution
sexting 78
sexual bullying 77–9, 80, 121, 233, 235
Sexual Paradox, The (Pinker) 148, 159, 178, 185
sexual violence 29, 33, 57–62, 104, 115; *see also* rape
Shapiro, Lisa 63–4
Shore, Michael 133
Singh, Suraya 27
Smith, Jacqui 121–2, 212
Smith, Zadie 117–18; *On Beauty* 117–18
Smuts, Barbara 197
Snodgrass, Sara 172
sociobiology 203–4
Span, Anna 102–3, 117
Spare Rib (magazine) 150, 205
spatial skills 148, 163, 175–6, 184–5, 194, 206
Spears, Britney 71
Spelke, Elizabeth 155, 159–60, 162, 165
Spencer, Stephen 205
Spice Girls 41–2, 43
Steele, Claude 205
stereotypes 199–230; 'stereotype threat' 205–8
Stevens, Rachel 36
Strassmann, Burkhard 141
Strictly Come Dancing (TV) 122
Sugababes 42
Sugar (magazine) 77
Sullivan, Andrew 153–4
Summers, Lawrence 152–6, 174
systemising 147, 158, 162, 170, 174, 179, 184, 186, 211

'Tania' 20–5
Tannen, Deborah 170, 173
'Taylay' 64
von Teese, Dita 43
testosterone 147, 148, 149, 180, 184–7, 206, 210, 211
Thatcher, Margaret 212
Theakston, Jamie 54
There's a Good Girl (M Grabrucker) 139
Thirlwell, Adam 104; *Politics* 104
Thomas, Imogen 30
Townsend, Catherine 95
toys 1, 4, 63, 129–35, 150, 222, 232, 237; *see also* Barbie, Bratz, Disney, Mattel
trafficking for forced prostitution 58

Vadera, Baroness 214
Valian, Virginia 215
VaVoom, Vivienne 43
verbal skills 12, 137, 154, 165–70, 200, 205
Vindication of the Rights of Women, A (Wollstonecraft) 3, 96–7
Vivid (magazine) 26
Vogue (magazine) 67

W.I.T.C.H. 69
Wahlsten, Douglas 191–2
Walker, Lea 31
Ward, Helen 55
Washburn, Sherwood 195
Weinberg, Katherine 164
Wetlands (Roche) 105
White, Hannah 78
White, Terri 32–3, 37
Whiteley, Carly 73–6, 82–3, 98, 120
Whole Woman, The (Greer) 44
Why Mars and Venus Collide (Gray) 149, 191
Why Men Don't Listen and Women Can't Read Maps (Pease) 195–6

Widdecombe, Ann 120–1
Wilson, Edward O 203–4
Wolf, Naomi 3, 7, 221;
    Misconceptions 221
Wollstonecraft, Mary 3, 96–7;
    Vindication of the Rights of Women, A 3, 96–7
Woman: An Intimate Geography (Angier) 197
Womankind Worldwide 78, 235
Women for Refugee Women 234
Women's Resource Centre 235
Women's Room, The (French) 85

work: inequality at work 8–10, 13, 148, 150, 169, 178, 208–17, 228–30; domestic work 9–10, 209, 218–30
Wynn, Karen 155

York University 26

Zack and Miri Make a Porno (film) 104
Zola, Emile 50